The Northeastern Outdoors

The Northeastern Outdoors

By
Steve Berman

PHOTOGRAPHS
ADAM LAIPSON

ILLUSTRATIONS
PHYLIS SATIN

Maps
Pamela Solar Mills

STONE WALL PRESS   BOSTON   MASSACHUSETTS

ACKNOWLEDGEMENTS

The author would especially like to thank Mrs. Dorothy Cook at the Fryeburg, Maine Public Library, Dick Krasker at Forest Acres, Jeff McQueen — "Tarzan of The Bear Pond Trail", Steve Forman, Stan Berman, Mom, Vee Wee, Muffin, my publisher — Henry Wheelwright, and everyone else who's brains I picked along the way.

Contents

The Northeastern Outdoors

INTRODUCTION

Before I tell you about this book — its uses, design, and intent — there are a few things I think you should know about its author.

I grew up just outside of New York City. And like many young urbanites, nature was never a part of my early childhood. My family lived just a few hundred yards from the Atlantic Ocean; but somehow that distance could have been a few hundred miles. There was the beach — with its smells, its sand, and surf; but nothing — not even a poorly reproduced seascape — ever adorned any of the homes in my neighborhood. The house I lived in — like the houses we all lived in — simply had little to do with our natural surroundings.

I remember a wall — a low concrete wall — that defined the boundary line between the sandy beach and the asphalt streets. Kids used to sit atop it in summertime to watch firework displays from a nearby amusement park. That wall, hindsight now tells me, was like a buffer zone, a DMZ that separated the *forces of nature* from the more *civilized* transpirings of our suburban community. And only a hurricane, when it riled the ocean's waters — pushing gray-blue seawater over the top of the wall and then pouring it out onto the streets — could ever make the mighty Atlantic a community concern. Otherwise, the ocean was just a slightly chilled, much enlarged bathtub; a place to cool off on hot summer days.

So nature's violence — those torrential September hurricanes — unfortunately, was needed to make us all a little appreciative of her ways.

As for appreciating nature's beauty, only the black-and-white pages of my elementary school textbooks were ever assigned that task. And not once did anyone ever have the enlightened notion to show me a flower, or to point my eyes towards a tree, or my ears to a bird. I was a city kid: and city kids, by some strange contortion of values, just weren't meant to listen to birds. Bizarrely, what city kids **were** meant to do, I later learned, was earn admission to some prestigious university and there train for a career in one of the biological sciences. Kids, strangely enough, then, with little or no exposure to the wonders of nature — to the very movements of life — were the very kids who later on were to serve as life's maintainers and protectors. But social commentary isn't what this introduction is to be about. So it wasn't until my eighteenth year that I finally was 'flowered'. Let me explain.

Naturally, I had seen flowers. As in many suburban mini-estates, tulips, roses, and geraniums grew abundantly in my parent's garden. But never, never, had I seen a **wild** flower. And never had I ever really **looked** at a flower (tulips, roses, and geraniums included). Never, what I'm really trying to say, had I ever **adored** a flower — listened to droplets of spring rainwater drumming on the large leaves of the false hellebore — an early spring wildflower, or watched a bee, exquisitely choreographed, busily extracting nectar from the small white flowers of a mountain mint. I had never even so much as smelled a wild rose atop a hillside.

My 'flowering' happened this way: I was in upstate New York — a hot, moist June day. A friend of mine, kneeling about twenty feet away from me, started yelling to me — his voice tight with excitement. I hurried over to where he was crouching — with just two thoughts filling my head: either my friend was experiencing some excruciating bodily pain or else he had just attained a lofty spiritual ecstasy. All he said, though, as I neared him, was "Look", as his two hands excitedly pointed to the ground. "Columbine!" he screamed, then repeating it twice. "Columbine. Columbine." My eyes quickly dropped to where he was pointing and there, dangling from two, long purplish stems, was a cluster of drooping violet-blue flowers.

Again, he urged me to look, this time imperiously pushing the back of my head towards the flower. "Just get right down next to it," he shouted, "and **look**!"

. . . And there, the moment of my 'flowering'. The moment — the very flash when nature decided to suffuse my vision with her awe, with her mystery, her grandeur. The very moment when looking at that flower somehow started me thinking about the planet Earth, of how the Earth was just one of many planets, the Milky Way — one of many galaxies. That reverent, deeply religious, epiphanous moment when looking at that flower was all there "**is**" . . . when the "**doors of perception**", as Aldous Huxley once described them, were all-of-a-sudden flung open, leaving only the present moment to somehow magically elongate — stretching out towards infinity.

Look, really look, at a bird, a flower, or a human being. And somehow begin to see/feel the thousands of years of evolutionary activity that preceded it: It's a pure moment — a moment the Buddhists call *'enlightenment'*. A moment, unfortunately, rarer and rarer in our future-obsessed world.

My love affair with nature had its seeds in that moment: the sort of moment that launches inspired naturalists — like Aldo Leopold or Loren Eiseley — onto lofty careers in science, or that catapults poets — Emerson, Wordsworth, and Bly — onto even loftier artistic ventures. It was the **stuff** — the very moment, I knew — that rendered substance to all the world's great religions.

For me, it was all slightly less complicated. It was simply the moment that made me want more of those moments. Which is to say that today I walk in the woods, study the wildflowers, eat all the wild mushrooms I can safely identify, and climb mountains, because of/and for that moment. It's what (and I'm almost hesitant to say it, fearing it'll sound too trite) — it's what gives meaning to my life.

By no means, though, should you now think of me as being one of nature's most torrid lovers. Nor her most diligent. In fact, I must confess that I'm probably one of the laziest lovers Mother Nature ever had. Her Latin names bore me. Rarely do I learn them. Her chemical transformations intrigue me — but never enough to make me want to study them. And her thousands of species — over a thousand different species of trees in North America and more than 5,000 flowering plants and ferns in the northeastern corner of the continent alone — while an admittedly overwhelming panoply — has never once entrapped me into learning them. Again, I'm one of nature's most indolent lovers . . .

. . . Which is precisely why I wrote the sort of book about nature that I did.

* * * * *

The book you now have in your hands is really "*A CHEAP AND LAZY PERSON'S GUIDE TO NATURE*". (My publisher and I chose not to emblazon that title across our front cover, fearing it would alienate all our potential buyers. After all, even now, who among you can overtly admit that he or she's either cheap and/or lazy.) So instead, we euphemistically entitled our book *THE NORTHEASTERN OUTDOORS* and saved our original title for this introduction.

Why the book's a *cheap* person's guide to nature is easy to explain. The final section of our book is an explicit travel guide (with maps, diagrams, and photos) describing well over 100 **free and open-to-the-public** locales — places where nature can still be enjoyed in her most uncorrupted best . . . New Hampshire's White Mountains, with literally hundreds of rare alpine wildflowers atop dozens of four-thousand-foot peaks; or Maine's mountain lakes, with water so crystal clear you can see straight to the sandy bottoms; or New York's Adirondacks, stocked with enough animal and wildlife vegetation to keep any nature lover — lazy or diligent — busy for a lifetime.

Explaining why the book's also *A LAZY PERSON'S GUIDE*, though, is a bit harder task.

It's long been my idea that to appreciate nature you didn't have to exactly **know** her — know her names, her chemistry, or her thousands of species (though none of that sort of knowledge can ever hurt). Rather, appreciating nature has always meant for me the ability to genuinely **see** her — to see her colors, her shapes, her changes. And as a person began to really see nature, I was convinced, then they'd almost automatically begin to know her — to know her formulas, habitats, and patterns. But it was always the **seeing** that was the main ingredient, what always was essential.

Much of this book, therefore, deals with *'how to see nature'* — which was why I began this introduction with an account of my own first glimpses of her. And while the book includes a lot of the sort of information needed for **knowing** nature (information like the ten most common birds, wildflowers, mushrooms, ferns and edible plants), the book's real function is to offer some useful, eccentric, and hopefully mind-expanding hints on how to see the outdoors.

Since most people consider seeing something — anything, a person or a plant — a lot easier than knowing it, I initially decided to call the book *A LAZY PERSON'S GUIDE TO NATURE.* But as I got more and more into the book, that common assumption — that seeing an object is somehow easier than knowing it — began to crumble. So much so, in fact, that by the time the book was completed, I felt the very opposite to be true: that seeing an object may be easy — easier than knowing it. But **really** seeing — seeing "through time" as William Blake once said, is a lifetime pursuit.

Really seeing, I finally came to realize, is really knowing.

Sight is a faculty. Seeing is an art.
—George Perkins Marsh—

Man can not afford to be a naturalist, to look at Nature directly, but only with the side of his eye. He must look through and beyond her.
—Henry David Thoreau—

We pattern life in such a way that never allows us enough time to actually see it. There is continual busyness, continual searching for the next moment. But the point of life is just to see things as they are ... or to see the 'nowness' of the very moment. For when we see the nowness of the very moment, there is no room for anything but openness and peace.

—Chögyam Trungpa—

As a kid, I used to watch fireflies. They'd blink their yellow lights on my parent's porch, and I'd usually just stand around and watch these strange, little luminescent visitors. I remember, too, counting the intervals of time that elapsed between each of their blinks. And I remember that a lot of the time they practically seemed programmed to blink their blinkers once every six seconds. It was the sort of observation a kid sometimes makes out of a moment of boredom. So I used to watch these fireflies — really observing them.

Years later, reading a book about insects, I came across the following paragraph: *"Fireflies flash their signals to one another as a sign that they're ready to mate. But several species may be flashing at one time, posing a problem to a male on the prowl. The way the male can tell, though, that a receptive female is of his own species is by the time interval that elapses between her flashes. One common species flashes at* **six-second intervals** . . . ."

That corroboration of my childhood observations sent warm flutters throughout my body. They were, for sure, small flutters — little moments composed of pride and joy; but they were moments, I knew, that nature had given me for once having observed her so diligently.

"In the universe," Stephen Gaskin, a contemporary how-to/do-it-yourself theologian, has said, *"you always get more of whatever it is you put your attention on."*

20

So paying attention is a lot of what **seeing** nature is all about. But paying attention, unfortunately, isn't quite as easy as it sounds. Try this experiment: Go into the woods, preferably on a clear spring day, and find some colorful flower — say a painted trillium or a small, veined violet. Now sit next to that flower — nestle yourself right up to it — and then start staring at it. And stare at it not for just a minute or two but let's say for ten minutes. That's ten **whole** minutes, ten complete revolutions on your watch's second hand. And really stare at that flower — observe the delicate purplish lines on the petals of the violet, a network of lines as fine as any meticulous pen-and-ink drawing. Or run your eyes across the casual ruffles of the trillium's petals. And as you're observing these flowers, try to simultaneously note just when it is that a mosquito or an enticing bird or a moment of boredom distracts you from your staring.

I suspect that very few people will be able to keep their attention fixed on that flower for our agreed time. In fact, most people, I'd be willing to bet, will probably have lost their concentration in just a matter of seconds — certainly within a minute.

So keeping your concentration affixed to a single object isn't quite as simple as you might have initially expected. In fact, it's probably one of the hardest things we as human beings can ever learn. But it's the very skill that later on will make all of your field trips into nature (as well as into Life) that much more rewarding.

Staring at a flower, incidentally, is an age-old and proven form of mind-control. Medieval Christian monks, sequestered in 'hermetically-sealed' monasteries, as well as ancient Buddhist cave dwellers and Hindu ascetics, all once practiced this very same meditational technique. It's a technique, too, that's still 'flowering' as it were, among the modern-day followers of these various religions.

Observing nature, observing her for extended periods of time, is like living in a new dimension. Things are quieter, slower, clearer here. Soft, subtle, calm. Growth and decay — the two poles between which nature executes her cyclical and varied dance — are never constant. Each sunset is a little different from the one before it; each flower slightly different from its neighbor, each bird — a new form. As you look at nature, as you observe her 'religiously', what you'll be seeing will always be new.

Allow your eyes to be expansive. Try to sometimes look at nature **unitively, holistically** — as one massive conglomeration of interlocking parts. (For truly she is that.) Temporarily suspend your mind's tendency to see things as isolated events, as discrete units, and just let trees-soil-flowers-leaves-clouds all merge together. Or maybe just sit and watch how the leaves of a particular tree arrange themselves to allow in the optimum amount of sunlight on the forest's floor. Or rather than just staring at a small cluster of mushrooms, step back for a moment and allow your eyes to observe what's known as 'Fairy Rings' — those slowly widening circular patterns that some mushrooms form when they're growing over a wide lawn. (The largest 'Fairy Rings' recorded to date have been more than fifty feet across!)

. . . Play with your eyes: Try to use your God-given zoom lens, telephoto lens, and fish-eye lens.

Then sharpen the focus of your eyes and move into a marsh of grasses. Pick up a few of the grass stalks and start observing them. No doubt, some will be tall, with dark stems and pendulous black seeds. Others — a rich silver color. Still others — distended golden plumes. Or maybe just look — and look so scrutinizingly that your eyes can practically feel the waxiness of a buttercup's enameled yellowish color or until your eyes can almost smell the spicy stench of a wild ginger plant.

The idea is really to enlist each of your senses in your appreciation of nature: taste the lemony flavor of a sorrel leaf, touch the smooth, powdery bark of a white birch tree, mush the gummy resin of a pine tree in your hands. Or just close your eyes some night and listen by the side of a pond to the strange, avant-garde orchestrations of the crickets, katydids, frogs, and grasshoppers.

. . . Seeing nature means eating her, smelling her, hearing her, and tasting her. And it means doing each of those things in every combination.

(Remember, too, that field glasses and magnifying glasses are very useful tools, each extending your visual appreciation of the outdoors. And you can usually pick up a pair of cheap binoculars or an inexpensive magnifying glass at some weekend tag-sale or auction.)

Nature knows no "off" season. You shouldn't only walk in the woods on a clear spring day or on a fall morning when the leaves are changing colors. The winter woods, for instance, have a mystery all their own: a cold, clear quietness, with the wind creaking the trunks of the maples, spruces, and firs; and the snow — an undisturbed covering — patterned only with the pawprints of an occasional pine mouse or weasel.

I remember one March morning taking a walk in the foothills of the Catskill Mountains, in upstate New York. It was a particularly sunny day which caused the snow to reflect hundreds of iridescent beads of every imaginable color. It was also a cold day, and I remember stopping near a stream where I noticed that some snow had prematurely begun to melt. Kneeling down, wondering why the winter's snows should be disappearing from just this one spot, I instantly could feel a dramatic change in the temperature. It was maybe twenty degrees hotter at this one spot than anywhere else in the forest. Looking for an explanation, I fortuitously eyed the emerging broad leaves of a skunk cabbage plant — one of the earliest springtime wildflowers. And touching the plant, I could then actually feel gusts of hot air radiating from the skunk cabbage's coiled leaves.

Later that day, after calling every amateur naturalist/ friend I knew, a plausible explanation for the phenomenon was finally given. Skunk cabbage, I was eruditely informed, in the very early spring, begins to convert the starches of its thick taproots into sugar. And that conversion process, it was explained to me, emits relatively large amounts of heat. In effect, the skunk cabbage, as I later read in Richard David's delightful little nature book — *HOW TO TALK TO BIRDS AND OTHER UNCOMMON WAYS OF ENJOYING NATURE THE YEAR ROUND* (Knopf, 1972) — were "small starch-burning stoves" — causing the snows of winter to melt around them.

. . . Every month/day/hour/moment in nature has its own little mysteries, its own beauty. And all any of us ever have to do is make the time and effort to see and appreciate them.

Hopefully, this introductory field and travel guide to the northeastern outdoors will help you to see some of nature's colors, patterns, and shapes. If the book so much as gives you one moment where the miracle of life becomes real for you — where you're momentarily awed by it all — then none of my efforts will have been wasted.

. . . . . Enjoy the book.
And enjoy nature.

And always remember: you and nature are not two, but one.

Hadley, Mass., September, 1976

Steve Berman

Read Nature not books. If you study Nature in books,
when you go out-of-doors you cannot find her.
—Louis Agassiz—

SOME NOTES ON HOW TO USE
THIS FIELD GUIDE

First off, this is a *LAZY Person's Guide to Nature*. So don't expect to find in these pages an exhaustive listing of all the birds, flowers, ferns, and mushrooms of the Northeast. What you will find here, though, besides all the common varieties of wildlife, are lots of off-beat facts — the sort of facts that will make your appreciation of nature something other than blandly scientific.

For example: The structure of a geodisic dome, created by Buckminster Fuller and adopted by hundreds of commune dwellers for their homes, is really the very same as the cell structure of a tiny animal who inhabits the ocean's bottoms. Fuller simply observed the strong molecular structure of this sea creature and then decided to construct his own much enlarged version . . . . Or another similarly eccentric natural tidbit: that the wildflower *smilax herbacea* (its common name being the 'carrion flower') exudes a really raunchy odor in the early springtime — the sort of overpowering dead-mouse smell of decaying flesh. Small flies and insects are consequently allured to this fetid flower . . . . Or that two common wildflowers of the Northeast — *bloodroot* and *hawkweed* — were both aesthetically employed by the American Indians. The orange colored juice of the bloodroot flower was used to paint fierce designs on their warrior's faces, while the hawkweeds (also known as *paintbrushes*) supplied a variety of colors for less military and more artistic activities.

* * * * *

Nature is vast. Too vast for any one person to know all her species. In the Museum of Natural History alone, in New York City, there are well over 11 **million** natural specimens on display — over 800,000 bird skins, more than 3,450,000 insects, and somewhere around 150,000 mammals and reptiles. So just enjoy nature. Enjoy seeing her. But don't, because in the long run it'll ruin it for you, become obsessed with knowing her.

It can never be satisfied, the mind, never.
—Wallace Stevens—

. . . And now onto the birds and the bees.

BIRDS

Bird watchers are pale, emaciated, and bespectacled. They wear baggy safari shorts, high knee socks, and styrofoam pith helmets. And they're usually either decrepit golden-agers or precocious science-fair-winning adolescents.

To be truthful, I have no idea how that stereotype of a bird watcher ever found its way into our American collective unconscious. (But I do suspect that an old, now defunct television show — *The Bob Cummings Show* — was at least partially responsible. The show had an occasional walk-on character — a daffy, British woman who was always clad in a pair of baggy shorts and a styrofoam pith helmet. She carried around a pair of binoculars, and if my twenty-year-old television memories are still intact, her "shtick" was that she birdwatched indoors. A ludicrous character. But very possibly the progenitor of "The Bird Watcher" — that stereotyped and enfeebled nature-lover.)

Now just why bird-watching has received such a bad image is beyond me. As a sport, while it's admittedly tame — not exactly what you'd call a contact sport — it nevertheless does manage to be mildly suspenseful, mildly invigorating, and mildly challenging — everything a sport's supposed to be. It even has its national heroes — Ludlow Griscom, the greatest of the field identifiers and Roger Tory Peterson, our own modern-day Audubon. And it also has its own very carefully kept world records: 497 still standing as the greatest number of North American birds ever seen by a single person in a single year, and 131 being the most species ever seen within a 15-mile radius on a winter day.

But what really makes 'birding' so challenging — challenging in the way a solitary game of golf is challenging — is what's known as a 'life list'. This is a compilation of every bird species a birdwatcher has ever watched. And understandably, by the time someone's in the four or five hundred life-list bracket, any new bird added to their list is an event as orgasmic as say a hole-in-one.

As a beginner, you should be content with a life-list of roughly a dozen common birds. And in the process of becoming familiar with just a few of these more common species, you'll also be developing the skills — patience and a focused attention — that'll later be necessary for racking up a five-hundred life-list tally. **But start off slowly.** Fanatics, it's been my experience, tend to burn-out quickly.

Besides watching birds, you can also feed them. (I usually serve my winged customers white millet, a cheap and abundant grain.) And you can also paint birds, record them, study their nests, or simply listen to them. Listening to birds, in fact — actually trying to decipher their language — today occupies hundreds of amateur and professional ornithologists. I even know of some birders so attuned to the various bird songs that they can pinpoint just where they are by simply listening and then noting the regional differences in a meadowlark's song.

Cornell University offers an album entitled "*An Evening in Sapsucker Woods*". It's a long-playing record consisting of more than twenty well-recorded bird songs. As an introduction to bird listening, it's a must. For a copy, write: Laboratory of Ornithology, 159 Sapsucker Woods Rd., Ithaca, New York 14850.

And the nicest thing about birds is that wherever you are — a foreign country, a remote island, or just a wintry city — there'll always be some birds around for you to listen to, feed, paint, watch, or record. (If, however, for some reason you can't find any birds, try playing your bird call record on a portable tape machine out in the woods. I guarantee flocks of curious birds will fly over to see just what in the woods is going on.)

1. ROBIN

It seems as if robins are social climbers. The last one I saw was swimming at Newport, bathing himself in an expensive marble bird-bath. (No doubt, he winters in Palm Beach.) These are very common and very friendly birds, about ten inches long — as measured from the tip of their bill to the tip of their tail.

2. ENGLISH SPARROW

As Roger Tory Peterson in his *Field Guide to The Birds* — the birder's bible — says of the English Sparrow, "it's distributed widely about civilization". Now I don't know quite why but there's something vaguely and cosmically comforting about a bird that's 'distributed widely about civilization'. It almost makes the world sound like some small, friendly farm community. (The English Sparrow, incidentally, isn't really a sparrow at all. It's actually a weaver finch.)

3. STARLING

Along with the appropriately named mockingbirds, the yellow-billed starlings are the 'Rich Littles' of the bird community. They can perfectly imitate the songs of nearly a half-a-dozen other species. And these starlings, of all the other black-colored birds — grackles, cowbirds, and rusty blackbirds — are the only ones with yellow bills.

1

2

3

4

5

6

7
8
9

4. BLUE JAY

Larger than a robin and much larger than a bluebird (which is about the size of a sparrow and has a distinguishing reddish breast), the Blue Jay has a really harsh cry — a jeering **jay** sound. With its sky-blue plumage, this bird is easy to identify in the field.

5. CROW

At dusk, in long lines, great flocks of crows can be seen moving across the sky, heading for their favorite roosting areas. (The expression — 'as the crow flies' — no doubt derives from this linear pattern of their flight.) These are large, all-black birds, about nineteen inches long. "Scarecrows", of course, are built to *scare crows* out of cornfields and gardens.

6. BALTIMORE ORIOLE

This orange-and-black intensely hued bird looks more like some tropical species than one of our own pedestrian northeasterners. (The gregarious oriole does, in fact, winter in Central America.) The females of this species, by weaving plant fibers and grasses, are the builders of those remarkably sturdy hanging nests, nests that somehow stay intact on bare, ice-encrusted tree branches all winter long.

7. GREAT BLUE HERON

Here's the tallest of all our native birds, standing about four-feet high. When the herons' young are developing, the areas near where they nest resemble New York City's Lower East Side; they're crowded, noisy, and smelly. (The smells are the result of the decaying remains of infertile eggs, food particles, and various wastes.) But since I've always managed to enjoy walking around New York's Lower East Side, being in eye-shot distance of one of these fetid and frantic heron communities is one of my more perverse outdoor pleasures.

8.   HERRING GULL

More commonly called the "Sea Gull", this two-to-three-foot-long coastal bird breeds from the Arctic all the way down to Long Island. I've watched sea gulls and listened to their querulous shrieks for hours at a time. They're probably the easiest of all the birds to inspect at close range — excepting, of course, for the domesticated city pigeon.

(Franklin Russell's *THE SEA HAS WINGS* — E. P. Dutton Co., 1975 — a book about all the Northeast's seabirds, has to be one of the most magical and inspired nature books around. As a poetical introduction to all the coastal birds, this book is unsurpassed.)

9.   PURPLE MARTINS

Americans, especially New Englanders, have long been trying to make the Purple Martin a permanent resident. Since Martins are insect eaters — and that means eaters of noisome mosquitoes — people have constructed elaborate bird houses hoping to interest these birds in northeastern real estate. Unfortunately, too often have sparrows and starlings (definitely lower-class birds) moved into these homes, quickly transforming a martin neighborhood into a trashy slum.

10.   LOON

Up in the "North Country", while canoeing along the glassy surface of some Maine lake, you'll probably hear the utterly insane cry of the loon; a high, strange sound that the Cree Indians used to think was the cry of a dead warrior — a warrior who was forbidden entry to Heaven. Our expression — a *loony bird* — meaning someone who's not quite all there, originates with this nutty-sounding bird. Loons are fish eaters, but unlike many water birds they don't go after their seafood platters by merely skimming along the water's surface. Rather, these birds dive, submarine-like, hundreds of feet beneath the water's surface — their wings tucked rigidly against their bodies, their feet frantically paddling away — and then dine on either young salmon or trout. At the end of one of their foraging dives, a loon can have as many as *fifteen* trout in its stomach.

11. BALD EAGLE

Though the Bald Eagle certainly isn't a "common" bird, the fact that it's America's national emblem — its talons clutching an olive branch and thirteen sharpened arrows on every U.S. dollar bill — makes it hard to ignore.

Bald Eagles mate for life and they cling tenaciously to their nesting sites; which is just about right for how the American Dream is supposed to operate. But the fact that these birds rob smaller birds of their food is, depending on your politics, either a very accurate or a terribly inaccurate symbol for how our American foreign policy has been operating these past few years.

That the bird is on its way to extinction, though — and this, regardless of your politics — is hopefully not at all symbolic of America's future.

A WORD ON ENDANGERED SPECIES

As we all begin to look at nature more carefully and more lovingly, hopefully we'll all begin to look more seriously at the abuses we've caused her. In the U.S. alone, in the past fifty years, over **50** native American animal species have been obliterated. In just a little more than a century, we've exterminated 5 **billion** passenger pigeons. And bisons, once numbering in the tens of millions, were so brutally and methodically slaughtered that today only a few dozen of just one species remains. The list of endangered species is today distressingly long: the Great Blue Whale, Polar Bears, Northern Swift Fox, Mexican Grizzly Bear, Giant Otter, Vicuna, Whooping Crane, California Condor, Red Wolf, Kabib Squirrel, Alligators, American Egrets, Bald Eagles, Ospreys. And the list, unfortunately, doesn't even stop there.

The brutal slaughtering of thousands of birds and animals by trophy-crazed murderers (no longer do many of them deserve the appellation 'hunter'), the promiscuous and deleterious use of insecticides, our fume-spewing automobiles, this society's consumptive penchant for furs, alligator shoes, whale oil perfumes, and fancy bird plumage, and a morality that puts profit before life — are all threatening to kill off every one of our natural resources — our fish, mammals, birds, wildflowers, and insects. By the year 2000, some of our more Doomsday conservationists have predicted, we'll all be left with "a world where polluted continents and oceans are the almost exclusive domain of men, livestock, and rats."

As each of us begins to get closer to nature— as we all actually start to see and love her — hopefully no longer will we be able to abuse and exploit her. She **is** us. And destroying her, we must begin to see, is simply our own global suicide.

BEES

(Insects)

The insect does not belong to our world. The other animals, the plants even, notwithstanding their dumb life and the secrets which they cherish, do not seem wholly foreign to us. In spite of all, we feel a certain earthly brotherhood in them. They often surprise and amaze our intelligence, but do not utterly upset it. There is something, on the other hand, about the insect that does not seem to belong to the habits, the ethics, the psychology of our globe.
—Maurice Maeterlinck—

Maeterlinck's words are really a somewhat orotund way of saying that insects are "creepy" — scary, little outcasts that Creation could have done without. Yet these bizarre, *six-leggeds* (a number of American Indian tribes used to call human beings "two-leggeds", animals "four-leggeds", and insects "six-leggeds") are, despite their essential 'creepiness', the most visible form of life on earth — in both the number of existing species (over a half-a-million!) and in the number of individuals. (Canadian entomologists have estimated the world's insect population to be 1,000,000,000,000,000,000: now assuming the weight of each of these insects is a not unreasonable 2.5 milligrams — which is less than one ten-thousandth of an ounce — then the total weight of the earth's insect population exceeds **by a factor of twelve** the total weight of all its human inhabitants.)

As a group of fauna, the insects are probably the most interesting to study. If you're a 'name freak' — someone who's narrowly content to know only the names (and not the habits) of nature's flora and fauna — then the insects, being so preponderant a life form, are ideal. But it's really the thoroughly weird, almost science fiction-like habits and life styles of many of these insects that makes them so singular. These are truly strange, little creatures. Nature's bizarrest.

For instance — during winter, honeybees gather into great golden balls in their hives, and there the bees in the interior of the ball begin a ritualized dance — a dance that serves to radiate heat throughout the circular mass. The bees on the outside of the ball eventually get to exchange places with the interior dancing bees — thus insuring an adequate winter heating supply for everyone.

Or a number of insects nightly find room and board in flowers (like poppies) that close their petals at sundown. In addition to being protected from the damp, the temperatures within these enclosed blooms are often higher and more comfortable than the outside air.

Or ants communicate to one another by tapping on each other's antennas. And a slightly becrazed German scientist actually spent his life compiling an "Ant Dictionary" — offering his speculations on just what these different tapping-patterns meant.

Or certain wasps, a husband-and-wife team of entomologists have ascertained, employ landmarks when flying home. (The wasps got lost when their landmarks were removed.)

Or unlike birds, whose wings move in a rowing motion, an insect's wings, when in motion, form elongated figure-eights. Aerodynamically speaking, insects are incredibly sophisticated. Their flight techniques — which in some cases even includes the ability to fly *backwards* — makes the most complex manned flights seem trivial.

Or a number of insects, among them the common monarch butterfly, will actually feign death for long periods of time in order to ward off predators.

Or some insects, like the appropriately named "bombardeer beetle", when threatened, will spew jets of a repelling, foul-smelling gas.

Or finally, a housefly (and this is one of those classic and mind-blowing facts naturalists love to tell) who originally laid only about 100 eggs at the beginning of a summer, could, under ideal conditions, be the progenitor of an eight generation housefly clan by the end of that very same summer. And an eight generation clan of houseflies would include somewhere around *1,875,000,000,000* adult members.

. . . It's these sort of eccentric habits of the various insects that makes studying them so fascinating.

Stephen Dalton's photographic work, exhibited in *BORNE ON THE WIND — THE EXTRAORDINARY WORLD OF INSECTS IN FLIGHT* — Reader's Digest Press, 1975 — is a classic. Color plates of green lacewings doing their balletic loop maneuvers, of rhododendron leafhoppers soaring Nureyev-like through space, and of mythic, positively extraworldly-looking desert locusts readying for flight — all take you powerfully and surreally into the strange and quiet world of insects. Unfortunately, (but justifiably because of the production costs), the book is practically prohibitively priced at $18.50. I strongly suggest, though, spending a few mind-boggling hours with *BORNE ON THE WIND* at your local public library.

SOME COMMON INSECTS OF THE NORTHEAST (AND SOME UNCOMMON ESOTERICA ABOUT THEM)

1.   MAY FLY

There are approximately 550 species of May Flies on the North American Continent. And truly, these are weird members of the insect fauna: they never eat, their life spans rarely exceed 24 hours, and their mating rituals are about as uptight as a bunch of twelve-year-olds playing "Spin The Bottle". Like human beings, they often mate at dances — really swarms — where all the males huddle together (again like human beings) and salaciously wait for a few intrepid females to step forward. Once on the dance floor, these females are quickly seized and are then even more quickly escorted away from the crowd by some of the more rakish males. A strange nuptial dance — one whose efficacy, though, can't be denied: these May Flies are among the most numerous insects in the Northeast.

1
2
3
4

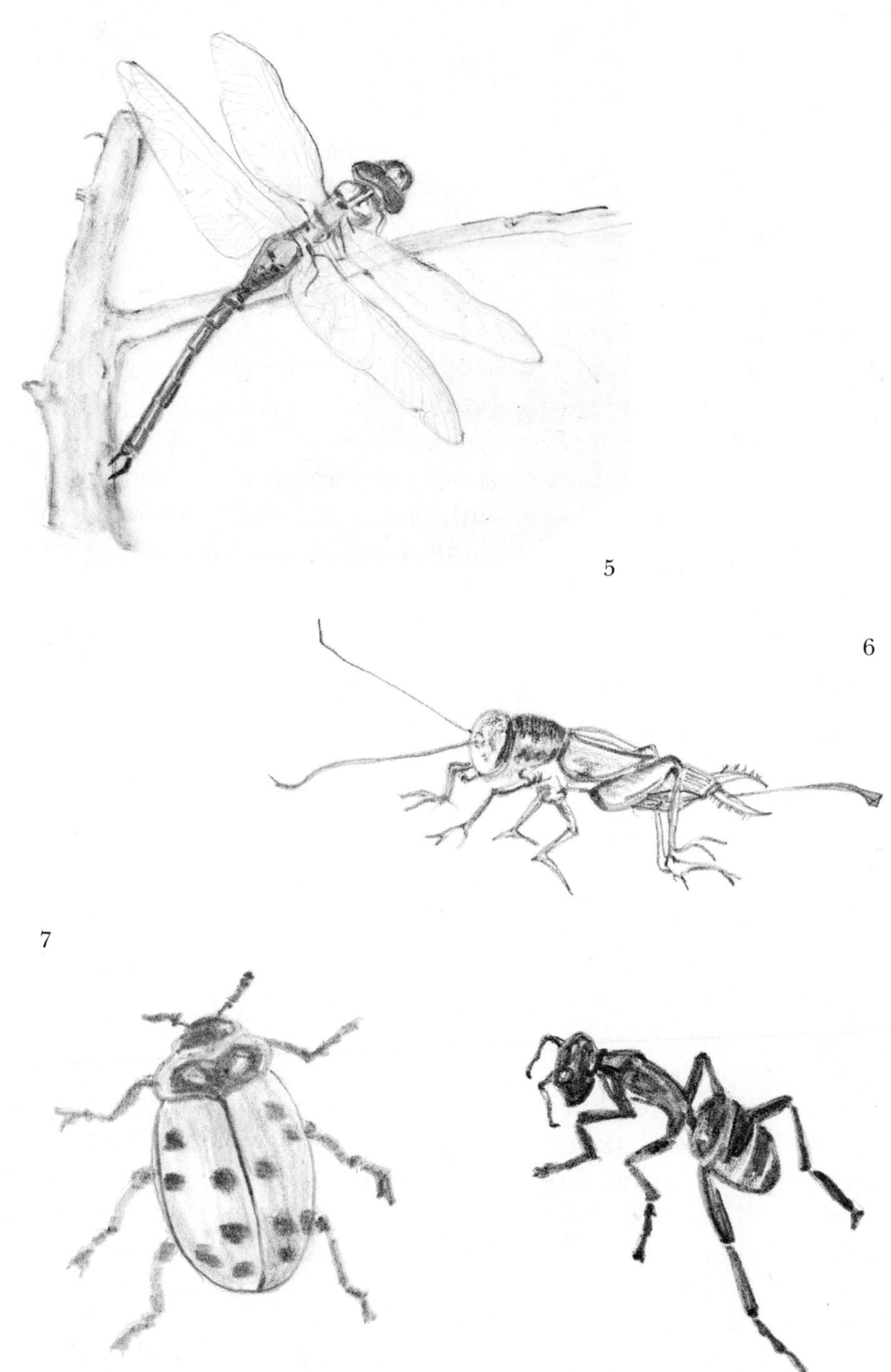

5

6

7

8

2. HOUSEFLY

Every forest, butcher shop, pizza parlor, and picnic table has, as unwelcomed guests, too many of these all-black and consummately creepy Houseflies. From Man's standpoint, Houseflies are thoroughly unredeeming creatures. A single Housefly, in fact, can offer free transportation to as many as **6 million** disease-causing germs. And the pathogens of such dreaded diseases as amoebic dysentery, typhoid fever, leprosy, gangrene, and bubonic plague have all been carried on the bodies of these filth-loving Houseflies.

Houseflies are equipped with six hairy legs which terminate in feet outfitted both with claws and sticky pads. These pads, which excrete a glutinous fluid, are what enables the Housefly to walk upside-down along window panes and ceilings. Grossest of all the Housefly's traits, though, is its table manners. In order to eat, it has to first soften its food; a digestive maneuver it disgustingly accomplishes by regurgitating the fluids of a previously digested meal into whatever victuals it wants to eat. . . . . . Truly *the creepiest* of all the insects.

3. MONARCH BUTTERFLY

If the Housefly is the garbage-picking, regurgitating derelict of the insect fauna, then the Monarch Butterfly is its much adored prince. And the story of the Monarch's birth and maturation is probably one of nature's most princely tales. From eggs that resemble tinted dewdrops, to striped caterpillars that regally feast day and night on the cells and tissues of Milkweed — a wildflower common to the Northeast, to a rich green-colored, silken chrysallis that looks like one of the family jewels, the black-and-orange winged Monarch Butterfly finally emerges. This dramatic metamorphosis — from a bland caterpillar into a butterfly whose wings resemble the intensely hued stained-glass windows of a medieval church — is, as one naturalist has remarked, "about the best proof for the existence of God I know."

Like the female-attracting fancy plumage and the melodic songs of many male birds, all male Monarchs come into the world with an equally alluring trait — a smell that resembles the perfume of a faraway honeysuckle. And equally ingenious is how the Monarch protects itself from predacious birds. It simply has a horrible tasting and nauseating blood that no bird would ever go after. (Another butterfly, the Viceroy, though it has no bird-repelling blood, shrewdly manages to avoid being preyed upon because its wings look like the Monarch's.)

Monarchs are among the few insects that migrate in the winter, often covering over a thousand miles in one of their annual southerly jaunts. Travelling in flocks — flocks that sometimes are over **a mile** across — these butterflies leave New England, follow a path along the outer coastal reaches of Long Island, and then finally cross over to the New Jersey mainland. (This, incidentally, is the identical route taken by many of the Northeast's migrating birds.)

4. SPIDER

Spiders really aren't insects. They belong to the class of animals known as *Arachnids,* which also includes scorpions and "daddy-long-legs". The fact that spiders have four pairs of legs technically excludes them from the *six-leggeds* or the insects.

It's the silken, geometric webs woven by spiders and used to ensnare their prey (though not all species of spiders weave webs) that are among nature's most lauded wonders. And it's the orb-webs or cart-wheel webs — those mandala-like constructions that glint with droplets of dew in the early morning — that have received the most attention. Unlike butterflies and moths whose silk factories are located in their mouths, spiders have their silk-producing 'spinnerets' attached to the hind end of their abdomens.

What's really so fascinating about the spider's silken web — besides its symmetrical design — is the utterly stealthy way in which it's employed. The common Garden Spider (recognizable by the white cross on its brown back) will usually leave the web's hub during the day and retreat to a nearby hide-out. Always attached to one or two of its forelegs, though, will be a silk signal-thread that runs from the hub of the web to its hide-out. And any victim who lands in the web will have to jingle the signal thread, immediately bringing the Garden Spider to the web's center. Then, by meticulously wrapping its prey in a swathe of silk, the spider, after a successful capture will move quickly along the threads of its web, anxious only to return to its hide-out for a leisurely supper.

5.   DRAGONFLY

Every year the mature Dragonfly competes with the butterflies and moths in my private "Ms. Nature Pageant". Along with the *Damseflies* — which are simply smaller and more fragile dragonflies — these sleek, glowing-eyed, rainbow-colored creatures always take the pageant's 'swim suit competition'. And for their little talent-revealing skit (can you surreally imagine Bert Parks, Miss America's chronic emcee, introducing amidst a drum roll and an ensuing suspenseful hush, the three remaining insects in the "Ms. Insect Pageant") the Dragonflies will perform their ooh-and-ah-eliciting aerobatics. Of all the insects, these are perhaps the most skilled flyers. With their veined and transparent wings — wings that may vibrate as many as 1600 times a minute — these barnstorming pilots can outdistance swallows, execute exotic loop patterns, and if they really want to win the "Ms. Insect Pageant" they can give the judges a look at their perennial show-stopper — flying backwards for five non-stop minutes.

6.   CRICKETS

The glistening black field cricket, whose body is between three-fifths of an inch and one inch long, is the Northeast's most popular twilight serenader. Only the males produce the cricket's characteristic shrill chirps, chirps heard so frequently near a grassy field or a marshy pond. These mating calls are the result of a roughened, file-like vein on the underside of the cricket's wing that's rubbed by a small scraper attached to the wing's upper side. And just how engrossed these insects become in making their music is often dependent upon the weather. In warm weather, they'll blow all night. But on cool nights, their style is to uninterruptedly "take five".

7. LADYBIRD BEETLE

Beetles, with more than 26,500 species in North America, are by far the most widely distributed of all the insects. And Ladybird Beetles, also called Ladybugs, would, if some civic organization were to offer a 'good insect samaritan award', be the hands-down recipient. These bespeckled beetles consume all varieties of noxious agricultural pests — including plant lice, potato beetle eggs, and scale insects.

Ladybugs, from Man's vantage point, have always been the least creepiest of all the insects. In colonial America, in fact, a ladybug living in your house was considered a good luck charm. In Central Europe, too, young girls, by letting ladybugs crawl along their palms, were supposedly increasing their chances for marriage. And some pioneer Americans even felt that if you ever came across a seven-spotted ladybug, you could crush it, stuff it into your teeth, and thereby relieve an aching toothache.

8.   ANTS

When we consider the habits of ants — their social organization, their large communities, and elaborate habitations; and even, in some cases, their taking of slaves, it must be admitted that they have a fair claim to rank next to Man in the scale of intelligence.

—John Lubbock, 1881—

Along with the honeybees, ants probably have the most complex social order of any of the insects. Their colonies — really vast underground cities — are matriarchical societies: the Queen Ants being regally catered to by both the males and neuter workers. (Where bees have only one queen per hive, ants have several.)

Smell, or what H. G. Wells called *"the patriotism of smell"*, is what keeps an ant colony together. The sensitive olfactory organs located on their antennas are what enables ants to recognize the members of their own species.

As with human beings, ruthless intercolonial wars are popular with ants. Red Ants will often viciously attack the fortresses of Black Ants, hoping to capture the Black Ant's maturing pupae or young ones. If triumphant, these Red Ants will march home trundling hundreds of cocoons filled with young Black Ants. Once mature, these Black Ants are then disciplined into becoming the slaves of the Red Ants — the rest of these Black Ants' lives spent gathering food and cleaning the colonies of their captors.

FLOWERS

(Wildflowers, Ferns, Grasses)

America's wildflowers, like America's people, are almost all immigrants — and only a very small handful of our common wildflowers — *asters, goldenrods, milkweed,* and *robin's plantain* — deserve to be called native northeasterners. The rest — *daisies, clover, Queen Anne's Lace, hawkweed, chicory,* and the common *dandelion* — arrived here from Europe, then quickly put down their roots into America's welcoming and fertile soil.

Immigrants traditionally settle near where they "get off the boat". My own grandfather, a turn-of-the-century Russian emigré, for example, settled near the docks of Lower Manhattan. Similarly, flowering immigrants will usually establish themselves around wharves, railroad embankments, and roadsides — wherever it is they happen to land.

Historically, these wildflowers, in the convenient forms of stowaway seeds, made their transatlantic journeys either in the stomachs of cows (who were being fed old country, home-grown fodder during their eighteenth-century sea-crossing voyages), or in some hay-packed cargo shipment (or maybe even in the cuffs of my grandfather's overalls). These seeds all arrived 'strangers in a strange land'; but like many young and enterprising immigrants, they were soon flourishing in the new world.

Indian paintbrushes — a small, orange, dandelion-like flower and *purple loosestrife* — another common, magenta-pink marsh dweller, both came to America under the roguish alibis of being choice garden flowers. But just when everyone thought these two rakish foreigners had been domesticated, they jumped every garden fence and escaped as "pioneers" into the wilderness; there to live wildly ever after.

There are around 5,000 species of flowering plants and ferns growing in the Northeast. Of these, almost 1,300 of the more common ones are described in Roger Tory Peterson's *A FIELD GUIDE TO THE WILDFLOWERS* (Houghton Mifflin Company). It's by far the clearest and simplest of all the identification manuals. Whereas some of the more academic botanical texts — *GRAY'S MANUAL OF BOTANY* and *THE NEW BRITTON AND BROWN ILLUSTRATED FLORA* — are occasionally useful in their exactitude, it's Peterson's guidebook (which is organized by color, and not by some arcane morphological system) that's best for beginners.

Immigrants, of course, never have it easy. They often have to populate areas where the more established natives won't or can't live. Consequently, many of our naturalized wildflowers are today found in such unlikely places as dump-heaps, roadside ditches, barnyards, gardens, and cultivated fields — all places where our more aristocratic native flowers wouldn't even deign to visit, much less live.

THE SPRING WILDFLOWERS

1. BLUETS

The smallest of the pasture wildflowers, bluets have a delicate pale blue bloom and usually form large clusters in the early spring. *Innocence, Quaker Ladies, Nuns,* and *Blue-eyed babies* are all local names for this ubiquitous vernal flower.

2. TRILLIUM

The leaves, petals, and sepals of all the **trilliums** (painted trillium, red trillium, prairie trillium, and sessile trillium) are always in whorls of 3. The large, parallel-veined leaves also tell you that this woods dweller is a member of the lily family.

3. WOOD AND RUE ANEMONE

Both of these members of the Buttercup family (a family characterized by an abundant amount of stamens and pistils that form bushy clusters in the flowers' innards) are whitish in color. Wood anemone closes its five petal-like sepals at night, whereas rue anemone keeps its six (and sometimes eight or ten) sepals open. Sepals are the tiny, modified leaves near the rim of a flower, usually located behind the petals. To see sepals, along with all the other small parts of a wildflower, a magnifying glass is helpful.

4. WOODLAND HEPATICA

Richard Cabot, describing the sometimes purple woodland hepatica, wrote: *"the white ends of its stamens shining against its purple cup, like stars in a summer night."* Stamens and pistils, of course, are a flower's genitalia.

1

2

3

The ancient Athenians used the common blue violet as a medicinal tea. It was believed to "moderate anger", "procure sleep", and to "comfort and strengthen the heart". Pliny, the Roman naturalist, encyclopediast, and writer, was convinced that if a garland of these violets was worn about the head, a hangover could be avoided. And the ancient Brittons, by steeping violets in goat's milk, concocted a 'guaranteed-to-make-you-look-ten-years-younger' facial cream.

4

5

SUMMER WILDFLOWERS

6.   QUEEN ANNE'S LACE

Umbrels are umbrellalike flower clusters. And it's the decorative umbrels of Queen Anne's Lace that gives this flower its name. I've been told that back in eighteenth-century England, women used to adorn their dinner tables with the flattened heads of these 'wild carrots' — this flower's other common name. And not surprisingly, the roots of these wild carrots are edible.

7.   DAISIES

During July and August there's hardly a field or roadside not exhibiting the common ox-eye daisy. With its yellow disc depressed in the center, and all its thin white petals, this summer wildflower is hard to miss.

8.   BLACK-EYED SUSAN

Unlike most of our European "immigrants", Black-Eyed Susans arrived to the Northeast via the grasslands of the West. I've seen its yellow flowers on thin stems sometimes as high as three feet. Its *chocolate*-colored center disc makes its 'black-eye' a slight misnomer.

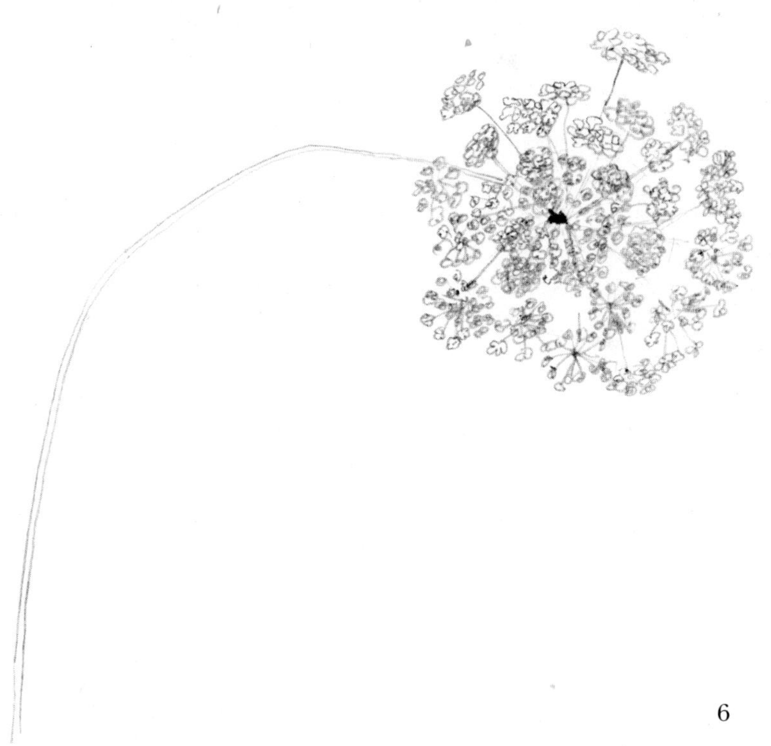

6

7

8

FALL WILDFLOWERS

9.   GOLDENROD

According to *GRAY'S MANUAL OF BOTANY* there are more than 130 different types of goldenrods growing in the Northeast. In the fall, the polleny yellow goldenrods become alfresco nectar bars, with bees and migrating monarch butterflies spending entire afternoons boozing away on them.

10.   ASTERS

GRAY lists more than 150 of these fall bloomers. Many of them are violet-blue and all of them, being in the Daisy family, have flower heads that are actually clusters of small flowers growing together.

9

10

MOUNTAIN FLORA

The flora on any mountain range, because of the varied climatic conditions atop a 4,000 foot peak, comprise a thoroughly distinct sphere of nature. In fact, there are botanists who only study these 'alpine' regions.

It's a lilliputian realm, this above treeline region: bright green and rust colored mosses, yellow crusty lichens (which are actually two unrelated plants — an alga and a fungus — living in a mutually supporting union), slender-branched horsetails, ancient clubmosses, aquatic quillworts, and dozens of ferns, grasses, and sedges. All these in addition to the more than 250 common alpine wildflowers. A book that's useful when studying the botany of these alpine zones is the Appalachian Mountain Club publication entitled *MOUNTAIN FLOWERS OF NEW ENGLAND.*

The words *botanist, ornithologist,* and *zoologist* are all fairly common. But how many people know what a *pteridephist* is? Chances are only a ten-thousand-paged dictionary would be able to define it. So to relieve what I hope isn't an already too rapidly mounting suspense, a pteridephist (or a pteridologist) is someone who studies ferns.

Ferns, as Boughton Cobb, the greatest of the pteridephists once commented *"are the perfect examples of the architectonic design found in plants"*. Which in other and more contemporary words means that the geometry of a fern is mind-blowing. And while there are about 10,000 species of ferns listed for the world, someone could learn about 100 of them and thereby know almost all of the species that are common to the Northeast.

I've included illustrations of five of our region's most common ferns: the polypody, spinulose woodfern, Lady-fern, Long Beech fern, and the Bracken. And hopefully this brief introduction to both the ferns and the other smaller inhabitants of the forest (the lichens, mosses, and quillworts) will start you looking at these less conspicuous floral coverings.

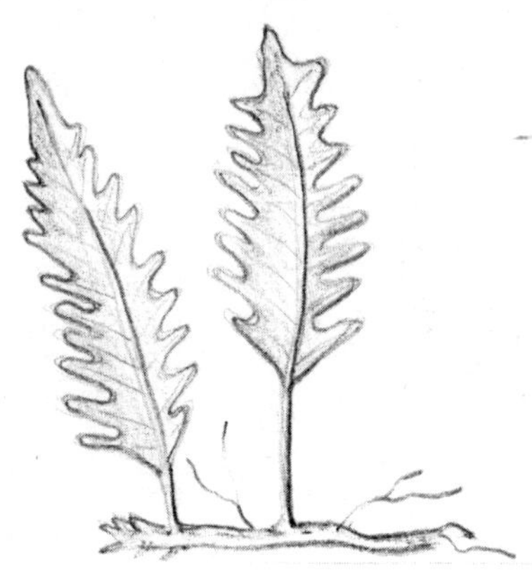

1. POLYPODY

2. SPINULOSE WOODFERN

3. LADY-FERN

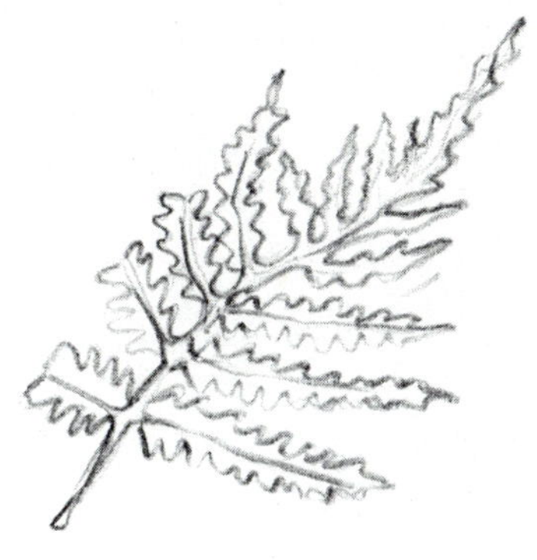

4. LONG BEECH FERN

5. BRACKEN

One more thing: If cultivated eccentricity is your thing, then do what my most cultivatedly eccentric friend once did. He listed his name in the Yellow Pages under "Pteridephist". (An old woman once called him, asking him how much he'd charge to remove a foot wart. She apparently confused pteridephist with podiatrist.)

TREES

(AND SOME COMMON SHRUBS)

The Northeast's landscape is actually a "treescape"; with more than seventy-five per cent of its land being covered with trees. And while there are approximately 1,100 species of trees growing on the North American continent, a familiarity with just a dozen of the more common species is really all the beginning tree-gazer needs to know.

There's a universal experience all of us undergoes when we're outdoors. As we stand atop a mountain or by the shores of some tortuous river, our imaginations inevitably wonder — 'what was it all like before *McDonald's* golden arches got here'. Or maybe our phraseology is — 'what did the first white settlers see when they finally stepped off their transatlantic boats'. Or, in recent years, a more popular phrasing has been 'what did it all look like when just the Indians lived here'. But, regardless of the wording, there's something in all of us that yearns for that pristine state of nature — for that vision of nature before she was ever exploited and corrupted. But without a vivid imagination, I'm afraid that yearning can never really be fully satisfied in the Northeast: too many men and too much greed has simply lived here too long.

Consequently, the woodlands and forests we see today as we zoom along the Northeast's interstate highways are almost all of recent vintage. Ruefully, only a very few stands of virgin forest remain in the Northeast. In another section of this book I include some of the precious few areas where century-old trees still stand.

So the Northeast's landscape has and continues to be a kaleidoscopic treescape. Pine, hemlock, cedar, and spruce — the *evergreens* — often and quickly establish themselves on land that formerly was used for pasturing animals. And especially in New England, where dairy farming has just about had its day and where ravaging nineteenth-century lumbering techniques were popular, have expansive stands of red cedar, white pine, and spruce flourished.

Nothing in nature, though, is permanent. And in time these evergreens, too, lose their heartiness; being destroyed by either sweeping fires, lumbermen, insect plagues, hurricanes, or money-crazed bulldozers (as they carve out the blueprints for some suburban heaven). Young oaks, maples, beeches, and birches — the *deciduous* or *hardwood* trees (trees that annually shed their leaves) — then take over the land.

The dance of the Northeast's treescape is an ongoing and complex choreography; its movements forever being affected by such factors as climate, soil, water availability, and the schemes and plans of men.

Every forest, then, that you'll be seeing in the Northeast is in some stage of recovery — is at some point in its own evolutionary transformation. Some forests, mainly those in southern New England and New York State, will be predominantly of oak and hickory. Others, in slightly more northern regions, will be populated with birch, beech, sugar maple and white pine. Still others, located in the northernmost sections of Maine, New Hampshire, and Vermont, will almost exclusively be of spruce and balsam fir. Very few forests, however, will ever be homogeneously inhabited by just a single species.

THE CONIFERS

These are the needle-leaved, cone-bearing evergreens — often (and sometimes mistakenly) called the "softwoods". "Hardwoods" or *deciduous* trees, being the other major grouping of trees, all have broad leaves (leaves that shed every autumn). The hard sugar maple and the birch are both trees with hard wood. Likewise, the white pine and the hemlock both have genuinely soft wood. But, and this is where some confusion may arise, there are some "soft-woods" whose wood is actually harder than some of the so-called "hardwoods"; and conversely, there are some "hardwoods" whose wood is quite a bit softer than many of the "softwoods".

1

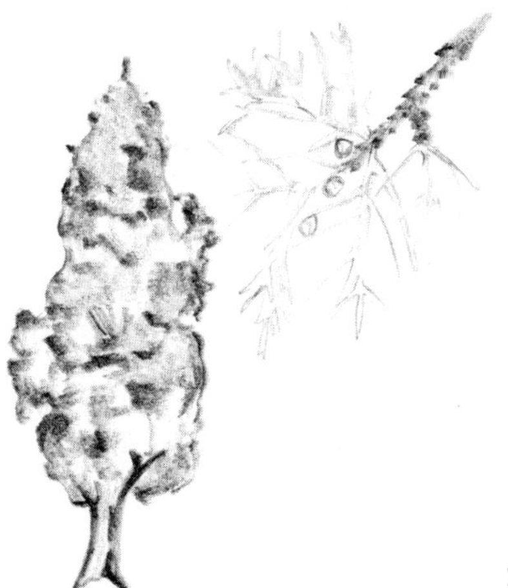
2

3

4

5

1.   THE WHITE PINE

White Pine, found throughout the Northeast but most commonly sited in central New England, has an interesting historical significance. Back in the 1600's, the British Navy wanted to use all of America's largest pines for their ships' masts. These trees, being light, durable, and reaching heights exceeding 150 feet, made perfect shipbuilding materials. As a result, an official decree issued by the King of England made it illegal for any colonist to cut down any pine tree whose diameter was greater than 24 inches. No doubt, the resentments this proscription generated amongst the early colonists helped fuel the desire for American independence.

To help you differentiate pine trees from some of the other conifers, just keep in mind that the needles of a pine tree are always in clusters or bundles — bundles consisting of anywhere from 2 to 5 needles.

In *THE MAINE WOODS*, the account of his journey to the north country, Henry David Thoreau remarked about the already begun lumbering of the mammoth white pines: *"It's as if individual speculators were allowed to export the clouds out of the sky, or the stars out of the firmament, one by one."*

2.   RED CEDAR

These are the trees used to make aromatic "cedar closets" and "cedar chests". In the more southerly regions of the Northeast, it's very often these red cedars that first appear in a neglected pasture. (As you head a bit farther north, however, it's the white pine that becomes the first pasture infiltrator.) Along with the pitch pine — another northeastern conifer — the red cedar is the most common tree to be found on Cape Cod, Massachusetts' southeastern beach area.

3.   RED SPRUCE

Spruce needles are usually short, slightly curving, fairly stiff, sharp-pointed, and are always and thoroughly covering the trees' extended branchlets. This needle analysis is what you'll need in order to differentiate the spruces from the hemlocks and firs — two other common northeastern conifers. Spruces, like the red cedar in New York-Connecticut, and like the white pine in Massachusetts-southern New Hampshire, is the tree that first invades an abandoned field in northern New Hampshire-Maine. Along with fir, about one-fifth of the entire land mass of Vermont, New Hampshire, and Maine is a solid spruce-evergreen forest.

Spruce, too, is the pulp industry's main tree. Huge piles of these small logs can be seen waiting to be processed all throughout northwestern Maine.

Where evergreens or conifers predominate the treescape, offering year-round shade to the forest floor, sun-loving wildflowers simply won't thrive. More often than not it's in these evergreen forests where mosses, ferns, and Indian Pipes (those bizarre and slender chlorophylless flowers that resemble a cluster of inverted calumets) will grow. And conversely, in the hardwood forests, which have only a smattering of evergreens and where the sun is better able to penetrate, the forest's undergrowth will include many of the more flowery plants — e.g., bunchberries, dogwoods, clintonias, and an occasional Lady's Slipper.

4. BALSAM FIR

The Balsam Fir is our common and redolent 'Christmas Tree'. The tree very much resembles a spruce, making it difficult for beginners to tell the two trees apart. But the easiest way to differentiate them is by examining their seed-bearing cones. The cones of all the firs will be growing upright along the branches; whereas the cones of the spruces always grow downwards.

Spruce-Fir forests are common in northern New England. But since both these trees are fairly thin-barked (and because none of the conifers, excepting pitch pine, can regenerate from just their stumps), tens of thousands of acres of evergreen forests have been destroyed by fires. The last great holocaust, back in 1947, destroyed more than 17,000 acres of spruce, white pine, and fir in the Bar Harbor region of Maine. Today, the hills of this coastal area are covered with a much less spectacular tree growth — a scraggly covering of birch, poplar, and wild cherry.

5. HEMLOCK

This is probably the most common and easiest tree to identify in the entire Northeast. The approximately ½″ long needles that spread out from both sides of the branchlets (see illustration) gives the Hemlock's leaf spray its characteristic "flat" appearance.

DECIDUOUS TREES

The deciduous or broad-leaved trees of the Northeast can be conveniently divided into two general groupings: the *Oak and Hickory forests*, which appear primarily in the southernmost regions of the Northeast, and the *Northern Hardwood Forests*, being composed mainly of birch, beech, and maple trees. While there is an overlapping of the two groups, separating the "hardwoods" into these two categories is a useful (and more or less accurate) technique for learning the more common trees of the Northeast.

6. OAK

The southern woodland stretches of New York and New England are composed mainly of oak and hickory trees with a smattering of red maples. The oaks are a large grouping of trees but for our purposes, we can divide them into two general categories — the White Oaks and the Black (or Red) Oaks. The trees in the White Oak group lack the tiny, hair-like bristles which protrude from the leaves of the Red Oaks.

Oak leaves are tough and leathery, and contain large amounts of tannin — a chemical substance that's used to harden and preserve leather. Consequently, the fallen leaves of oak trees don't readily decompose into the soil, as do the softer leaves of the maples, ashes, and basswoods. The undergrowth in an oak forest, therefore, is meager compared to the undergrowth in any of the other hardwood forests. Traditionally, a heavily-matted oak forest will have partridgeberry, Canada Mayberry (also called 'Wild-Lily-Of-The-Valley'), blueberry, and huckleberry growing on its floor; while a typical maple forest, with its rich "mull" soil, will exhibit a panoply of flowering plants — Dutchman's Breeches, Bloodroot, Anemone, and Toothwort. This interrelationship existing between the various trees and the types of undergrowth they encourage to grow is just one of nature's utterly mind-blowing, utterly miraculous, and utterly interdependent processes.

7. HICKORY

The Shagbark Hickory exhibits one of my favorite and re-
curring geometric patterns in all of nature. The tree's five
leaflets, all of them tightly affixed along a leaf axis, increase in
size — subtly and uniformly — as they near the terminal
leaflet. (See above illustration.) On a much smaller scale, this
same type of progression — where the size of a plant's leaves
will gradually increase as they ascend or descend the stem —
manifests itself in the delicate Northern Bedstraw — a small
and slender summer wildflower.

8. WHITE BIRCH (CANOE BIRCH)

The Birches (Black Birch, Yellow Birch, Red Birch, Gray
Birch, White Birch, and Blue Birch — all differentiated by
their bark's faint color variations) are the most valuable of the
Northern hardwoods. White Birch, whose velvety, almost
powdery white bark — a bark that's strong and waterproof and
was used by the Indians to build their canoes — is probably the
Northeast's most common birch. (*THE SURVIVAL OF THE
BARK CANOE* by John McPhee — published by Farrar, Straus,
Giroux — is a beautifully written book about a New Hamp-
shire craftsman who still uses birch bark to build canoes.)

9. BEECH

Thoreau, who is always both deservedly and profusely
being quoted in just about any book on nature, called the
beech's sharp-pointed winter buds, "the spearheads of
Spring". The smooth, light-gray bark of the beech makes it one
of the simplest trees to identify. Its wood is used in making
salad bowls, tool handles, and furniture.

7

8

9

10

10. MAPLE

Hockey fans, if they're at all familiar with one of the National Hockey League's top teams — *The Toronto Mapleleafs* — will have little trouble in identifying this popular tree (including Sugar Maples, Black Maples, Red or Swamp Maples, Silver Maples, and Ash-leaf Maples). Besides their distinctive broad, 5-lobed leaves (*The Toronto Mapleleaf's* team emblem), the maple's "keys" — being two-winged seeds that are joined in growth and which spin helicopter-like from the trees to the ground — makes these trees simple to identify.

All the maples (and not just the Sugar Maples) contain that alchemical sap that when boiled transmogrifies into one of Mother Nature's sweetest gifts — maple syrup. By boring a 3″ hole into a maple tree with a half-inch bit and hammering a *spile* or spigot into the hole — (these metal spiles can be bought from a number of maple sugaring outfitters) you can collect the diluted sap in metal buckets the size of wash-pails.

In February and April in the Northeast, when the days are sunny and warm but the nights still freezing, this watery sap begins to gush out of the maples. And by boiling about forty gallons of sap you'll eventually be able to produce about a gallon of golden syrup.

It's a sweetener that astronomically retails for around $13.00/a gallon precisely because of this 40-to-1 sap-to-syrup ratio.

On a sunny February afternoon, standing outdoors by a billowing wood fire, the maple tree's sap boiling away and slowly turning into a thick, golden syrup — your mustache just about coated with the sweet, viscous syrup — it's somehow hard not to applaud whoever or whatever it was (and is) who thought this whole universe up.

ECDYSIASTS — ARBOREAL STYLE

Despite that word — *Ecdysiast* — sounding like some thoroughly arcane and rarefied scientific babble, it really has a very earthy meaning: Ecdysiasts are strippers — stripteasers. And nature's autumnal striptease show, when her trees annually shed all their leafy vestments, has to be one of the best free shows around. (This colorful show, incidentally, occurs nowhere else on our planet except in the northeastern United States and in China.)

Now if your elementary and junior high school memories could be reactivated, you'd no doubt recall *chlorophyll* — that versatile chemical substance your biology teachers used to speak about. Chlorophyll, you'll remember, is the substance present in leaves that makes them green and that, in the presence of sunlight, enables them to convert carbon dioxide and water (what we human beings are all the time exhaling) into sugar — the food that plants can utilize.

Allow this very brief refresher course in basic biology: Carrying food in the form of sugar from the leaves of a tree into its branches, and in turn, supplying the leaves with all the substances it needs to replenish its waning reserves of chlorophyll, are tiny tubes. The flow in these tubes, which run along the leaf stems, are regulated by a tiny furrow at the base of the leaf stem — a furrow that acts as a cut-off valve. And in the fall, when nature — by a miraculous temperature-control device — moves this valve to its "off" position, all production of chlorophyll is stopped. And without chlorophyll, the leaves begin to lose their green hue. Yellow and browns, being the colors of certain other chemical substances that are always present in the leaves (but that are usually eclipsed by the chlorophyll's more potent green) then start appearing. (The appearance of these brilliant autumnal yellow and browns is most strikingly seen on the birch trees.)

Now as the sugars that are being produced in the leaves begin to pile up (since they're being blocked at the cut-off valve from travelling into the tree's branches) a new substance is also being produced — a substance that's responsible for the pinks and purple hues of the autumnal color show. The scarlet sugar maples and the purple ashes and dogwoods are all brought out by the interacting of this new substance with the acid or alkaline liquids that are in the leaf cells. (So frost, it should here be noted, while it may hasten the whole process, is not, as many claim, the cause of the divinely-ignited fall foliage.)

Which brings me to one last point: If by telling you all this scientific blather you now feel that you understand just why the leaves turn color in the fall, then I'm afraid you're deluded and I'm responsible. For no matter how much knowledge I or anyone else can ever impart to you, always remember that ultimately it's all — this whole contraption we call Life — a downright mystery. We can talk about plants and leaves all day. But — and this, regardless of how technical and convoluted our talk ever gets — the basic and underlying mystery of just what is a plant will never budge. We can name something and even begin to see how it works. But never can we know it. Its essence will forever elude us.

No matter what you touch and you wish to know about, you end up in a sea of mystery. You see, there's no beginning or end, you can go back as far as you want, forward as far as you want, but you never get to it, it's like the essence, it remains. This is the greatest damn thing about the universe. That we can know so much, recognize so much, dissect, do everything, and we can't grasp it. And it's meant to be that way, do y'know. And there's where our reverence should come in. Before everything, the littlest thing as well as the greatest. The tiniest, the horseshit, as well as the angels, do y'know what I mean. It's all mystery. All impenetrable, as it were, right?
—Henry Miller—

SOME COMMON SHRUBS

The *Heath Family* — (sounds like a new BBC dramatic television series) — contains many of the Northeast's most common shrubs: *azalea, rhododendron, mountain laurel*, and *blueberry*. (Shrubs are simply small, thin-stemmed trees.) And commonest among all these shrubs is the mountain laurel — a dark green shrub that prefers the acidic soils found in oak forests.

Rhodora, a reddish-purplish spring wildflower is by far the most popular of the azaleas; and the rosebay rhododendron is the Northeast's only wild species of rhododendron.

Blueberries and huckleberries, also members of the Heath Family, both grow on dry woodlands, beneath pine and oak trees. They're about the only shrubs that will grow after a forest has been destroyed by fire. So if forest fires are good for nothing else they'll at least supply you with enough blueberries and huckleberries to glut yourself for a year with blueberry pies, blueberry muffins, blueberry ice cream, and my favorite — a mushy serving of blueberry cream-cheese cake.

RHODORA

RHODODENDRON

BLUEBERRY

ANIMALS

"Man also is a part of Nature, not a miraculous intrusion."
—from the letters of Robinson Jeffers—

Chances are, unless you've been brought up on a farm or in the country (and by country I don't mean suburbia or exurbia), you're going to be at least vaguely frightened when you first encounter a wild animal. Not so with birds or insects but with animals — porcupines, deer, raccoons — the adrenalin almost always starts pumping.

What we all tend to forget (and what many of us want to forget) is that Man, too, is an animal. And what we all don't know (and can't know because we've been taught the very opposite) is that nature's animals are harmless; not some wild stampede of irrational beasts lurking in the forest, waiting for their human prey. **Animals — and this applies to every species of animal known to inhabit the Northeast — are harmless — unless they're riled by outsiders.**

If you walk in the woods respectfully, unobtrusively, and observantly — not as "a miraculous intrusion" but as "a part of Nature" — you'll see dozens of species of animals; see them caring for their young, foraging for their food, or just playing near a mountain freshet or an old, decaying tree stump. Just sit quietly and watch these animals: watch some beavers building a dam or a mother opossum carrying her young on her back or a deer nibbling at the bark of a cherry tree in wintertime. And because these animals are so much like us, we always have the same option that we have with members of our own species: we can either fear or love them. And fearing, while easier, never is very much fun.

Love is the action of being in the same space with other beings, which means that love is real, as real as we are. Love is not a limited idea, it is something we do, ultimately with our whole selves . . . And that is all we need to do: Give full, permissive, loving attention to absolutely anything that we see in our minds, in our bodies, in our environment, or in other people.

—Thaddeus Golas—

1. OPOSSUM

Opossums are our only native North American Marsupial (marsupials are mammals who carry their young in a pouch). These not particularly intelligent animals are night travellers who are forced to rely on their senses of hearing, smelling, and touching since their sight is so poor. 'Playing possum', whereby in dangerous situations these animals will feign death — they actually lie rigid on their backs for long periods of time — is probably the most clever act executed by these otherwise dim-witted mammals.

2. BATS

The 'big brown bat' is the bat you'll most likely see hovering about your head — as they try to entrap, either in their mouths or in their scoop-shaped tails — a swarm of mosquitos. These are the only mammals capable of flight, generally flying at night.

Bats utter very high-pitched supersonic squeaks (as many as 50 per second) that are inaudible to man. And by listening for the echoes of these sounds as they ricochet off of insects and nearby obstacles, most bats can deftly maneuver in nearly total darkness.

3. COTTONTAILS

Hugh Hefner's Playboy Bunnies derived their name from the well-known fact that rabbits, reproductively speaking, are prolific. Female rabbits often produce 4 to 5 litters a year; each litter consisting of anywhere from 4 to 7 babies.

1

2

3

4

5

4. WOODCHUCKS

Woodchucks have justifiably paranoiac eating habits. Practically every gardener and farmer whose crops are eaten by them wouldn't mind blowing their little heads off. Consequently, as they nibble away on a milkweed leaf or on some green apples, their heads are constantly and cautiously peering about.

Woodchucks live in burrows that are sometimes sunk to a depth of five feet (and which can extend 30 or more feet). At the end of one of these amazingly engineered underground chambers the ground is often elevated, so that water can't rise into them. And it's here, on this elevated mound, with wall-to-wall grass and leaves, that the woodchuck hibernates every winter.

Often, woodchucks will cleverly allow grasses and other herbaceous plants to grow around the entrance to their burrows. These plants effectively camouflage their homes from uninvited guests. And because their eyes are set high on their heads, woodchucks can inconspicuously scan — periscope-like — the terrain around their homes from the mouths of their burrows. Some woodchucks have even been known to frame the portals of their tunnels with roots and rocks: both excellent deterrents for interloping invaders.

5. SQUIRRELS

The three common squirrels of the Northeast are the gray squirrel, the red squirrel, and the flying squirrel.

Anatomically speaking, it's a squirrel's bushy tail that makes this mammal so unique. Squirrels can use their versatile tails as steering rudders when they're making their dramatic arboreal leaps, as balancing parasols when they're scampering across a network of fine twigs, and as a parachute to cushion their occasional falls. Squirrels, because of this parachute, have been known to plunge fifty and sixty feet without injury.

6.   RACCOON

Raccoons make a bizarre sight if you catch them at their dinnertime. With their deft forepaws — almost as useful as the forepaws of a monkey — they'll take a piece of food, dip it into a brook or stream, swish it around, carefully inspect it, then swish it again, and finally down the hatch. Watching a raccoon's dainty eating habits is one of nature's cutest shows.

7.   PORCUPINE

The approximately 25,000 ½″ to 5″ quills that erect themselves on a porcupine's body when the animal is in danger are painfully lethal. Wolves, mountain lions, and bears have all been found dead — their bodies riddled with the barbed quills of some frightened porcupine.

Porcupines love salt. They've even been known to chew on old, sweaty ax-handles, trying to get whatever taste of salt they can from the wood.

8.   BEAVER

Beavers are nature's dam builders. And while a lot of the tales we hear about their engineering feats are apocryphal (for instance, that beavers transport to their dam sites bundles of wood that are tied together with strips of bark) still, many of their building techniques genuinely are miraculous.

To transport saplings and branches to their dams, beavers will sometimes build elaborate canal systems (some of these canals are as long as 750 feet). And a "busy beaver", in just one night's time, can cut down a half-a-foot-thick tree, reduce that tree to neat 6-foot lengths, and then tote all the lumber to the communal dam site.

6

7

8

9

10

9. SKUNK

Skunks are generally placid, friendly animals. But the two large glands found on each side of their anus — their malodorous scent-throwers — have given them the reputation of being less sociable creatures than they really are. When they finally do get mad enough, though, to spritz their sulphide (this spritzing is almost always done as an act of self-defense and is almost always preceded by a cautionary head-lowering and stamping of their forefeet) **watch out**. They discharge only about a twentieth of a teaspoonful of this raunchy liquid but it's ejected under a great pressure. The resulting fine carrying spray (a spray that can travel anywhere from 10 to 15 feet) is, to put it mildly, an unpleasant stench.

Some people claim that skunk spray can blind human beings — or at least, cause temporary blindness. Edwin Teale, however, the Pulitzer Prize winning naturalist and photographer reports quite the contrary: a neighbor of his, he said, who had been sprayed in the eyes by a skunk actually had his vision temporarily cleared. "In fact," Teale says, "under certain conditions, the fluid of skunks has been used by oculists for aiding eyesight."

10. FOX

Both red foxes (which live around farms) and gray foxes (swamp and forest dwellers) are found in the Northeast. The red fox is quite a bit larger and more cunning than its gray cousin; but gray foxes are by far the better tree climbers.

11

12

13

11. BLACK BEAR

Bears range in color from black to pale cinnamon and they usually have a white spot on their chests.

An adult bear will range in length from 4½ to 6½ feet and will usually weigh between 200 and 300 pounds — though super ursine specimens have been known to tip the scale at 500+ pounds.

Bears, unless they're seriously provoked, usually won't breakup a human campfire. Nor will they break our bones in some mythical vice-like "bear hug". If a bear's going to do us in, more than likely it'll be with a powerful forepaw wallop, quickly followed by its ravaging teeth and claws. Ugh.

12. DEER

The White-tailed Deer is the prized quarry of most of our northeastern hunters. In late November, day-glow-colored hunters begin their annual deer round-up. For me (a vegetarian), this is when I stay as far away from the woods as possible.

The American Indians, because they were hungry, used to wear swatches of deerskin on their bodies and then go after the forest's deer. Today, hunters in plastic and vinyl outfits (and usually not out of a physiological hunger but out of one that's psychological) enter the woods during the deer's mating season with highpowered rifles. In their mating season, deer obviously aren't their usual cautious selves.

Vermont has an estimated 150,000 deer; Massachusetts 20,000; and Connecticut 7,000. Starvation can quickly diminish a thriving deer herd. In the winter of 1970-71, about 40,000 of Vermont's deer died of malnutrition.

Moose are the Northeast's largest mammals; some of them weighing as much as 1,400 pounds. They're solitary roamers with a maximum life expectancy of twenty years. These mammoth beasts usually prefer the northern coniferous forests of Maine — where they spend their time voraciously consuming anywhere from 40 to 60 pounds of food daily. It's been estimated that around 15,000 moose are now glutting themselves up in the Maine woods.

If you plan to spend any time hiking in Maine, you're bound to run into fellow hikers with storehouses of adrenalized tales about the time they were chased and nearly killed by a moose. Nearly is here the crucial word . . . . . I've heard lots of "close-call" stories about run-ins with moose. But never — never — have I heard a story that didn't have a "and-they-lived-happily-ever-after" ending.

ANIMAL TRACKS

Identifying and following animal tracks is a skill that once developed offers a year-round and perfectly harmless excuse for getting out into nature. Snow in winter, loam in fall and spring, and sand in summer are all equally suitable turfs for tracking down both animals or birds.

Naturally, stories of master trackers abound. One American Indian during the time of the Civil War was said to have known by the tracks alone that "a tall soldier riding a lame roan horse" had passed a certain spot. By observing the fine pieces of horsehair that stuck to the bark of a tree (that the soldier's horse had brushed against), and by observing both the hoof tracks of the horse and the boot imprints of the soldier, the Indian was able to offer his accurate deductions.

What follows are illustrations of a few of the tracks (deer and moose) and traces (fox, rabbits, and porcupines) of some animals you'll likely be encountering in the northeastern outdoors.

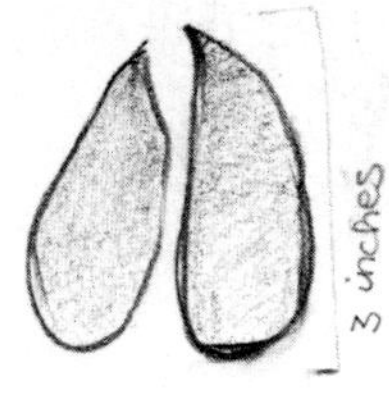

1

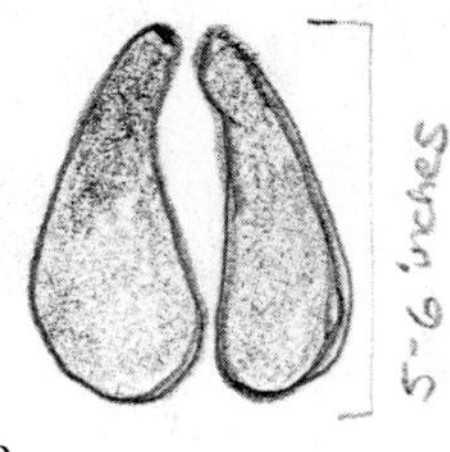

2

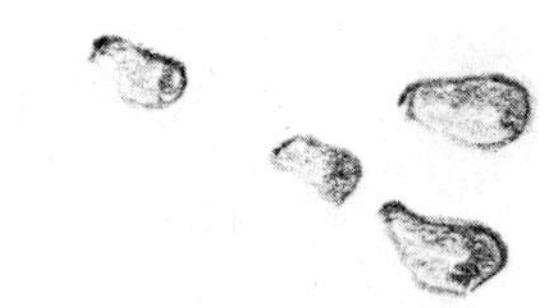

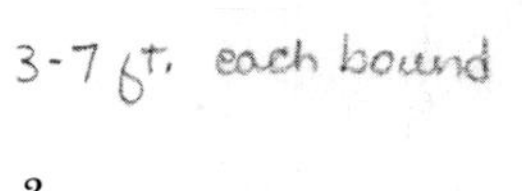

3

4

1. DEER

Of the big game animals, the deer leaves the smallest tracks. Assuming it's walking leisurely, the two toes of the hoofs will leave a closed imprint. But if it's fleeing and jumping (and some of these deer can jump up to 25 feet), its tracks will then be like a jumping rabbit's.

2. MOOSE

Moose, being large animals, have hoofed imprints that are apart from one another. They walk as if straddling a straight line.

3. RABBIT

Rabbits, as well as squirrels, are both small game animals equipped with paws. They walk on both the soles of their feet and their toes, often leaving clean imprints (revealing the entire sole and toe).

4. PORCUPINE

Porcupines have toenails or claws that leave identifying marks along the earth.

VEGETABLES

(EDIBLE PLANTS AND MUSHROOMS)

One way to get to know nature is to eat her. Really, there's just about no better way to learn how to identify a large number of plants than going out into the woods and foraging for your dinner. Certainly, before you put anything down your esophagus, you'll have examined it and re-examined and re-examined it — examined it cautiously, repeatedly, and with a few justified trepidations. Remember: EATING WILD FOODS MAY BE HAZARDOUS TO YOUR HEALTH. So don't foolishly risk your life for some mushrooms you thought were puffballs but turned out to be a poisonous amanita. Be 100% sure of your identifications.

. . . And Bon Appetit.

* * * * *

Euell Gibbons, of course, was America's popularizer of wild foods. He himself was popularized by all the inane jokes Johnny Carson used to make about him on *The Tonight Show*. "I was walking to the NBC building this afternoon," Carson used to quip in one of his nightly monologues, "and there — right in front of the building — was Euell Gibbons — half-starving, on his hands and knees — looking for some food between the cracks in the pavement." Everyone in the audience (and probably everyone in America) would then laugh (on cue) at the thought of a middle-aged man foraging for food in the middle of Manhattan. But Gibbons, on many occasions, had, in fact, successfully foraged in a number of America's cities. In Philadelphia, for example, he once found eighteen different edibles; in Chicago, near a vacant lot, he came across fifteen; and in just one afternoon strolling near the Chesapeake Bay, he took eleven assorted goodies home for dinner.

All of Gibbon's books — *STALKING THE WILD AS-PARAGUS, STALKING THE HEALTHFUL HERBS,* and *STALKING THE FARAWAY PLACES* — are easy-to-use and easy-to-read guidebooks. Stone Wall Press also has a small il-lustrated booklet — *160 EDIBLE PLANTS COMMONLY FOUND IN THE EASTERN USA* by Joe Freitus ($2.95).

* * * * *

Of the roughly 250,000 species of plants populating the earth, thousands of them are potentially excellent sources of human food. I've chosen to here introduce you to five — *wild leeks, daylilies, cattails, dandelions,* and *watercress.* All are fairly common throughout the Northeast, and each has a wide variety of uses. (I'll even recommend a dinner menu later on using only these five ingredients.)

1. WILD LEEKS

These mild, garlicky onions are usually found in dense, rich woods in the early spring. You can always spot them by the small cylinder of tightly rolled leaves their bulbs send out. Similar to garlic cloves but much larger (and lacking the membranous cover of a garlic clove), the wild leek bulbs are sweet — "the best of the wild onion," Gibbons used to lovingly call them.

2. DAY LILY

The common orange day lily, which grows abundantly along roadsides and in abandoned fields during June and July, is, I confess, one of the more universally palette-pleasing wild foods. (Which, of course, is a rather circuitous way of saying that a lot of wild foods lack gastronomic pizazz. But like everything else, once you develop a taste for them, you'll be hooked.)

The day lily is truly versatile. In the spring, you can eat the sprouting stalks by first cutting them above the root and then slicing the tender inner portions. They're good in raw salads or cooked like asparagus. This same day lily also produces edible tubers underground. The tubers are small — about a half-inch to an inch in diameter — but when cleaned and cooked in boiling water for approximately twenty minutes, they become a mildly sweet-tasting vegetable. Since day lilies grow so profusely, don't be hesitant to dig up as many as you need.

The unopened flower buds, too, if you get them at the right time — when they're almost full-sized — are tasty treats when boiled and buttered. And even the flashy orange blossoms (which open only for one day — giving the plant its name) can be dipped in an egg-and-flour batter and fried to crispness.

1

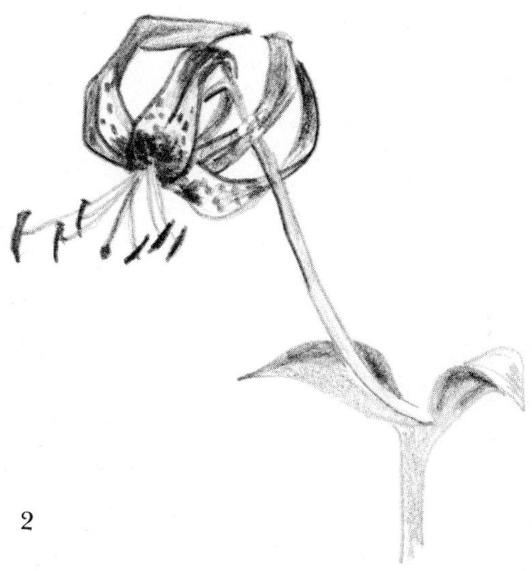

2

3

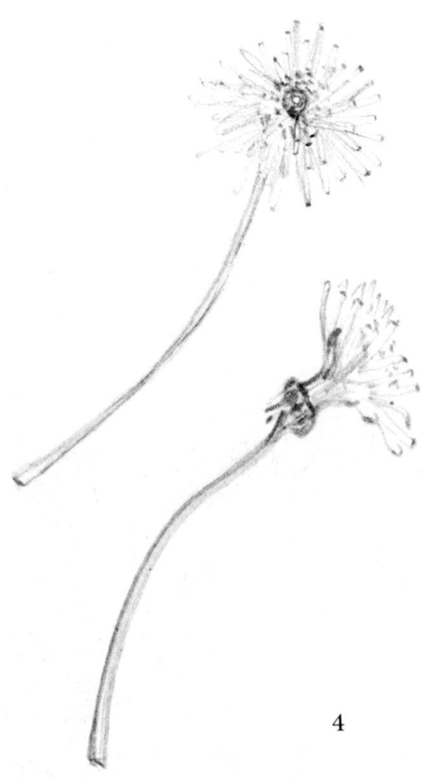

4

3.   CATTAILS

If you catch these marsh dwellers at the right time of the year — in late June or early July in upstate New York, and a bit later as you move into northern New England — you'll actually be able to prepare five different dishes from its various parts. The young green bloom spikes (these spikes are the ones that will have no yellow pollen on them) can be removed from their sheaths and boiled. Served with butter, they make a bizarre corn-on-the-cob substitute. The peeled white base of the young plants (young here means when the cattails are about two feet high) are what's known as "Cossack Asparagus" — a Russian delicacy. They're *almost* delicious . . . a two star rating.

The pollen that forms on the blooms that were too old to be eaten can be rubbed into a pail by hand, then put through a sieve, and used as a flour. The cattail's starchy root cores (I warn you beforehand — it's a messy affair to dig them up) can be roasted in a fire, smeared with butter, and gobbled down as a snack. (Some people even manage to make an excellent bread flour out of these roots: dry the roots, pulverize them, add some water and, for my limited patience, too many steps later — presto — a loaf of cattail bread.) Finally, the white sprouts at the end of the roots can be broken off and cooked like green beans.

4.   DANDELIONS

In retrospect, it was one of the most pyrrhic battles ever fought. Chemical warfare, hand-to-hand combat, an array of bayonet-resembling weaponry — all malevolently being used by my otherwise peace-loving father to eradicate from the face

of our suburban lawn the loathsome, villainous dandelion —
the killer-weed of middle-America's manicured 40′ x 100′ es-
tates: A war that to this day still persists; only now, mercenaries
(gardeners) have been hired to do the slaughtering.

Obliterating dandelions, I must here and now proclaim, is
ludicrous. **Suburban landowners of America — stop your war
on the lowly dandelion and allow just a moment's
moratorium** as I tell you about some of the uses of this most
extraordinary and most extraordinarily persecuted "weed".

Right before a dandelion sends out its composite yellow
flowers, you can gather its tender roots, peel them, cook them,
and then feast on a vegetable that's tastier than a parsnip.
These same roots can be dried — by roasting them in an oven
for a good 3 to 4 hours — then ground and used as a coffee
substitute. In addition, the crown of colorless leaf stems
situated atop the dandelion's root can also be eaten — either
raw or cooked.

And Dandelion Greens (the leaves of the dandelion), if
gathered early, have long been a popular spinach-like dish.
And, of course, there's the beloved 'Dandelion Wine' — that
potent alcoholic blower of minds — a brew first made in England but later quaffed by thousands of tongue-wagging
Americans during those terribly dry days of Prohibition. To
make 'Dandelion Wine', place about a half-gallon of dandelion
flowers in a covered gallon-sized crock filled with boiling water
for four days. Put the resulting liquid (minus the flowers) in a
big boiling pot, stirring in the rinds and juices of a few lemons
and oranges. To this, add about a pound of brown sugar and
boil for twenty minutes. Allow this brew to become lukewarm,
then spread some yeast atop a wafer and float it on the concoc-
tion. Keep the resulting mess in a warm room for a week, and
then strain off the wine into a jug. Cork it lightly (using some
cotton) and let it sit in a dark room for about a month. Then
carefully pour it off into a bottle and cork it tightly.

. . . Then, on Christmas Eve, pop her open, down the
hatch, and out your mind.

So again, belligerent suburban gentry: Make Love To The
Dandelion, Not War.

Here's an abundantly growing wild plant that almost inevitably costs a small fortune when you buy it in a supermarket. All you have to do, though, is go to practically any stream and collect as much of it as you want — all for free. You don't want the whole plant, though, when you gather watercress, just what's above the surface. So in gathering it, don't yank it from the ground; just try to snap it off at the water's surface.

In a salad or as a garnish for sandwiches, or cooked like spinach, wild watercress is truly a gourmet's delight — one that all of us plebians can now easily afford.

5

* * * * *

Wild plants + a dab of imagination = one 6-course dinner.

TONIGHT'S WILD FOOD MENU:

Cocktail	Dandelion Wine
Soup	A watercress soup: diced onions, grated watercress, milk, and flour — all heated and stirred for 20 minutes.
Combination Salad	Leeks, watercress, cattail sprouts, day lily tubers, dandelion crowns topped with a spicy oil-and-vinegar dressing.
Entrée	A cheese-smothered casserole of dandelion roots, leeks, cattail buds, and the tender flower buds of the day lily.
Vegetable	Buttered dandelion tubers
Bread	Cattail flour biscuits
Special Bonus Dessert	Strawberry Short Cake — made from freshly-picked wild berries.
Beverage	Dandelion coffee

. . . As you down that last sip of dandelion coffee, your stomach delightfully bloated, savor the fact that your lavish repast cost you not a single cent; just a few hours foraging in the woods.

MUSHROOMS

For twenty years of my life, I lived with the illusion that a mushroom was a mushroom. And never once, in all that time, did I even remotely suspect that the mushrooms I was eating (*Algaricus bisporus*) were just one of the more than 3,000 types growing in North America. I simply ate my mushrooms back then in ignorance; an ignorance unaccompanied by bliss.

Blissful mushroom eating didn't come to me until I was twenty-one. Accompanied by an amateur mycologist (a toadstool or mushroom collector) I finally saw my first *puffball* — a delicious tasting mushroom that looked like an albino basketball sitting under a tangle of bushes.

Visually, mushrooms are extraordinary — with their WW I combat-helmet caps and striated gills. And despite the fact that they're nutritionally inconsequential (being composed mostly of water), nearly all the edible mushrooms (approximately 250 of them) can make tasty and bizarrely cute additions to any meal.

Lots of "spook stories" abound in the mushroom literature. Stories of entire families ingesting *Amanita Verna* (or more commonly and forebodingly known as the "Destroying Angel") — a deadly mushroom that's especially cruel because its symptoms are delayed — (sometimes for as long as 24 hours). Personally, I've never known of any mushroom fatalities (though I have come across some pretty nauseous friends). Assuming you're colossally careful with your mushroom identifications, then eating toadstools can only be salubrious.

WARNING: The intention of this section on mushrooms is only meant to turn you on to their existence and to acquaint you with some of the more common varieties. In no way, however, is this brief introduction meant to be a substitute for a trustworthy mushroom field guide. Two books — one a pamphlet published by the Department of Agriculture and written by Vera K. Charles entitled *SOME COMMON MUSHROOMS AND HOW TO KNOW THEM* (write: Superintendent of Documents, Washington, D.C. to obtain this booklet) and the other, a University of Michigan Press Book — *THE MUSHROOM HUNTER'S FIELD GUIDE* by Alexander H. Smith (who, strangely enough, tells us he's allergic to many of the mushrooms) are about the two most useful field guides around.

1. GIANT PUFFBALLS

About the size of baseballs with smooth white exteriors, these popular mushrooms are attached to the earth by a cordlike structure. Before you eat them, check by cutting the mushroom in half — lengthwise — and ascertain that its interior is homogeneous and white — making sure you don't have a poisonous *Amanita*.

(I have purposely not included sketches of mushrooms in this section. It's my insurance policy, dear reader, that you can't and won't mistake my brief descriptions here for an elaborate mushroom field guide. Enjoy mushrooms — enjoy these tasty little fungi. But don't — I repeat — don't be foolish enough to let them enjoy you.)

2. SPONGE MUSHROOMS, OR MORELS

With its Latin name — *Morchella esculenta* — sounding like Xavier Cugat's latest songstress, this popular and easily recognizable mushroom is found early in the spring. It often appears in old apple orchards.

3. INKIES AND SHAGGY-MANES

The tall (6 in.) pointed stalk of the shaggy mane, along with the ring that encircles it, helps to identify this choice edible. It grows abundantly along the sides of asphalt roads. Inkies or Inky caps, in the same family as shaggy manes (Coprinus) appear both in the fall and spring during cool wet weather.

MINERALS

Once upon a time — about ten-thousand years ago — it snowed and snowed and snowed. And because it snowed so much and because it was so cold, everything — mountains, rivers, and trees — was soon covered by a thick sheet of ice. No ordinary sheet of ice, either; but a massive wall of mile-thick frozen snow that was several *million* square miles long.

This sheet of ice — this Great White Sheet — liked to slowly trudge — maybe just a few hundred feet a year — across the earth's surface. But like a silent and vicious sea monster, it had the nasty habit of gobbling up anything and everything in its path. So baby trees, grumpy old mountains, and even scaly reptiles all got eaten by this Great White Sheet.

The Great White Sheet was born in the Arctic Circle and as it matured it began to float southward — over New Hampshire's White Mountains, and over Massachusetts, Rhode Island, and Connecticut, and finally floating all the way down to the northern side of Long Island. There it — *puff* — melted away, disappearing into the flooding waters of the Great Blue Sea.

The Great White Sheet, of course, like everything else, eventually died. But even written as a fairytale such as this, you'll never really be able to understand the vastness of this Great White Sheet or the vastness of the geological changes it wrought.

It does read like a supernatural tale, this story of the continental glacier. The glacier literally hurled boulders that weighed over *four-thousand tons*, first ripping these massive chunks of rock from mountain sides, then depositing them about the countryside. (Just a few miles south of Conway, New Hampshire is the famed *Madison Boulder* — a 4,000-ton block of granite measuring 83 x 37 x 23 feet). The random depositing of gravel, sand, and mud, as well as thousands of smaller-sized boulders — (these being the materials that were carried by the moving ice sheet and then deposited when the ice sheet finally melted) — changed — drastically, cataclysmically — the earth's topography: lakes and swamps were formed, vast mounds of sand and gravel created, and large grooves or 'glacial striations' — the result of the earth's bedrock being gouged and scraped by all the floating-in-ice boulders — appeared. (Today, especially throughout the White Mountains, and especially on the upper ledges of Mount Kearsarge, these 'glacial striations' can be observed). Cirques, too, or vast hollows were yanked out of the Northeast's mountains by the advancing glacier. (*Tuckerman's Ravine* is probably the best-known cirque in the entire Northeast). And *notches* (like *Franconia Notch, Pinkham Notch*, and *Crawford Notch* — all in New Hampshire) being wide, U-shaped valleys, were randomly sculpted by these glaciers as they flowed and pounded their way through previously narrow, stream-cut areas.

Besides lakes, cirques, and notches, the activity of the glacier also brought about a number of other geological formations in the Northeast. As you drive or hike throughout the region, you'll probably spot some of these other glacier-formed formations:

1. MORAINE

This is a glacial deposit of *till*, or unsorted mud, sand, and gravel. These moraines, being in the shape of irregular, hummocky ridges, often mark the terminus of a glacier. The hilly northern side of New York's Long Island — consisting of many small irregular hills — is a moraine that reveals the southernmost limit where our region's most recent (10,000 years ago) glacier ended. And beyond this moraine (to the south of it) is an area that was never covered with ice; an area, called an *outwash plain*, that today consists of just sand and gravel.

(The northern hilly part of Cape Cod is also a moraine.)

2. ESKER

Near Bangor, Maine (in the low country to the east of the Penobscot River) are steep-sided, narrow-topped ridges that resemble railroad embankments. This sort of continuous, winding ridge, which runs in a north-south direction for a number of miles, is called an "esker". These eskers were formed by streams that somehow flowed through or under all the massive sheets of glacial ice; these streams actually depositing large amounts of till between the walls of ice. (When the ice walls eventually melted, these till deposits remained as ridges.)

3. KAME

Kames are similar to eskers in that they were formed during the Ice Age by accumulating till deposits. They are steep-sided conical hills, many of them actually formed when a stream filled in a hole of the Great White Sheet with till.

116

GROUND
MORAINE
DRUMLINS

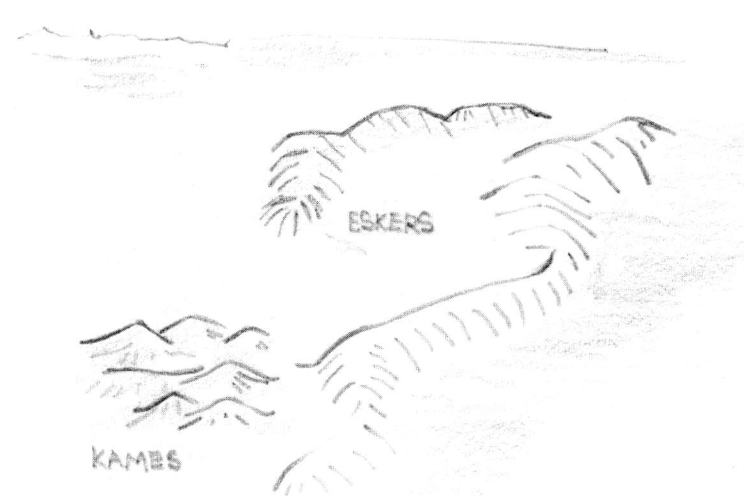

ESKERS
KAMES

Drumlins, like eskers, kames, and moraines are heaps of sand, gravel, and mud. They're really elongated hills, anywhere from one-quarter to one-half mile long, and anywhere from fifty to a hundred-and-fifty feet high. Boston Harbor, where the sea actually drowned the land (indeed, much of the Northeast's coast is what's known as a "drowned coastline") reveals many of these *drumlins*. In Boston Harbor, the bases of these drumlins have been flooded by the sea; but their uppermost portions — appearing today as islands in the harbor — are easily visible.

A VERY BRIEF APOLOGIA

I am a dabbler. Not a scientist. I study nature because, for me, studying her has become a religious act; the same as eating a Eucharist wafer or being *bar mitzvahed*. I'm reminded of how inexplicable and how magical everything is when I'm in the outdoors, when I'm kneeling on the ground, examining a wildflower or a mineral.

But I don't really *study* nature. I don't watch her, that is, with the precision of a scientist. That sort of precision, I'm afraid, bores me. Always has.

Now those mildly self-lacerating, admonitory remarks were no doubt provoked by my just having skimmed James Dwight Dana's nineteenth-century tome — *A SYSTEM OF MINERALOGY*. Dana's gargantuan opus, filled with a dense academic foliage of chemical formulas, complex drawings, and elaborate scientific descriptions, reminded me of my own "dabblerism". So as you read all my introductory remarks about the Northeast's birds, bees, flowers, trees et al., bear in mind that these are all terribly sketchy introductions — sketchy introductions to fields that both deserve and require lifetimes of study.

SOME GENERAL AND BRIEF REMARKS ABOUT THE ROCKS AND MINERALS OF THE NORTHEAST

Rocks and minerals make up the Earth's crust; and everything else — soil, water, plants, and animals — would be homeless without them. Minerals are composed of elements: quartz, for instance, consists of one part silicon to two parts oxygen. And rocks (remember that this introduction is a very general one) are really extensive mineral bodies, composed in varying degrees of one or more minerals. (Granite, for instance, is mainly composed of two minerals — quartz and feldspar.)

A very easy way to determine what rocks are common to a specific area is to note the type of rocks used for gravestones in the region's oldest cemeteries. (New cemeteries now generally import stones.) In the Connecticut Valley, many of the old headstones were made of red sandstone. In Vermont, marble head and foot stones predominate. And in New Hampshire, it's granite that's most abundant.

Other common rocks in the Northeast are *mica schist* (which comprises the bedrock in New York City's Central Park), *basalt* (which makes up the Palisades sill on the west side of the Hudson River at New York City; the Palisades being a well-known geological formation formed thousands of years ago out of volcanic lava), and *dolomite* (a rock resembling limestone that's found largely in Vermont).

Rocks are drab in comparison to minerals. The angular shapes taken by minerals (when they solidified thousands of years ago from molten states) are exquisite. These various crystal formations of the minerals — the long slender prisms of an amethyst quartz, the red-colored trapezohedral crystals of garnet, or the bright yellow orthorhombic crystals of sulphur — make these specimens the most desired among collectors.

Collecting rocks and minerals or "rockhounding" is a popular hobby. With just a prospector's pick, a sledge hammer, some cold chisels, a magnifying glass, and a collecting sack, you'll be ready to visit the Northeast's abandoned mines and quarries. To locate these old mines — mines where you can hunt for specimens by picking through vast heaps of dynamited rubble — a number of worthwhile guidebooks and pamphlets are available. *THE MINERAL LOCALITIES OF CONNECTICUT AND SOUTHEASTERN NEW YORK* by Ronald Everett Januzzi is probably the most comprehensive guide for that section of the Northeast. And by contacting the geology departments of a region's colleges and universities, you'll be able to get some additional information on the collecting sites and common minerals of that area.

Remember: Always have **written** permission before visiting a mine. Otherwise you're a trespasser and subject to arrest.

To be honest, it's hard to unearth worthwhile specimens at most of these mines. Too many rockhounds for too many generations have been picking through too many rubble heaps. So if you become discouraged, visit the mineral collection at the Museum of Natural History in New York City. It's a consummate collection.

WIND

(THE SKY AND THE WEATHER)

Charles Darwin once remarked that in our everyday lives very few of us ever gaze higher than fifteen degrees above the horizon. Our eyes seem to be earthbound; as if by looking upwards — upwards at the immense expanses of sky — we'll vaguely fear being reminded of our own insignificance, our own cosmic *drop-in-the-bucketness*. Most of us seem content to merely keep our eyes safely peering along the ground — where all we can ever see are the plants we eat, the insects we step on, and the smaller mammals we too often feel superior to.

Looking upwards at the clouds or at the stars or at a rainbow is somehow threatening to us.

It doesn't seem right, though, that the skies were created to humiliate us. Possibly to sometimes humble us; but never, I think, to humiliate us. "Just as sure as the eye is designed for seeing," Eric Sloane, the well-known illustrator, has remarked, "it seems logical that there must be things designed to be seen. And I am certain," Sloane deductively reasons, "that the sky was designed to be seen by man."

This sky — which is above us — possibly was created to elevate us, to spiritually uplift our otherwise earthbound souls. And as long as we don't fear looking upwards and sometimes being reminded of our human *smallness*, then very possibly it'll be our human *bigness* that we'll find.

Just the lighting of the outdoors is uplifting. The rich, metallic blue of a late night fall sky, the changing and shifting cloud formations after a windy, summer rainstorm, or the utterly sacred light that sometimes pours curtain-like over the ocean at twilight. . . .

In the day sky it's naturally the clouds that are most eye-catching. And a good way to learn some of the more common cloud formations is to first learn a few of the more popular and time-tested weather forecasting proverbs and verses; sayings that were written hundreds of years ago which use the cloud patterns to predict the weather.

*"When white clouds cover the
heavenly way
No rain will mar your plans
that day."*

or

*"If woollen fleeces spread the heavenly way,
Be sure no rain disturbs the summer day."*

The "white clouds" and "woollen fleeces" alluded to in these two verses are *Cumulus* clouds — a name derived from the Latin word for "pile". These are dense and sharply outlined clouds, and unless they become extremely tall during the course of a day, they won't bring any rain.

*"Mackerel skies and mare's tails
Make tall ships carry low sails."*

The "mare's tails" of this verse refer to the delicate, featherlike plumes of *cirrus* clouds — another Latin word whose literal translation is "curl of hair". These clouds, by themselves, do not lead to rain; but they can presage a distant storm whose fringe winds often create the conditions in which cirrus clouds form.

*"When the clouds are upon the hills
They'll come down by the mills."*

Stratus clouds often form on hilltops, the result of a fog drifting over the warmed surface of the hilltop and then gently rising above it. These flat, gray clouds are the lowest and most uniform-appearing of all the clouds. And while there are plenty of summer mornings when a capping of such clouds brings a fine day, more often than not these clouds foreshadow rain. *Stratus* means "spread out" in Latin.

These three main types of clouds — *cumulus, cirrus,* and *stratus* — (all of them first named back in 1803 by Luke Howard, an amateur British meteorologist) are merely the building blocks for a much more involved system of cloud identification. Other cloud families include *cirrocumulus, cirrostratus, altocumulus, altostratus, nimbostratus, stratocumulus,* and *cumulonimbus.* (The prefix *cirro* denotes high clouds, clouds occurring at altitudes ranging from 20,000 to 40,000 feet. The prefix *alto* denotes mid-level clouds — those ranging from 8,500 to 20,000 feet. And the other prefixes denote low clouds — up to 8,500 feet.)

The changes in the weather, to recapitulate, can many times be predicted by the constantly changing formations of these various cloud families. When cumulus clouds, for instance, build up in the summertime to form cumulonimbus, a thirty-minute thunderstorm is often the result. Or in the winter when Nimbostratus clouds start appearing in the sky, then a snowstorm is probably in the making. The Appalachian Mountain Club sells (at a nominal charge) a clearly written and well photographed pamphlet entitled *BE YOUR OWN WEATHER PROPHET.* As an easy-to-use cloud guide, it's perfect for beginners.

Besides the clouds the sky's color also offers prognostic possibilities. Two of the most trustworthy "color" verses used in predicting the weather are:

> *"Evening gray and morning red*
> *Sends the traveler wet to bed*
> *Evening red and morning gray*
> *Sends the traveler on his way."*

And in the Bible (Matthew 16:2-3) this very same idea appears in a slightly different form:

> *". . . When it is evening . . . it will be fair weather*
> *for the sky is red. And in the morning*
> *it will be foul weather today for the*
> *sky is red and lowering."*

Both sayings refer to the red-colored *stratocumulus* clouds (low water clouds) that appear at both sunrise and sunset. And just how all this predicting the weather by the sky's color operates is really not too complex a matter.

It's known that most of the weather on the North American continent travels from west to east; which is to say that both the warm and cold fronts (also called warm and cold air masses) move from the west coast to the east coast. These air masses travel at the rate of approximately 600 miles every 24 hours. And these air masses (more precisely, their interaction) are what's responsible for our weather.

Now when the sky is red at sunset that means that the air to the west of us is dry because in order for white sunlight to appear red (to us on earth) it has to first be scattered (like a prism) through a large number of small particles. And only in dry weather — which means sunshine — are there enough of these small particles in the atmosphere to do that. And conversely, if the western sky is gray at sunset, then with equal confidence we can say that the air to the west of us is moisture-laden (which means rain) because wet air simply contains particles that are too large to scatter red light.

(That semi-technical spiel on light diffraction, along with the quick refresher course I already gave you on photosynthesis are, I swear, the only two such technical ramblings in this entire field guide. Both recondite spiels, though, hopefully will inspire you to investigate some of the other scientific principles that are constantly at work in nature. But as I promised in the beginning of this guide, this is to be "A *Lazy* Person's Guide To Nature".)

TWO ADDITIONAL COLOR RULES FOR THE AMATEUR WEATHER FORECASTER:

In winter a pale yellow sky during the time of the sun's setting means that there's a 60 per cent chance of rain within 24 hours.

And if the sky above the western horizon is tainted with green soon after sundown, then the chances for rain the following day are 80 per cent or better.

SOME ADDITIONAL AND TRUSTWORTHY WEATHER VERSES

"When the moon or sun is in its house
Likely there will be rain without."
(A cloud cover is what's meant by the "moon's house").

"Rainbow in the morning
Travelers take warning.
Rainbow at night
Traveler's delight."

"If smoke and birds go high
There's no rain in the sky.
If smoke and birds are low
Watch out for a blow."

(Birds have an easier time flying high during the high pressure air of fair weather skies. And smoke from chimneys curls downward due to the blowing of pre-storm winds. The wind, of course, with its velocity and direction, is another important determinant of weather.)

"If frost or dew sees morning light
No rain will come before that night."

(And conversely, *no dew* in the morning is a sign of rain.)

"Short notice, soon will pass.
Long notice, long will last."

(This refers to thunderstorms that are carried by cool, fast moving winds. These storms come in quickly and leave just as quickly. But slow moving cloud processions always herald a rain of long duration.)

The weather — which is so all-encompassing — including the clouds, winds, rains, snows (like Eskimos, incidentally, have over a *hundred* compound words in their vocabulary to describe the many varieties and conditions of snow), the hail, sleet, sunshine, and the very air we breathe, affects everyone and everything. Ants travel in rows during a rainstorm while they scatter on clear days. Insects (because they can manoeuvre better when the air is a little heavy) usually cling and bite when the air is moist. The leaves of rhododendrons will always stand erect at 60°F, droop at 40°, curl at 30°, and blacken at 20°.

And people — well just about everyone's mood tends to vary with the weather, "Do business with men when the wind is from the Northwest," Ben Franklin wrote more than two hundred years ago. (Northwest winds, Franklin knew, are cool and clear; the perfect weather for closing otherwise heated business transactions.)

Everything, therefore, in nature is intimately involved with the weather. Every animal, flower, tree, bird — *everything* — is somehow profoundly affected by even the slightest change in the day's weather. Civilizations, romantic liaisons, mating rituals, sporting events, business deals, wars — everything — is influenced by the winds, clouds, rain, and sun.

To know nature is to both know and feel this ubiquitous matrix within which everything else transpires.

> *Praised be my Lord*
> *For our Brother the Wind*
> *And for Air and Cloud,*
> *Calms and All Weather.*
> —St. Francis of Assisi—

SAND

(THE BEACH)

Beaches and romances, thanks to Hollywood, have become synonymous: torrid lovers writhing on perfectly white beaches, forlorn suitors taking wintry, melancholy strolls, and paramours finally running — wildly and unnoticed — along the ocean's shoreline. The images are irrepressible: hundreds of yards of the film industry's celluloid have simply limned the beach for a "for lovers only" paradise. (Who can forget Burt Lancaster and Deborah Kerr passionately embracing on the beach in "From Here To Eternity".)

Probably because I grew up near the beach did I never understand it. I didn't have to. I experienced it. The geological upheavals that materialized the coast, those powerful glacial surges that pounded thousands of vast boulders into millions of tiny, powdery sand particles . . . or the incredibly strange habits of all the burrowing sand crabs I used to watch — some of them able to dig tunnels as fast and as deep as any man . . . or the extraordinarily bizarre, almost militaristic anatomy of

the dead horseshoe crabs I'd see sprawled on the beach, their spiked tails and tank-like carapaces turning brittle by the corrosive action of the sea water and sun. I observed all these things: crabs, tidal movements, seaweed, snails, whelks. But because these were things I saw every day, I never bothered learning their names.

Years later, as an adolescent, when I became interested in learning the names of some of these beach objects, I started reading different monographs written by the various well-known marine biologists. And after reading them I'd stare at a sand particle or a piece of seaweed under an inexpensive microscope, or I'd dissect (really mutilate) a crab with just a screwdriver and a hatpin for tools. I was a kid then and I wanted to know everything about the beach. Everything.

But my quasi-scientific efforts all failed. It seemed that the more I studied the beach the more bored with it I became. I'd just go there to collect some new specimen and then hurriedly return home, only anxious to analyze whatever it was I found under my microscope. (A converted bar in my parent's basement — complete with Pyrex beakers, flasks, and test tube racks — served as my childhood laboratory.) Until finally I was forced to just forget the whole thing. Something in me sensed that if I continued with my investigations the beach would somehow and forever be ruined for me. So I quickly disassembled my basement laboratory, returned all my father's displaced liquor bottles to their proper shelves, and miraculously (miraculously because it happened so fast) the beach and I once again resumed our never-again-to-wane romance.

The motto of this little story? To enjoy nature but to enjoy her without getting all hung up on trying to know everything about her. Just love nature. And then, if you still feel like studying her, let your love and appreciation guide you. But don't, don't over-analyze nature. You'll lose her.

Hopefully, the following few pages will make your strolls along the Northeast's beaches more rewarding. But if you feel — even slightly — that you can more fully enjoy your walks along the beach without knowing anything about what you'll be seeing, then by all means leave this field guide at home.

1. SAND

All the sand on the Northeast's beaches — and try to imagine what that means — was originally mountains. Our sands were and are produced by the fragmentation and abrasion of mountainous rocks. And not surprisingly, since granite is one of the most abundant rocks of the continental crust and since thirty percent of granite is quartz, most of our northeastern sand today consists of crushed quartz of various colors mixed with a number of minerals such as biotite, feldspar, magnetite (which will cling to a magnet), augite, and hornblende, as well as some semi-precious gems like garnet, and bits of the shells of snails and bivalves (oysters, clams, mussels). (On Martha's Vineyard, an island off of Cape Cod, grains of *sapphire* and *ruby* have even been found in the sand.)

Garnet sand, which is the result of the decomposition of red-colored garnet schists and garnet gneisses — two fairly common rocks — is an especially beautiful sand. It's often found in segregated rows along an otherwise quartz-sand beach. Charlton Ogburn, Jr., author of *THE WINTER BEACH* (William Morrow & Co., Inc., 1966) describes some of this garnet sand as resembling "a stain on the beach that looked as if black-raspberry juice had been spilled and then washed over by a retreating wave." (A pocket-sized magnifying lens, of course, is mind-blowingly useful when you're observing the fine sand granules along a beach.)

Now before I tell you about some of the flora and fauna that's to be found on top of the sand, let me briefly tell you about the microflora and microfauna that's actually found **between** the sand. These tiny plants and animals (called *thalassopsammons*) really do live on and between the grains of sand. And with a good dissecting microscope you can see the thin, flattened, colorless, and thread-like bodies of these bizarre interstitial species. (Mix some sand with a few inches of seawater, knead the resulting glop for two minutes, and then, in the excess water, with the aid of a magnifying lens, you'll be able to see dozens of these lilliputian creatures darting about.)

2. SEAWEED

Practically all the seaweeds are algae, which are among the simplest of the plants. The varieties of seaweeds found on our northeastern beaches include *dulse* — a highly edible, red-colored plant that's rich in iodine; *bladder wrack* — which looks like brown, flattened gloves; bright green *sea lettuce*; *sponge seaweed*; *palmated kelp*; and *laminaria* — a type of kelp that can grow up to twenty feet long. (One of the Pacific Ocean's kelps is said to have reached a length of a *fifth-of-a-mile*.)

3. JELLYFISH

Jellyfish are among the most common animals living in the shallow waters off of coastal New England. And the species that's most often seen washed up on our beaches is the "white sea jelly" or "moon jelly". Its body is milky white.

4. BARNACLES

Thousands of these multicolored animals (they can be white, yellow, orange, or red) often crowd our beaches. Unfortunately they also encrust the bottoms of ships and lobster pots — annually costing the U.S. shipping industry more than $100 million. Perhaps the best known biographer of these clinging crustaceans (they attach themselves by their heads to solid surfaces) was Charles Darwin. His monograph remains, to this day, the field's definitive study.

5. BLUE CRAB

The reason blue crabs cost you so much to eat is that they must be kept alive until they're cooked; and once cooked their meat will only stay fresh for a few days. These crabs, with their green shells, bright blue legs (the females even have a dainty, scarlet nail polish dabbed on their toenails) have the magical quality — called *autonomy* —of being able to re-grow any limb they might happen to lose in the course of their aquatic peregrinations.

BEAUTIFUL SWIMMERS (Little, Brown & Company, 1976) by William W. Warner is a strongly recommended book about both the blue crab and the multi-million dollar industry that's been built around it.

Two other common crabs of the Northeast are the *hermit crab* — a species of crab that appropriates for itself the protective shell of a dead snail or whelk — and the *mole* or *sand crab* — a small, light-brown-to-white-tinged-with-purple crab who survives on a diet of pure sand. Its internal organis sift through this ingested sand, extracting all the edible interstitial algae and animals that live on or between the sand granules.

5

Our society is convinced that anything stellar — superstars, Hollywood stars, Stars of Bethlehem — has to be good. But the common *Northern Starfish* is a "baddie"; its protruding stomach eats the shells-and-all of such human delectables as oysters, clams, and scallops. At the top of each of its arms the starfish's eyes are located. And as its arms swing about (while the starfish slowly climbs along some rocky surface) its eyes constantly scan its next prey.

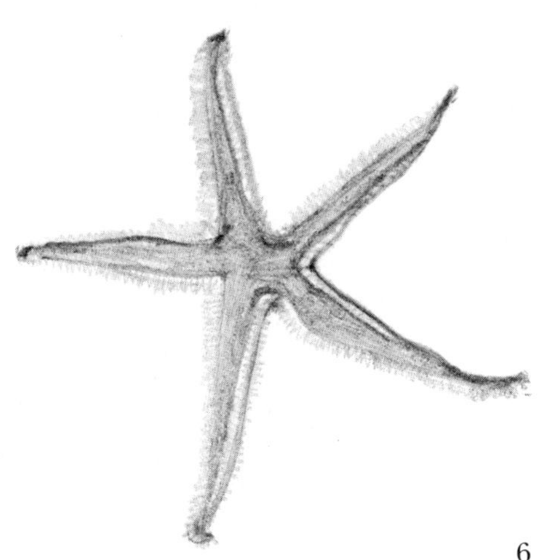

6

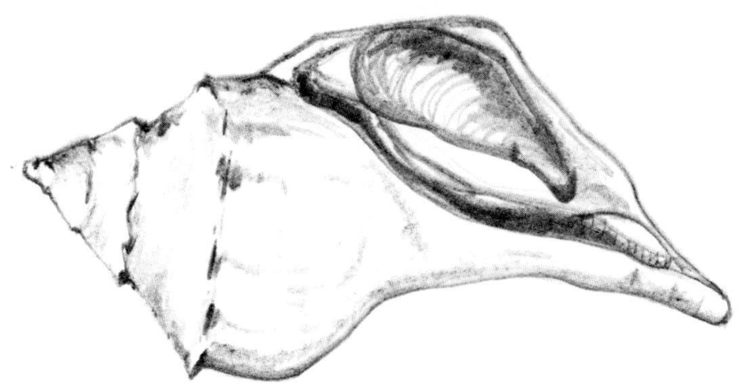

The Knobby Conch — this large, pear-shaped ashen-colored shell houses the *whelk*, a snail that's a delicacy in the West Indies.

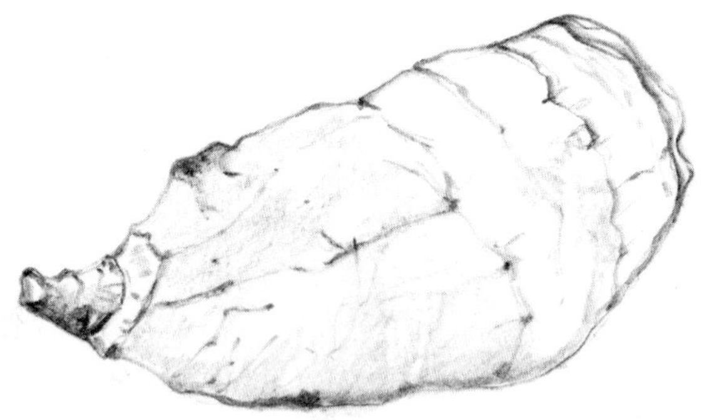

Oyster Shell — the oyster is the only bivalve mollusk with unlike shells. Its shell is often not smooth and is always ridgy.

The Surf Clam — these shells are largest and nearly triangular. The surf clam's shell, since the animal is the largest marine bivalve along our coast, makes excellent ash trays and paper weights. (A *bivalve* is simply a sea creature — an oyster, clam, or mussel — who has two shells hinged together).

Mussel — this is a smooth-shelled, blue-to-violet-to-black-blue, three to six inch mollusk. Often in clusters, its shells attach themselves by a *"byssus"* or beard to a stone or jetty.

A THALASSOPSAMMOPHILE COMMISERATES*

Rockaway, New York, where I amphibiously grew up — spending much of my early life swimming in the Atlantic Ocean and the rest of it on the mainland playing touch football, Ringolevio, and one-on-one basketball — has seen two natural tragedies in my lifetime alone: Its sand crabs have become extinct — those creepy, little burrowing beasts that all the neighborhood kids used to greedily dig for by the ocean's muddy shoreline — and its dunes have disappeared, razed by too many bulldozers greedily excavating house foundations.

Today, wisps of sand make their way from the beach, then over Rockaway's concrete walls and onto the asphalt streets. If left alone, this process (whereby fierce ocean winds hurl the beach's sand onto the streets) would eventually return to Rockaway all of her lost dunes. But instead, a Mr. Friedman — a truly conscientious and good member of the community — periodically takes a broom to the asphalt streets and sweeps all this accumulating, potential dune-forming sand back into the beach.

. . . I just wonder sometimes if Mr. Friedman, when he's out there cleaning the streets with his broom, ever thinks to himself that he's the only thing preventing the re-establishment of Rockaway's mountainous sand dunes.

**A beach lover

STARS

(THE MOON, SUN, AND THE CONSTELLATIONS)

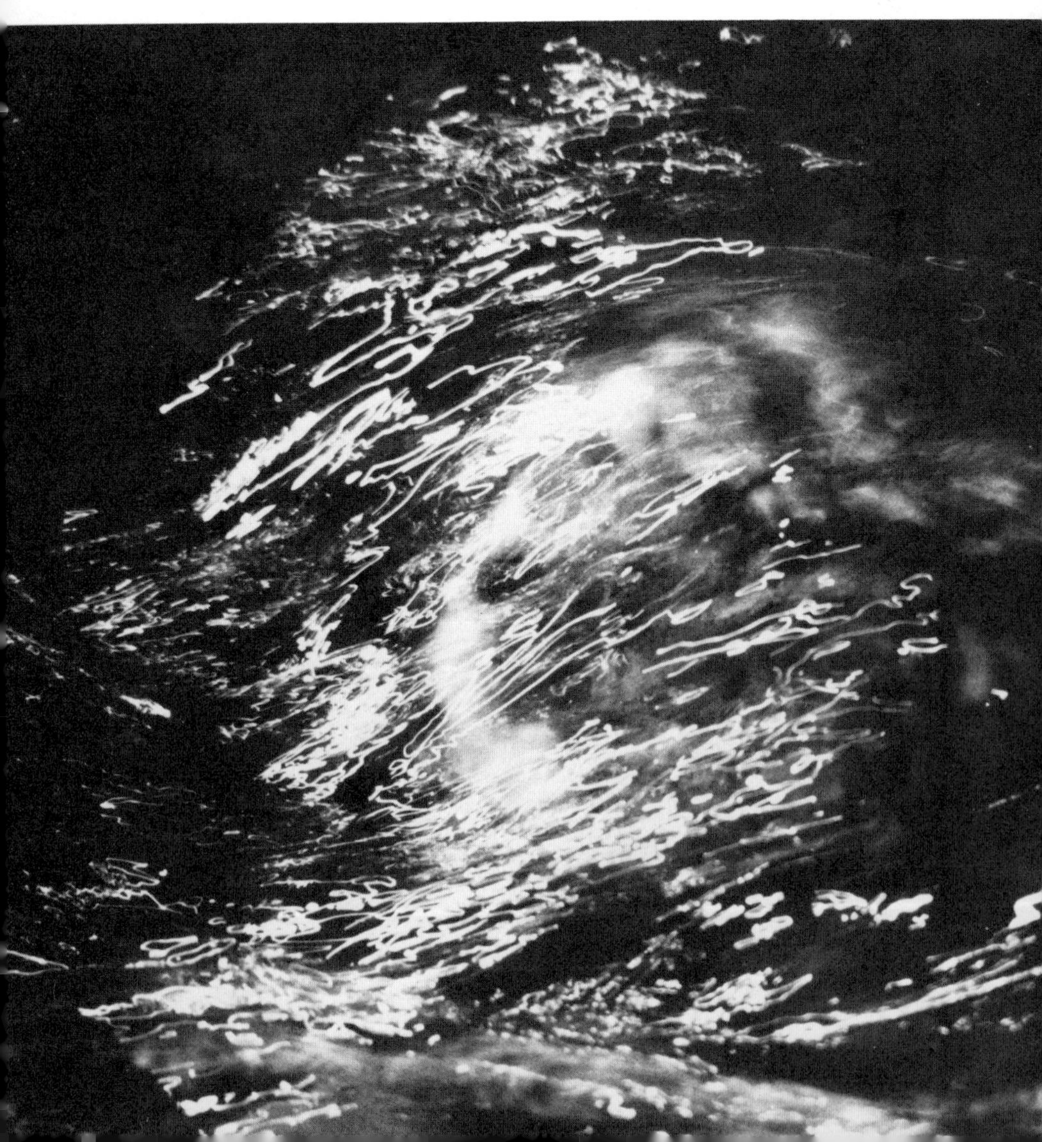

Just as I sat down and started to write about the stars the lights in my cabin blew; my electric typewriter stopping dead in its carriage. A genuinely profound coincidence because I had been thinking of beginning this penultimate chapter with a few mildly derisive comments about our society's near-total-dependence on the electric light bulb. (A very clever way, I thought, of introducing a section on the more natural sort of lighting afforded by the sun, moon, and stars.) It's dark, then, as I pen these words. But above me, beyond my study's windows, the moon and stars are shining.

THE MOON

Friends of mine, ardent astrologers, claim they have very valid insights into my personality as a result of their studying my astrological "chart" — a circular drawing of the heavenly bodies as they appeared at the time of my birth. I don't really doubt my friends' claims. The moon, I remember learning in junior high school, affects the ocean's tides; and I also remember learning in junior high school that our human bodies are composed of nearly 90 per cent water. Reasonable then that the moon should also affect our watery bodies.

Besides such profound glimpses into the human psyche, the moon can also supply us with a number of slightly more mundane insights.

First, the moon can be used as both a watch and a compass. If the moon is full and if you hold the hour hand of your watch so that it points directly towards the moon, then the direction South will always be at the halfway point between your watch's hour hand and the figure 12.

But if the moon isn't full (but is either waxing or waning), then the procedure for determining the North-South line is slightly more complex. (A *waxing* moon opens to the left, a *waning* moon to the right.)

When the moon isn't full and in order to determine the North-South line, you'll have to first determine whether the moon is waxing or waning. And in addition, you'll also have to estimate how many twelfths of the moon's face is visible. Then, for a waning moon, subtract however many hours from the actual time as there are invisible twelfths of the moon. For example, if it's twelve midnight and only one-quarter of a waning moon is visible — which means that three-quarters or nine-twelfths are *invisible* — then you'd subtract nine hours from midnight to come up with the figure three o'clock. Then simply align the figure 3 on your watch with the moon, and the North-South line will lie mid-way between the 12 and the 3.

With a waxing moon the procedure is identical except rather than subtracting the twelfths you add them.

Admittedly, those directions all sound very complicated. But once you follow them just a few times they'll become second-nature.

In addition, if you know when the moon rises and sets you can fairly accurately determine the time. A moon that's in its first quarter will rise at dusk in the south and will set at dawn in the west. And a moon that's in its last quarter will generally rise at about midnight in the east and will set at about dawn in the south. And by noting how close the moon is to either its rising or setting points, you can then estimate the time. Again, this procedure will only work if you know beforehand the exact times of the moon's rising and setting. These times are available from either a newspaper or a local observatory.

THE SUN

The sun, if we observe its daily rising and setting patterns, can also serve as a trustworthy compass. In the summer, the sun always rises in the northeast and sets in the southwest. And in both fall and spring it rises in the east and sets in the west. And regardless of the season, the sun is always in the southern sky at midday.

As with a full moon we can also use the sun to determine the North-South line. Simply align the hour hand of your watch with the sun and then locate the halfway point between the figure 12 and the hour hand. This midway point will always be facing south.

THE STARS

Before telling you about what you can see in the night sky, I think it'll be interesting if I first tell you about something you can't see. Look up at the Big Dipper, perhaps the most well-known of all the stellar constellations. This Big Dipper consists of seven stars, and if these stars were connected to one another by a pencil line they'd appear as either a question mark or as an old soup dipper. To the naked eye the bowl part of this dipper appears quite empty, nothing more than a blackened space. But viewed through large observatory telescopes, it's been ascertained that in just this small area of the dipper's bowl there are at least 1,500 galaxies of stars. Now conservatively estimating 10 **billion** stars to be in every galaxy, that means that in this comparatively small surface area located in the dipper's bowl, there's something like **10 million billion stars.** Bear in mind that many of these stars are **thousands** — yes thousands — of times larger than our own sun. This will remind us of our true place in the Cosmos.

The Greeks and Romans named the constellations, the British and Spanish explorers navigated by them, and all the poets, Indians, and lovers who've inhabited our planet have either praised or worshipped them. What follows are some brief, introductory profiles of the common stars and common star formations you'll be seeing in the heavens.

1. ORION

Orion is one of the most brilliant of all the constellations. In Greek mythology Orion was the ideal hunter, boasting Mohammed Ali-like that there was just no animal around he couldn't kill. Until his boast was successfully challenged by a scorpion; a scorpion that the Greeks later placed in the heavens as far away from Orion as possible. (The stars that comprise this scorpion constellation triumphantly rise when the defeated stars of Orion are setting.)

Orion is recognized by his belt; a straight, diagonal line consisting of three stars. (The middle star of Orion's sword, it should be noted, is really a *nebula* — a kind of cosmic dust cloud. It's one of the very few such clouds visible to the naked eye.)

2. URSA MAJOR (THE BIG DIPPER)

The Big Dipper is probably the most common of all the constellations. And its popularity derives from its serving as a "pointer" to Polaris, the North Star. (The North Star, of course, has been used by generations of navigators to guide their ships across darkened oceans and rivers.) More specifically, it's the two stars in the *bowl* of the Dipper that point to Polaris.

3.   CASSIOPEIA

On practically the opposite side of the North Star from the Big Dipper is another bright group of stars — the constellation *Cassiopeia*. Cassiopeia (who was an ancient Ethiopian Queen) is appropriately situated next to her husband, the constellation *Cepheus* and near both her daughter (the constellation *Andromeda*) and her son-in-law (*Perseus*).

The tiny, brightened cloud that's just barely visible to the naked eye near the belt of Andromeda is called the Great Nebula of Andromeda. This nebula — and here's another gentle reminder of our truly infinitesimal place in the Cosmos — contains about a *thousand million* stars.

4.   THE TWELVE CONSTELLATIONS OF THE ZODIAC

The *zodiac* is simply an imaginary line that traces the sun's path across the skies. And twelve constellations — the twelve signs of the zodiac — intersect this orbital path. These constellations have today become household words: *Aries* (the Ram), *Taurus* (the Bull), *Gemini* (the Twins), *Cancer* (the Crab), *Leo* (the Lion), *Virgo* (the Virgin), *Libra* (the Scales), *Scorpius* (the Scorpion), *Sagittarius* (the Archer), *Capricornus* (the Goat), *Aquarius* (the Water Carrier), and *Pisces* (the Fishes).

Vega is one of the brightest stars in the summer sky. Located near the constellation Lyra, it was the very first star ever to be photographed. The star's picture was taken back in 1850 on an old-fashioned daguerreotype plate at the Harvard Observatory. Sirius, the brightest star in the sky (about one-and-a-half magnitudes brighter than Vega) is located in the constellation *Cavis major* (the Greater Dog). The helical rising of this star (meaning the time when Sirius first appears in the eastern sky just before sunrise) served as a forewarning to the ancient Egyptians that the Nile was soon to flood. (The Nile's annual flooding deposited a rich soil on Egypt's fields; a rich topsoil that was responsible for ancient Egypt's agricultural hegemony.)

AURORA BOREALIS

Everything in nature is *seeworthy*. There's nothing in the skies, mountains, forests, or beaches that doesn't warrant our closest examination. But nature does have a few extra-special treats for her adoring observers: And certainly the *aurora borealis* — a celestial light show that only the Creator Himself could have choreographed — is one of these.

. . . Sheets of undulating, shimmering silver light moving across the darkened skies . . . shafts of red glowing light and frosty greens occasionally ascending from the horizon . . . the moon rising against a sometimes electric blue backdrop, lightning and falling stars gliding across this iridescent confluence of gossamer light.

These intermittent cosmic light shows are triggered by explosions on the sun. And they seem to materialize at about eleven year cycles. The early sixties, for instance, were "years of the quiet sun" and there were very few auroras during this time. But by the late sixties and early seventies these light shows again started appearing with more and more frequency in the Northeast.

146

Auroras are reverent spectacles. If you see one just lie
back and become absorbed in the subtle display. Let go of all
your frustrations and triumphs and just be there. Sit there and
be contented — humbled, awed, and reverent. And be thank-
ful for all this planet has given you.

PESTS

(AND WHAT TO DO ABOUT THEM)

When you learn to love hell, you will be in heaven.
—Thaddeus Golas—

Nature has her pests: poison ivy, poison oak, poison sumac, mosquitoes, wasps, no-see-ums, blackflies, chiggers, and black widow spiders. (Fortunately, the Northeast has very few dangerous animals and even fewer poisonous snakes.) And it's these annoying and sometimes nerve-racking plants and insects that are responsible for keeping a lot of people in their homes — their air-conditioned, television-blaring, artificially-scented homes — on warm summer days.

Now when the bugs really are pestiferous, when clouds of blackflies are menacingly roaming about, then I'd certainly recommend spending the day indoors. Read a good Dashiell Hammett novel or just spend some time with your wife/lover/kids/parents or friends. The Maine Indians, in fact, members of the Penobscot and Passamaquoddy tribes, used to leave the interior woodlands in the summertime and make their way towards the relatively bugless Maine coast — there to leisurely steam oysters and clams in hot seaweed.

But to allow nature's few pests to keep you narcotized in front of a T.V. on an otherwise perfect summer day is simply criminal. None of these pests are fatal. None even near fatal. Admittedly, they're all annoying; some, like a wasp's sting, even a little painful. But the Northeast just isn't some malaria-infested jungle, and nothing too terrible (other than falling off a high ledge or being gorged by a Maine moose — ugh) can befall you in the northeastern outdoors.

Personally, I've been bitten and stung by nearly every insect known to bite and sting in the Northeast. And I've tried — night after itchy night — not to scratch some terribly seductive poison ivy rashes. But to give up the years of enjoyment I've had in the woods just because of a few isolated rashes and bites would be utter insanity. (Somehow, too, as you begin to spend more and more time in the outdoors fewer and fewer of these pests will afflict you. It's almost as if Nature somehow decides to give you her seal of approval and then tells her pesty thugs to lay off.)

Poison Ivy is a shrub or a climbing vine easily recognized by its three shiny, dark green leaflets. These leaflets, one-to-four inches long, may be smooth-edged or bluntly-toothed. (These leaflets turn varying shades of red in the fall.)

Like the common cold, everyone has their own and often eccentric cures for ivy poisoning. Some people wash the exposed area with gasoline, others use only hot water and soap. The American Red Cross, in their *First Aid Text-Book* (a good book to own) suggests treating the itchy rashes with the following preparation: 5% Menthol, 2% Phenol, and 93% olive oil. (Any druggist will gladly concoct this preparation for you.) Perhaps most natural, though, of all the remedies for ivy poisoning is Jewelweed (also called 'snapweed' or 'touch-me-not'). Jewelweed, a wildflower often growing near poison ivy, secretes in its stem an orange-colored juice — a juice that (when rubbed on an exposed area) will almost always prevent poisoning. . . . So learn how to identify Jewelweed. It might someday save you from days and days of harrowing itching.

Jewelweed

2. POISON OAK

Poison oak is simply a variant on the same species as our more familiar poison ivy. Its leaflets are softer and more oak-like in appearance. (Treatment for poison oak is exactly the same as it is for poison ivy.)

3. POISON SUMAC

This is a rare pest — a shrub or small tree that reaches a height of 25 feet and that almost exclusively grows in or near swamps. Its seven to thirteen leaflets are two-to-three inches long, and are red-veined, smooth along the edge, and shiny. And Poison Sumac — (ask anyone who's suffered from its rashes) — is infinitely more infernal than poison ivy.

3

All the biting bugs — midges, no-see-ums, mosquitoes (only the female mosquitoes are culpable), blackflies, blood-sucking deerflies, houseflies, black widow spiders (rare in the Northeast), bees, and wasps — are among nature's most persistent pests. Thoreau, on his two jaunts into the Maine woods, used to wear a veiled hat to keep all of them out of his face. (He also burned wet leaves in a campfire, the resulting smoke serving as a bug deterrent.) Nowadays, we prefer to douse ourselves with various insect repellents of "fly dopes" — all of them smelling like oil of citronella. And, in fact, it's this citronella stench — and nothing else — that keeps the bugs away.

Now if you're going to be in the woods for an extended period of time, these small, commercial bottles of repellent (since everytime you sweat, swim, or wash they come off and then have to be reapplied) can become a costly item. So instead of buying these expensive, pre-packaged bottles, try making your own "dope" by mixing in a mortar:

> 1 ounce of pure pine tar
> 1 ounce of oil pennyroyal ›
> 3 ounces of vaseline

The resulting and economic glop should keep most of the varmints away.

For stings (wasp and bee stings) simply remove the "sting" (if it's still present) and place a soothing baking soda paste on the pricked area.

PREFACE

Now that you've been given some hints on how to see nature and have been shown some of the more common flora and fauna of the Northeast, it's finally time to get into your car and head for the beaches, mountains, and woods.

You won't need much in the way of supplies (contrary to what the sporting goods companies would have you believe): a canteen, a knapsack, some trail guides, a compass (in case you wander from one of the well-marked trails), a rain poncho, a warm parka, a good pair of walking shoes (with rubber Vibram soles that are screwed into the boot), and some quick-energy food — (either nuts or raisins — but no candy bars since all they'll ever do is give you a too frenetic sugar rush and then prematurely poop you out). And if you prefer overnight camping to day hikes, then you'll have to add to that list a tent, a sleeping bag, a backpack, an outdoor stove, and some additional food supplies. (A lot of people like to buy flashy fluorescent-orange tents and canary yellow sleeping bags. A more subdued shade of green, though — one that blends rather than clashes with the wilderness — is probably your best bet.) So for less than what you'd probably pay for fifty movies, you'll be able to equip yourself for years and years of hiking enjoyment.

This whole issue of just what to bring along on a hike can sometimes become ludicrous. Every sport, especially camping and hiking, has what's known as 'equipment freaks' — people who are obsessed with a particular sport's paraphernalia. They'll read every catalog with the avidness of a stock broker scanning the day's closing prices. Or they'll spend whole days in camping supply stores, meticulously checking out all the latest goods.

To keep your own 'equipment freak' proclivities within sane bounds, you might want to remember Milarepa, the 11th-century Tibetan saint, who used to wander around the Himilayas wearing nothing but a thin cotton garment, and carrying just a few religious objects and a bowl. Or John the Baptist, who traversed the wilderness of Judea in 'camel-hair raiment and leather girdle', eating locusts and wild honey. Or more recently, John Muir — the turn-of-the-century naturalist/writer/explorer — who used to hike with just a tin cup, some tea, a little sugar, and a bag of bread.

. . . *Travel lightly in the woods.* There's just no need to spend months deliberating about what you'll need for only a few days in the woods. (Only long expeditions warrant this sort of equipment exactitude.)

And please — don't become a dogmatic purist. Purists, in hiker's circles, are people who will refuse to bring along a bottled-gas stove on an overnight trek or who'll refuse to use a nylon tent, always insisting on building primitive lean-tos instead. But as far as I'm concerned, this sort of playing at being rugged wilderness men — being appalled at bringing any of the modern conveniences into the woods — is just a lot of atavistic baloney. Our American wilderness — which is now being used by more and more people every year — simply no longer has the wood to keep all of these mock Paul Bunyans deluded. We **have** to use portable gas stoves and we **have** to use nylon tents. Otherwise we'll only be further ravishing our precious woodlands. And certainly they've already been abused enough.

THE BACKPACKER, by Albert Saijo (distributed by Charles Scribner's Sons, New York) is a good primer for novitiate hikers. (*Novitiate* is a good word here — for in his book, Saijo treats backpacking as a religious discipline — a spiritually uplifting pursuit.) The book offers worthwhile physical, as well as metaphysical, advice of just what's involved in hiking.

Read through this *CHEAP PERSON'S TRAVEL GUIDE TO THE NORTHEAST* and then choose the sort of terrains you'd enjoy traversing. Some people will prefer near-wilderness conditions — tough, steep climbs across rocky ledges. Others — the less gung-ho of you — will opt for the easier walks — the beach strolls and macho-less mountain hikes. Whatever your preference, though, it's all here, included in the more than one-hundred recommended trips.

And one word of caution before you start your romance with nature. Nature, as much as we've all tried to tame her, has always stubbornly refused to become our gentle/never-harmful lover. She can sometimes be cruel — when, for instance, from seemingly out of nowhere — on a hot, June day — she'll all-of-a-sudden materialize near hurricane winds and freezing rains atop a New Hampshire mountain. (This, unfortunately, once happened to me — and my hands nearly froze; a pair of gloves being about the last thing I thought of bringing along on a June trek to the White Mountains.)

It's also times like these when a condition known as *hypothermia* can develop — a fatal condition that's especially wicked because of its sudden and furtive entry. The condition is the result of a too rapid lowering of the body's temperature (exhaustion, wind, and rain being the factors that bring it on); and unless it's administered to promptly (by adding heat to the victim's body — blankets and a fire) then it can too easily make a day of hiking a lifetime of mourning. So be extra careful and be fully equipped on strenuous mountain climbs.

One final caution: flowers, deer, rabbits, mosses, ferns, and just about everything else that makes his or her or its home in the woods, all deserve your absolute consideration. Enter the woods as you would a friend's home — expectantly, appreciatively, and respectfully. And always leave the woods in the same condition as you found it — alive, clean, and healthy.

. . . Drive carefully, enjoy yourself in the outdoors, and like a branch that bends but doesn't break in the wind, always yield to Mother Nature. Don't fight her.

The Creator made the world — Come and see it.
—Pima Indian Prayer—

98-101
102
103
96
95
NY
94
95
92
90
104
109
111
110
PA
106
114
112
108
116
115
107
117
113
89

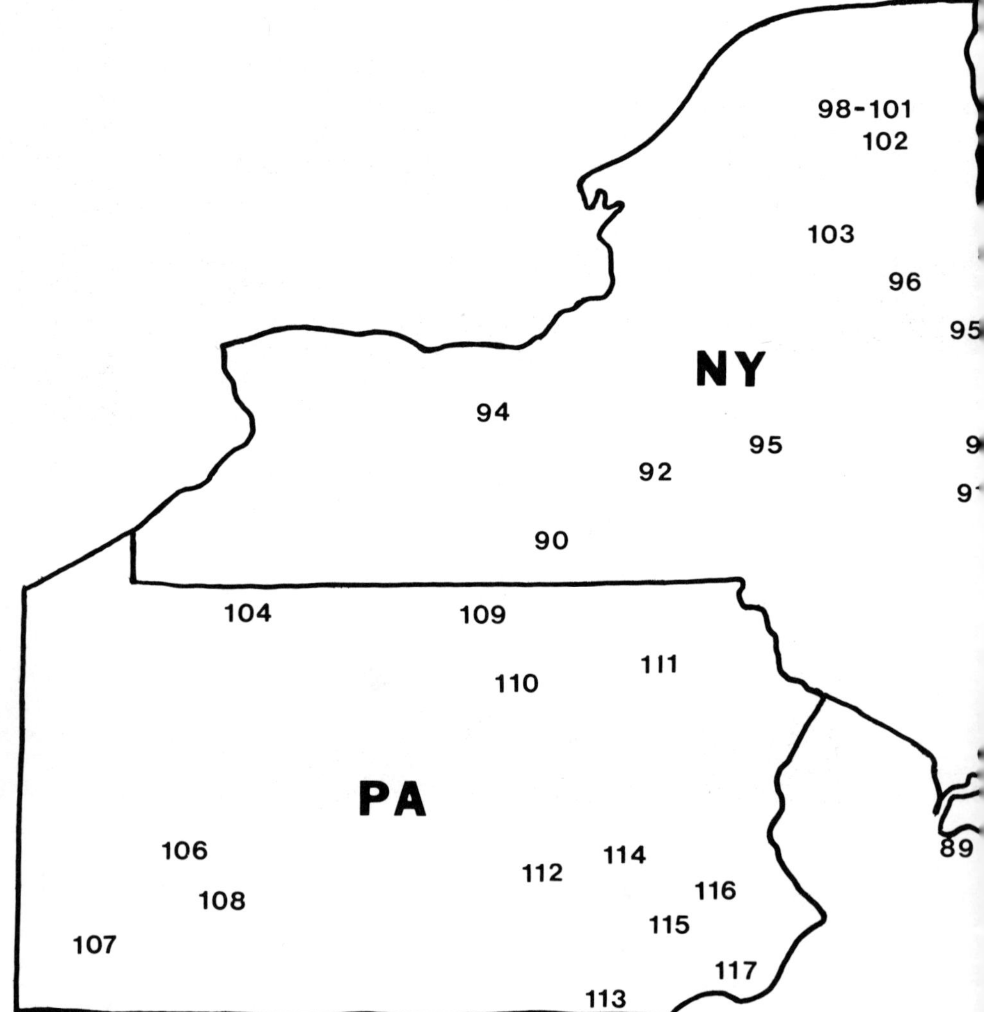

158

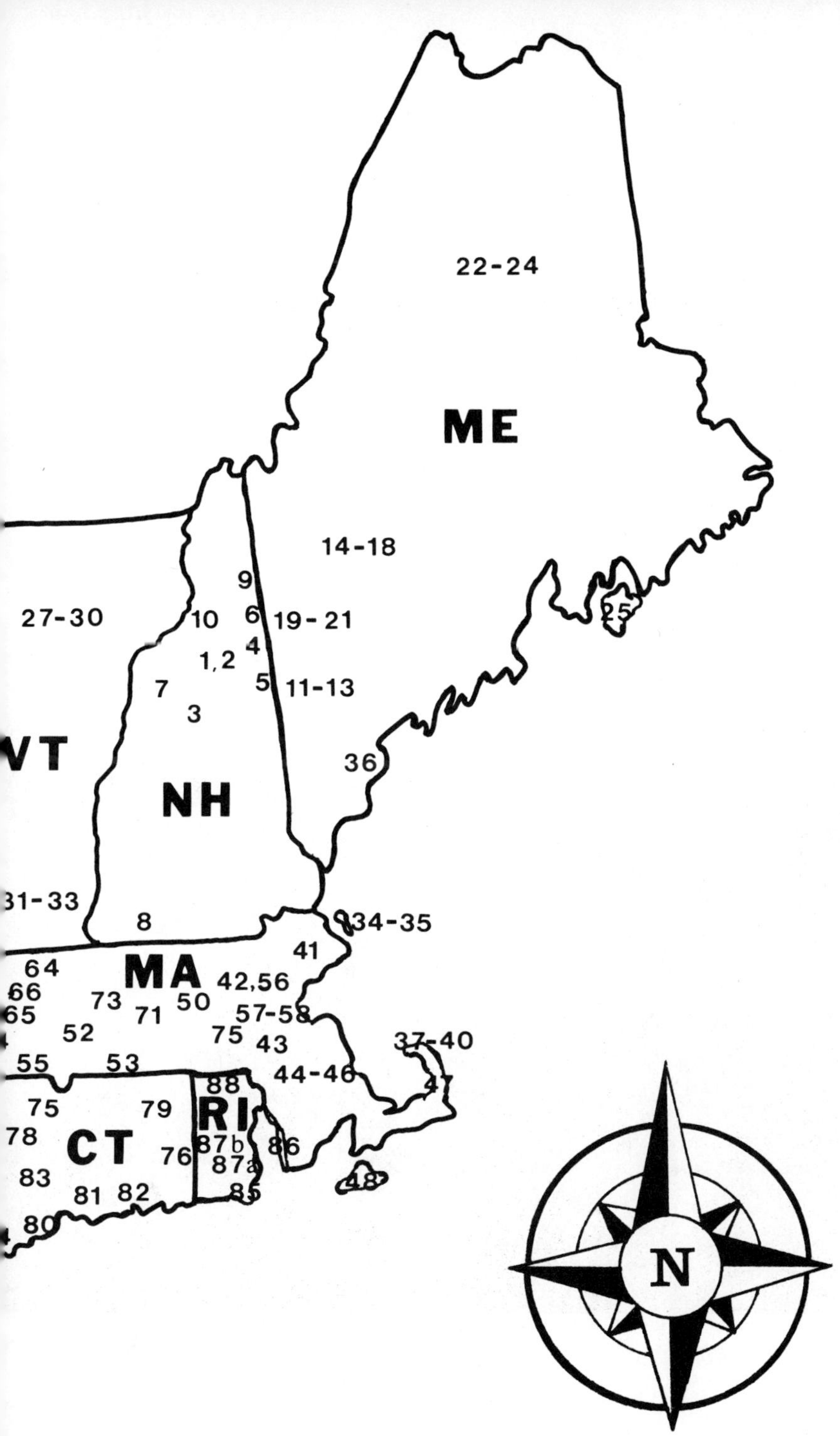

22-24
ME
14-18
9
27-30
10
6
19-21
4
1,2
5
11-13
7
3
VT
36
NH
31-33
8
34-35
41
64
MA
42,56
66
73
50
65
71
57-58
52
75
43
37-40
55
53
44-46
75
88
79
RI
87b
86
78
CT
76
87a
83
85
81
82
48
80
N

NEW HAMPSHIRE

Northern New Hampshire's White Mountains Region, covering more than three thousand square miles and extending one hundred miles north and south, is the largest area of public lands in the eastern United States. The White Mountain National Forest, traversing more than 700,000 acres, and including a number of impressive mountain ranges (among them the Sandwich Mountains, the Franconias, the Carter-Moriah Range, and the Great Presidentials) is one of the most accessible areas for viewing nature in all of New England. Hiking trails (developed and maintained by the Appalachian Mountain Club, the New Hampshire Division of Parks, and the White Mountain National Forest Association) take you deep into these federally-protected lands — down dramatic ravines, up steep slopes, above timberlines, and across remote, tundra-like topographies. And it's here, on the summits of New Hampshire's White Mountains, that a variety of rare alpine wildflowers are in bloom from mid-June to early July.

The twenty-first edition of the Appalachian Mountain Club's *White Mountain Guide* is practically indispensable for anyone planning to do any serious hiking in this region. You can write directly to the AMC, 5 Joy Street, Boston, Mass. and receive their complete catalog, along with their listing of events (guided hikes, AMC sponsored canoe trips, and seasonal lectures).

The ten hikes briefly described in this introduction to New Hampshire's White Mountain Region are all solid day hikes. So bring along a canteen or a plastic water bottle, some nuts, raisins, a loaf of bread, and enough stamina and enthusiasm to carry you all the way to the mountain's summit. Mind-blowing vistas and Disney-colored wildflowers await you up top.

(Two wilderness areas in the White Mountains National Forest — the *Great Gulf Wilderness* and the *Presidential Range-Dry River Wilderness* require permits to camp in them overnight. Write the Forest Supervisor, White Mountain National Forest, P.O. Box 638, Laconia, N.H., 03246 for further information.)

This is a day hike that those of you who are in slightly better-than-average shape should have no difficulty attempting. Most notably, the hike takes you into a remote virgin spruce forest — the virgin spruces lying on the upper reaches of Nancy Brook, a small stream that tumbles down into the Saco River. This hike begins on the west side of U.S. 302, 1.2 miles north of the Sawyer River Road and only a short drive from Crawford Notch, New Hampshire. (By using a New Hampshire road map, along with the maps put out by the AMC, you should have no problem reaching any of the sites listed in this book.)

The AMC guidebook is very explicit with this trail. You'll be crossing two brooks — Halfway Brook and Nancy Brook — and then, about 2.2 miles from the hike's start, you'll reach the base of Nancy Cascades. (Swimming here, in the clear, cool waters, is a must.) As you continue to climb from the base of the cascades — all the while with spectacular views of the falls — (these cascades being several hundred feet high) — you'll eventually reach the moss-carpeted virgin spruce forest. Finally, after hiking through this forest, you'll come to the northeast shores of Nancy Pond.

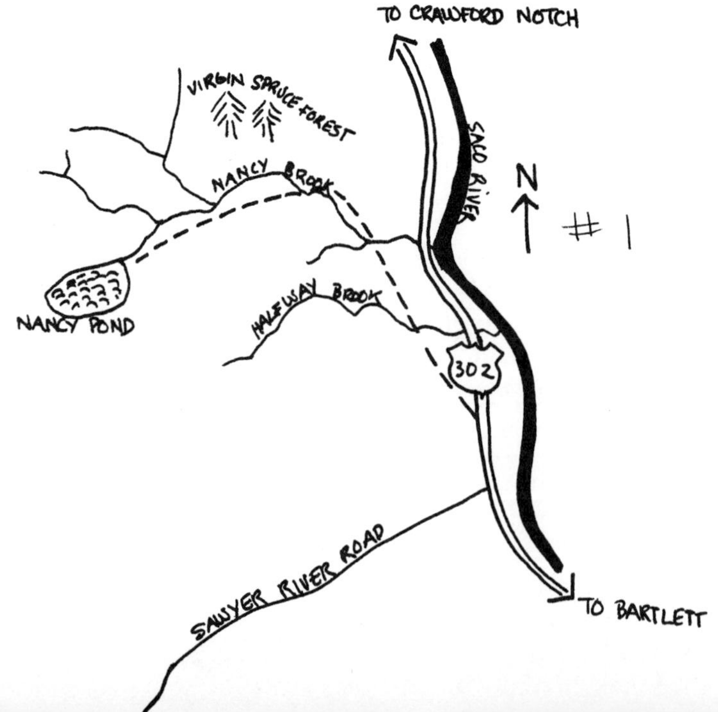

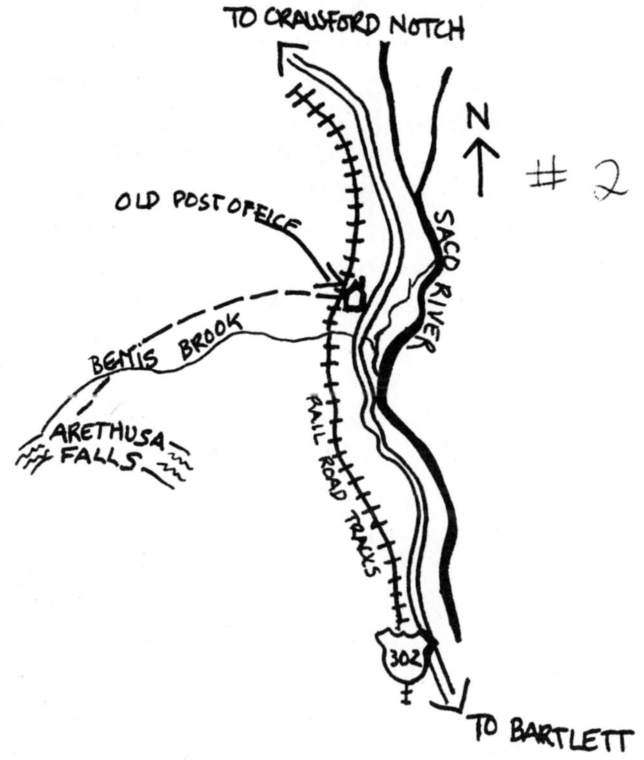

2.   ARETHUSA FALLS TRAIL

This is definitely a short beginner's hike. The trail starts at a parking lot near a former post office building, crosses some railroad tracks, and follows an old logging road above the north bank of Bemis Brook. 1¼ miles from the parking lot, you'll then reach Arethusa Falls — one of the highest falls in New Hampshire. The parking lot where this trail starts is located just off the west side of U.S. 302, only minutes north of the Nancy Pond Trail.

With lots of parking available at the nearby Lafayette Campground, the Falling Waters Trail (which leaves from the east side of US 3 — between North Woodstock and Franconia Notch, N.H., and ends at Little Haystack — a minor mountain peak high up in the Franconia Range) is an excellent day's hike. You'll be seeing waterfalls, brooks, forests (filled with yellow birch, beech, and maple), narrow ravines, gorges, Shining Rock Cliff — a massive granite rock that's over 200 feet high and nearly 800 feet long, and a wide variety of alpine wildflowers. The day I was there, *rhodora* — with its intense pinkish blossoms — was in full bloom.

Once you reach Little Haystack, assuming the day is clear and your body is up to it, you can connect from the Falling Waters Trail to the Franconia Ridge Trail and hike to the summit of Mount Lincoln (5,108 feet above sea level).

A "loop", in hiker's vernacular, is simply what its name implies: a series of hiking trails that loops around — so you eventually end up where you started from without ever having to retrace any of your original steps. If you're feeling vigorous, from Mount Lincoln you can loop back to where your car is parked by continuing on the Franconia Ridge Trail until you reach Mount Lafayette. At Mount Lafayette pick up the Greenleaf Trail, which eventually will connect into the 'Old Bridle Path' (literally an old horse trail). This 'Old Bridle Path' will then lead you out to Route 3 — just about a quarter-of-a-mile from where your car is parked.

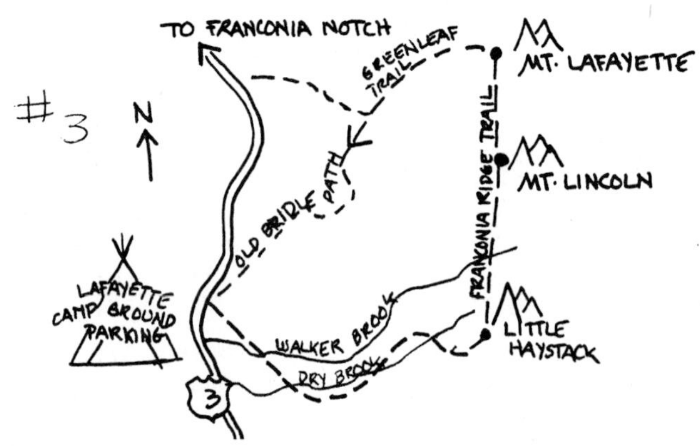

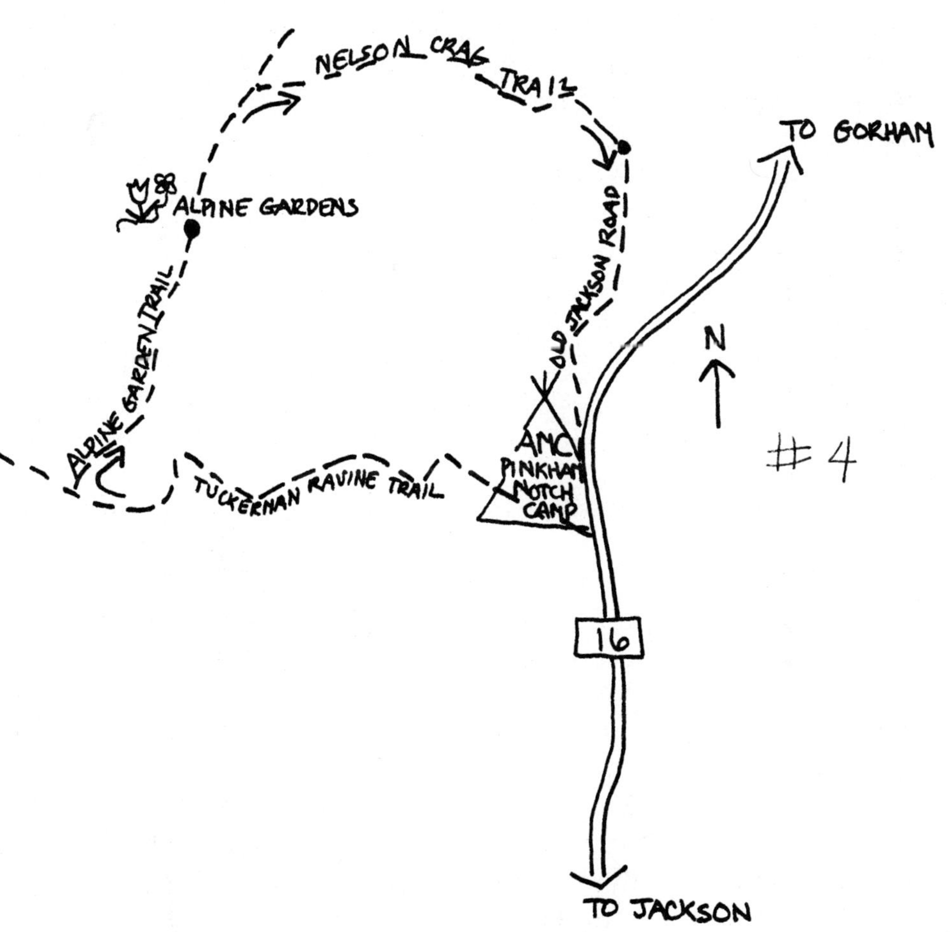

NELSON CRAG TRAIL
ALPINE GARDENS
ALPINE GARDEN TRAIL
OLD JACKSON ROAD
TUCKERMAN RAVINE TRAIL
AMC PINKHAM NOTCH CAMP
TO GORHAM
N
#4
16
TO JACKSON

It's a fact that every 400 feet in a mountain's elevation produces the same sort of climate that an area 100 miles farther north of it would have — which is just a fancy way of saying that the higher up you go, the colder it gets. The climate that exists, therefore, say 5,000 feet up on Mount Washington (which is about where the trees stop growing), is roughly the same climate that northern Quebec experiences. And it's here, oddly enough, above Mount Washington's timberline, on the largest mountain east of the Mississippi (6,288 ft.) that more than 110 species of rare flowering plants yearly bloom from June to early July. (Logical, then, that many of these same plants are also found on the arctic tundra of northern Canada, and at lower elevations in Alaska and Greenland.)

Spring, incidentally, travels north at a rate of approximately 17 miles a day, slowing up only when it has to ascend mountains and hills. Then it climbs at the considerably slower rate of a hundred feet a day. Consequently, spring arrives late on the top of Mount Washington — sometime around late May/early June.

Probably the best place in the Northeast to view this colorful display of mountain wildflowers is at "The Alpine Garden" — a flat area on the steep eastern slope of Mount Washington. Here, clusters of flowers sometimes 10 feet square — all of them of strikingly varied hues — thrive in the peaty mountain soil.

To reach the Alpine Garden you'll begin your hike at the Appalachian Mountain Club's Pinkham Notch Camp, which is 10 miles north of the town of Jackson, New Hampshire. The AMC's buildings are right off of NH 16. At the Pinkham Notch Camp, you can obtain trail maps explaining just how to reach the Alpine Garden. In addition, there are a few exhibits of the region's flora and fauna at the AMC-sponsored camp, as well as reasonably priced food and lodging. For further information write: Appalachian Mountain Club, Northern N. E. Regional Office, Gorham, New Hampshire 03581.

This walk begins just minutes outside of North Conway, New Hampshire. It's a good day's trek, taking you along a well-marked trail. The trail begins at Diana's Baths — a small water pool that's just a couple of miles outside of North Conway. The Baths are reached from North Conway by turning off the West Side Road, 1¼ miles north of what's known as the Lucy Farm. This farm, which will be on your left hand side (assuming you're driving from North Conway) has a well-kept white farm house. Turning off the road and parking your car along the shoulder of a dirt road, you should then follow the signs leading to Diana's Baths. And it's at the Baths, on a nearby tree, that an accurate trail map describing the terrain you'll be crossing is posted. The distance from Diana's Baths to the summit of North Moat Mountain (3,201 ft.) is 3¾ miles.

(All throughout the Northeast, you'll be running across small bodies of water — each of them with the name *Diana* appended to them: *Diana's* pool, *Diana's* brook, *Diana's* baths. Diana, by the way, was an ancient Roman deity, believed to be the goddess of the moon.)

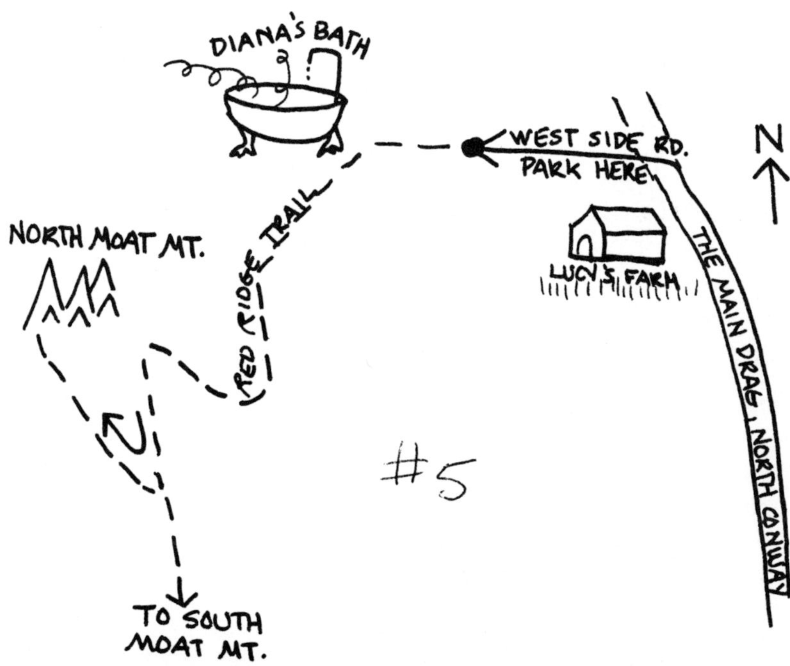

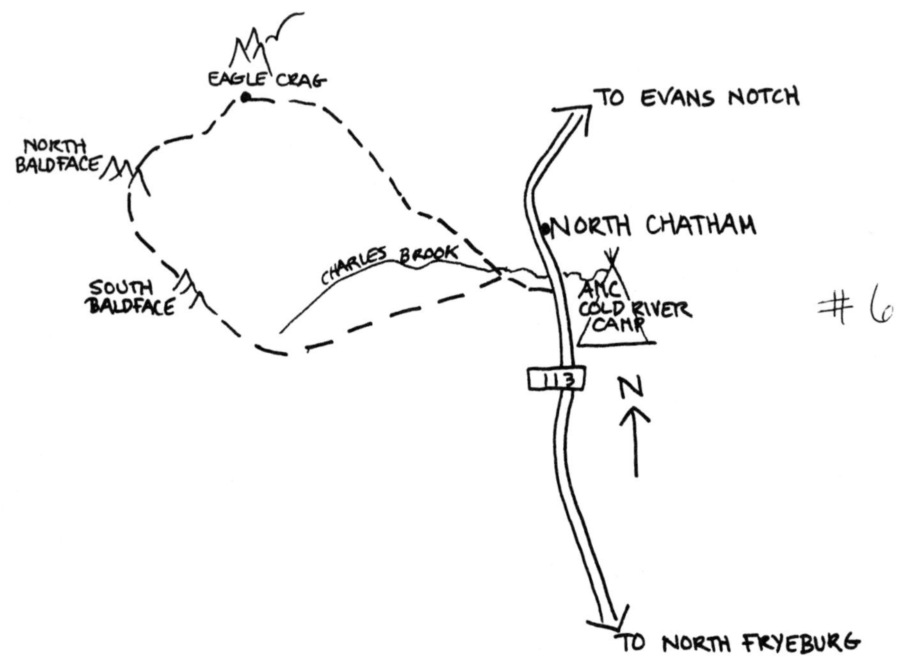

6.   BALDFACE CIRCLE TRAIL

Just south of the bridge going over the Charles Brook and
$1/5$ of a mile north of the Cold River Camp (see map) is the beginning of this approximately nine mile "loop" through the
North Chatham Region of eastern New Hampshire. (The
Baldface Circle Trail, incidentally, is the hike recommended
by the AMC as being this area's most attractive.)

Back in 1903, massive fires denuded many of the summits
here. As a result, miles and miles of unobstructed vistas, in
addition to countless brooks and pools, contribute to making
this trek one of eastern New Hampshire's "musts". Some of the
climbing on this trip, though, is steep. So if you're feeling lazy,
avoid the Baldface Circle Trail.

In the hiking world, as in the fashion, business, and show-biz worlds, everyone has different preferences. Consequently, some hikers like tough, steep hikes in the woods, while others prefer gradual climbs up eroded mountain sides. Still others simply enjoy leisurely strolls along well-travelled logging roads. My own preference is for water: tumbling cascades, icy springwater pools, winding brooks. Their sounds, smells, and beauty are what makes my days of hiking so extraterrestrially worthwhile.

The Beaver Brook Trail, in the Moosilauke Region of the White Mountains, is probably one of the most densely water populated trails around. Beaver Brook, which runs into Beaver Pond, and the Beaver Brook Cascades — being among the finest water displays in the entire region — make this hike a personal favorite. It's a solid four-to-six hour hike, covering about three miles of sometimes steep, always waterful terrain.

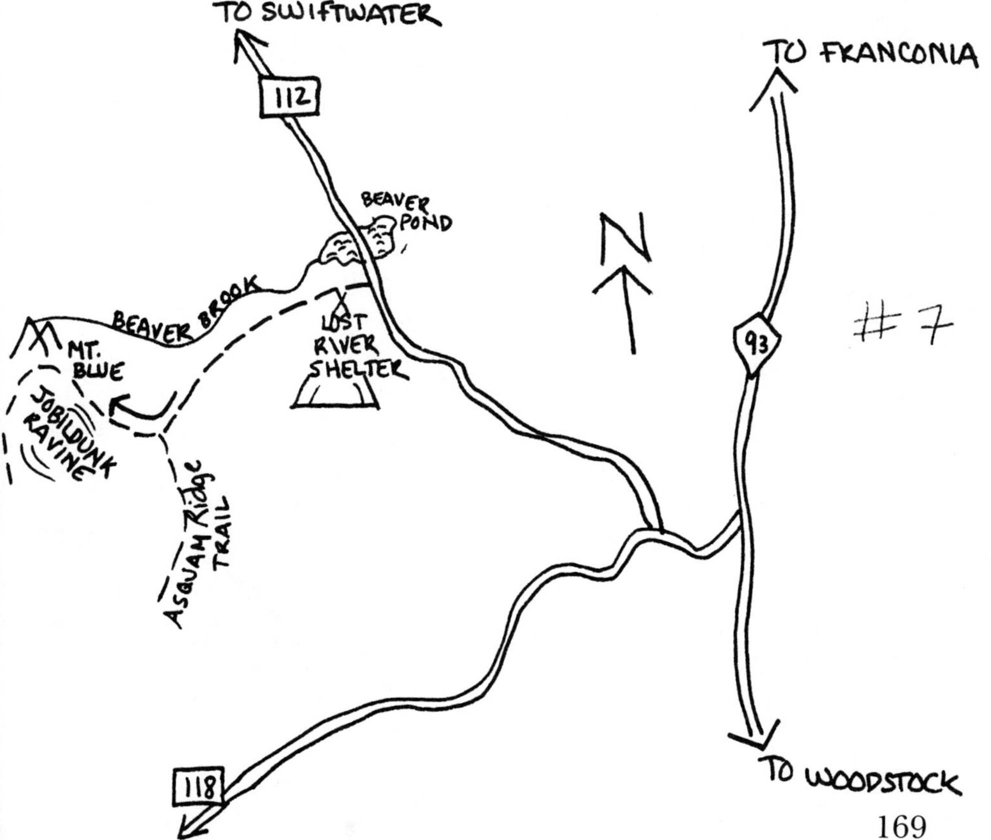

8. MOUNT MONADNOCK
"THE MOST CLIMBED MOUNTAIN IN AMERICA"

Located In Jaffrey, New Hampshire, Mount Monadnock is something of a protuberant freak. In the middle of an otherwise low and hilly terrain, this 3,165 foot peak dramatically extends the skyline. Geologists, of course, have their own explanation for this sort of isolated peak: hundreds of millions of years ago, they claim, after the earth's topography (previously ravaged and transformed by pounding glaciers and internal eruptions) had finally stabilized itself, God's sculpting knife — erosion — began its work of carving out our present-day landscape. Torrential waters, constantly and powerfully beating against the earth's rock layer, geologists theorized, formed our mountains and valleys — the very topography we know today. But in some areas, probably where the layer of the earth's bedrock was more resistant to the forces of erosion, a number of mountains simply refused to be razed. Mount Monadnock, in southern New Hampshire (just 10 miles north of the Massachusetts border) was one such stubborn area. (Geologists have even made the mountain's name a generic term — *monadnock* — today meaning any mountain that towers over its immediate surroundings.)

From Monadnock's summit, on a clear day, you can see to the north and east a sizable part of New Hampshire; to the west the expansive ridges of Vermont's Green Mountains; and to the south, the entire length of the state of Massachusetts — all the way from Boston's Prudential Tower to North Adam's Mount Greylock, near the New York border.

Because of ancient forest fires, which stripped the mountain's upper five-hundred-feet of all its tree growth, the resulting open ledges today offer hikers some of the best vistas in the entire Northeast. Six well-marked, fairly easy trails lead to Monadnock's summit; and each of them makes a more than satisfying hike.

172

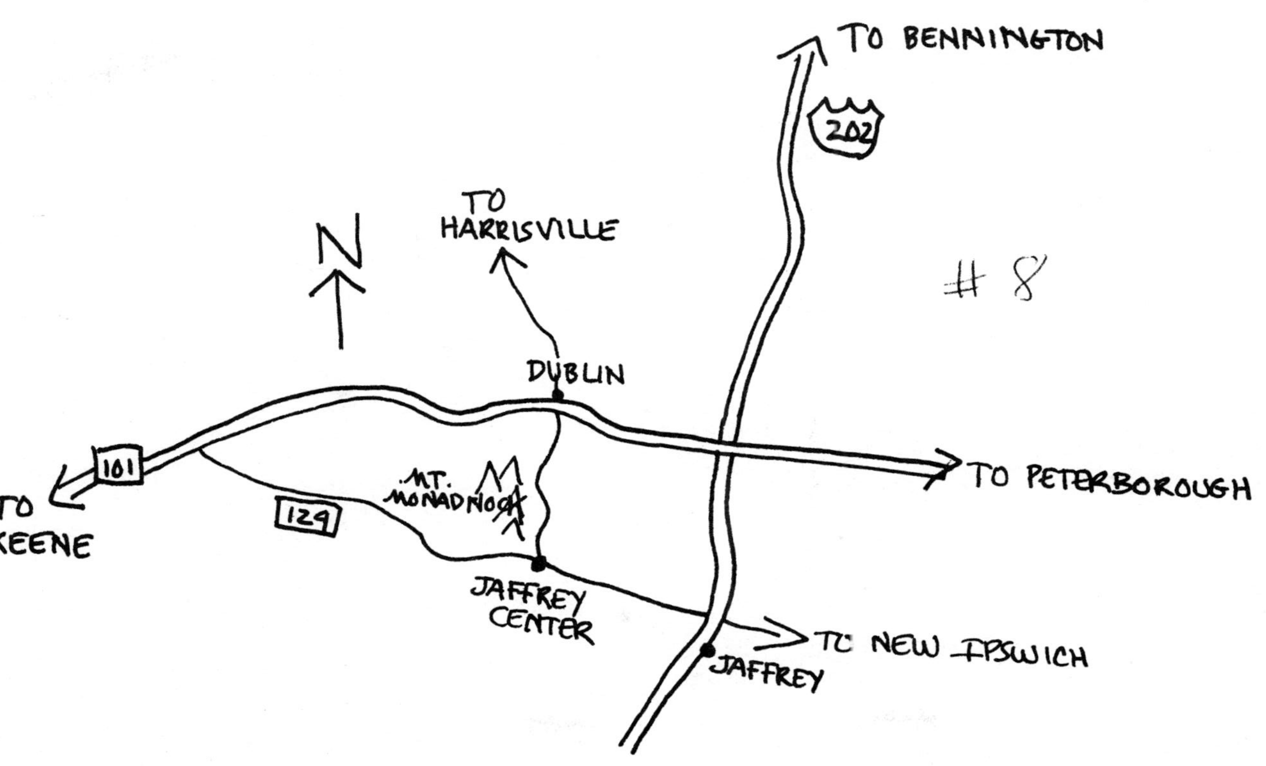

TO BENNINGTON
202
N
TO HARRISVILLE
DUBLIN
8
TO PETERBOROUGH
TO KEENE
161
129
MT. MONADNOCK
JAFFREY CENTER
TO NEW IPSWICH
JAFFREY

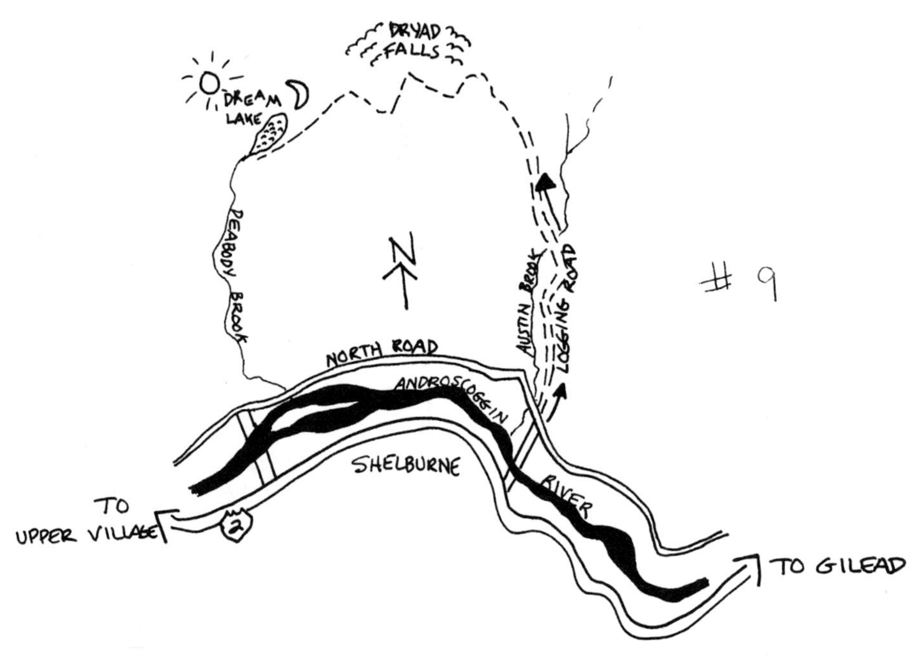

9. DRYAD FALL TRAIL

The *Dryad Fall Trail* is another of New Hampshire's waterful hikes. Dryad Fall, one of the highest cascades in the Mahoosic Range Region, along with Dryad Brook and Dream Lake are all included on this short (1½ mile) hike. To reach this trail's starting point turn off US 2 (northeast of Shelburne, NH) onto the road that crosses the Androscoggin River. Then turn left onto North Road until you reach a logging road. This logging road will finally take you to the beginning of the Dryad Fall Trail.

This approximately 2½ mile trek to the summit of the Presidential Range's third highest peak — Mount Jefferson — has been included here for those of you who really enjoy steep, steep climbs. Climbing up the "caps" or ledges of this trail will prove tough work; in fact, practically a quarter of the Caps Ridge Trail is a straight, vertical climb.

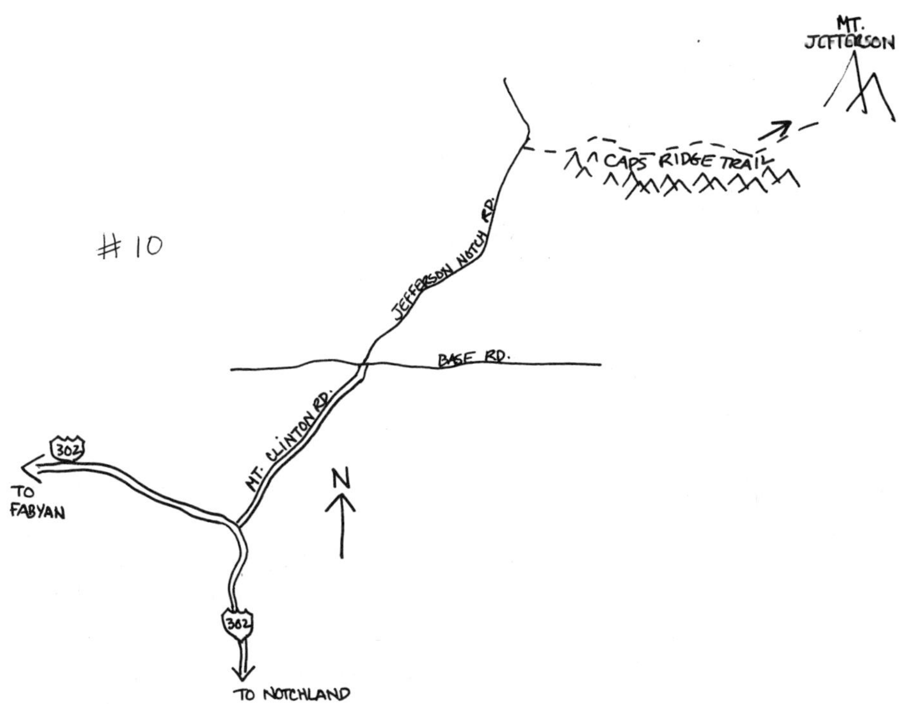

MAINE

In land mass, Maine is larger than New Hampshire, Rhode Island, Connecticut, and Vermont combined. Its more than 20 million acres presents one of the most variegated topographies in all the Northeast. Her rugged seacoast and sandy beaches, along with all her rolling farmlands and vast wilderness, makes the state of Maine, as the state's license plates proclaim, a genuine "Vacation-land". Over 2,200 lakes and ponds are listed on the Maine map, as well as 5,100 rivers and streams. *Cadillac Mountain* (1,530 ft.) in Acadia National Park, offers the highest elevation of any point along the entire Atlantic Coast (north of Rio De Janerio). And *Mount Katahdin* (5,267 ft.) in Baxter State Park provides some of the Northeast's most extraterrestrial vistas.

Two-thirds of Maine is owned by large timber corporations. (The state, incidentally, produces more than 26,000,000,000 toothpicks each year.) *Great Northern* owns 2.4 million of Maine's acres — which is more than twice as much land as both New Hampshire's White Mountain National Forest and Vermont's Green Mountain National Forest combined. *International Paper* 1.1 million. The *Scott Paper Company* 750,000. Traversing these corporate-owned lands (most of them are in northwestern Maine) are private roads that are usually open to the public. But along a number of these private roads are traffic control centers that are constructed and maintained by the various corporations. And each time you run into one of these toll booths, it'll cost you a couple of dollars. For additional and free information on northern Maine and her privately owned lands write: The Paper Industry Information Office, 133 State Street, Augusta, Maine 04330 and ask for their *Sportsman's Map of Northwestern Maine.*

Winter hiking in Maine (and winter cross-country skiing) is not as treacherous as you might imagine. With a pair of snowshoes, you can climb along many of the state's snow-covered trails. *Baxter State Park's* nearly 200,000 acres are especially popular for winter treks. (Permission to hike at Baxter is required from October 16 through May. For permission write: Supervisor, Baxter State Park, P.O. Box 540, Millinocket, Maine 04462.)

And besides winter skiing, I've also heard of people panning for gold (with limited but fun-filled success) in some of northern Maine's mountain streams.

11. A CANOE TRIP DOWN THE SACO RIVER

For canoeing, the Saco River in Southwestern Maine is probably one of the best beginner's trips around. The Saco (an Indian word meaning 'a snake-like stream running amidst pine trees') is a shallow and winding river whose shores are mostly sand-covered beaches. Starting from Swann's Falls, which is just north of Fryeburg, Maine (off of Route 5), you can follow the river downstream to the Walker's Bridge — a

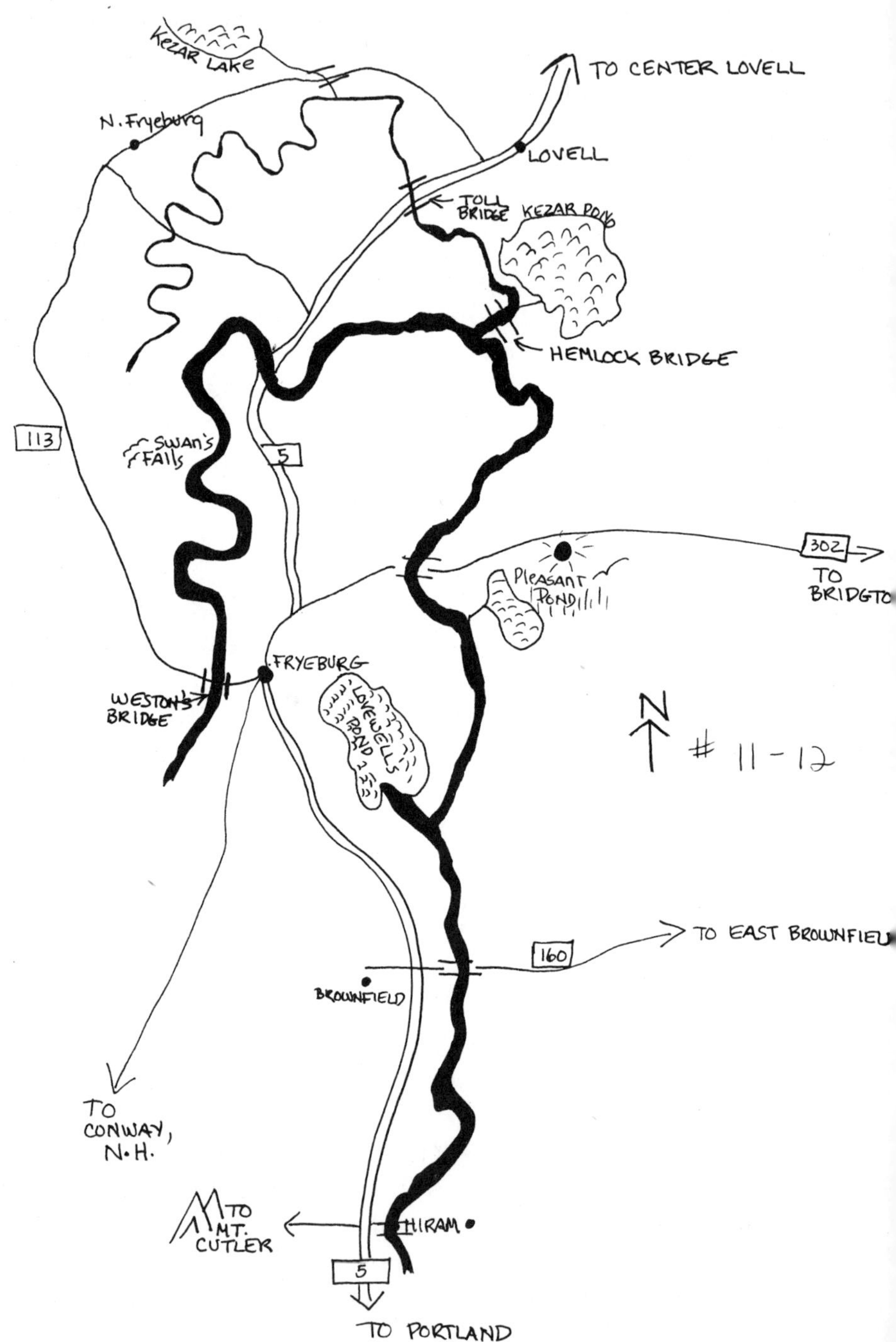
KEZAR LAKE
TO CENTER LOVELL
N. Fryeburg
LOVELL
TOLL BRIDGE
KEZAR POND
HEMLOCK BRIDGE
113
SWAN'S FALLS
5
302
TO BRIDGTO
PLEASANT POND
N
11-12
FRYEBURG
WESTON'S BRIDGE
LOVEWELLS POND
TO EAST BROWNFIE
160
BROWNFIELD
TO CONWAY, N.H.
TO MT. CUTLER
HIRAM
5
TO PORTLAND

12-mile run that makes for a solid day's trip. If you prefer to go out for two days, you can continue beyond the Walker's Bridge and paddle all the way down to Hiram, a small town that's nearly thirty miles from Swann's Falls. Side trips into historic Lovewell Pond (where white men brutally quelled an Indian uprising back in 1725) or Pleasant Pond are also easily navigated. (Fire permits are required for overnight camping along the river's beaches. They're available at no charge at several convenient locations in Fryeburg.)

Canoeing is one of the best ways to see and appreciate nature. If you start your journey just when the sun is coming up and then quietly float downstream, you'll probably be able to see more birds and animals along the river's or lake's shore than at any other time of day. A canoe moves unobtrusively through the water, allowing its occupants to be silent observers of the early-morning outdoors.

And certainly, you don't have to be an adventuresome sort of tough-guy to enjoy a canoe trip. As long as you're journeying along a relatively calm and rapidless river, then anyone can enjoy a leisurely downstream paddle. Along the Saco, I've seen parents, toddlers, and dogs all effortlessly and luxuriously floating downstream.

Canoes are lightweight, inexpensive (a used canoe can often be bought for less than a hundred dollars), and durable. So even if you invest in a new canoe (somewhere around $200.00), the years of enjoyment you'll be deriving from it will quickly eclipse your initial investment. (Canoe rentals, too, are reasonable. *The Saco River Canoe & Kayak, Inc.*, for example, on Route 5 — north of Fryeburg — rents out canoes for around $11.00 a day.)

A LANDLUBBER'S RESPITE

12. MOUNT CUTLER

See previous trip's map.

After your overnight canoe trip down the Saco, and in walking distance from the Hiram Bridge (see map for trip #11) is *Mount Cutler*. The open ledges of this 1,180 foot summit provide excellent views of the White Mountains. You can take your canoe out of the water at Hiram — shoring it on the west bank of the Saco — and then hike along Mountain View Road (a narrow blacktop road that abuts Cotton's Variety Store). The trail ascending Mount Cutler will then start off of Mountain View Road — at the site of an old railroad station.

Along the trail, not far from an old picnic area (you'll see remnants of a group of old picnic tables here) is an abandoned gold mine. The mine, however, isn't as dramatic as you might imagine: it's just a large hole that's been dynamited out of the rock.

Finally, from atop the eastern ledges of Mount Cutler, you'll be able to see your canoe — docked near the Hiram Bridge. . . . As a landlubber's respite from your canoe trip down the Saco, Mount Cutler is a worthwhile divertissement.

13.   JOCKEY CAP

This is a "gentleman's climb". It's an easy quarter-mile stroll to *Jockey Cap's* 600-foot garnet-studded top — a summit overlooking Lovewell Pond. The ledge, which rises perpendicularly some 200 feet above the surrounding plain, is just east of Fryeburg, Maine on Route 302. At the top of Jockey Cap is a circular bronze reproduction of all the surrounding summits that was etched by Robert E. Peary, discoverer of the North Pole. Jockey Cap, local residents perhaps mistakenly and self-aggrandizingly claim, is the largest boulder in the world.

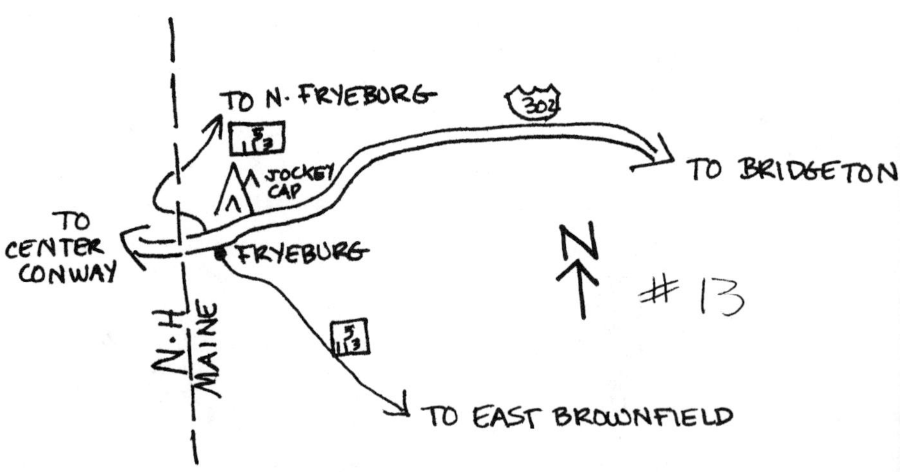

180

FIVE HIKES IN MAINE'S LITTLE-KNOWN WELD REGION

Weld is a small village in western Maine that's completely encircled by mountains. Though most guidebooks either overlook or underplay Weld's hiking areas, the region — being relatively isolated — is probably my favorite hiking area in all of northern New England.

14.   PARKER'S RIDGE TRAIL

This is probably the easiest trail to the summit of Tumbledown Mountain (3,035 ft.). The first mile of this approximately 2-mile hike isn't too steep. As you climb towards the open ledges of Parker's Ridge, though, the incline will sharpen; and I guarantee you the backs of your legs will start to feel a commensurate strain.

From the open ledges of Parker's Ridge, the trail then descends to Tumbledown Pond — a crater lake that's 2,250 feet above sea level.

15.   THE BROOK TRAIL

This is the shortest trail to the crater lake. This "Lake In The Clouds", Maine's highest lake, is probably the biggest drawing card to the entire Weld region. Surrounded by acres of mountain laurel, the lake is a deserved and sumptuous reward for any hiker finally reaching its shores. And once at the lake, be sure to swim out to the lake's island. The view from this small island is transcendent.

LITTLE JACKSON MT.
TO PHILLIPS
TUMBLEDOWN MT.
CRATER LAKE
PARKER RIDGE TRAIL
BROOK TRAIL
TO BYRON
MT. BLUE
156
LAKE WEBB
N
14-18
TO WILTON
BALD MT.
TO DIXFIELD
142
142

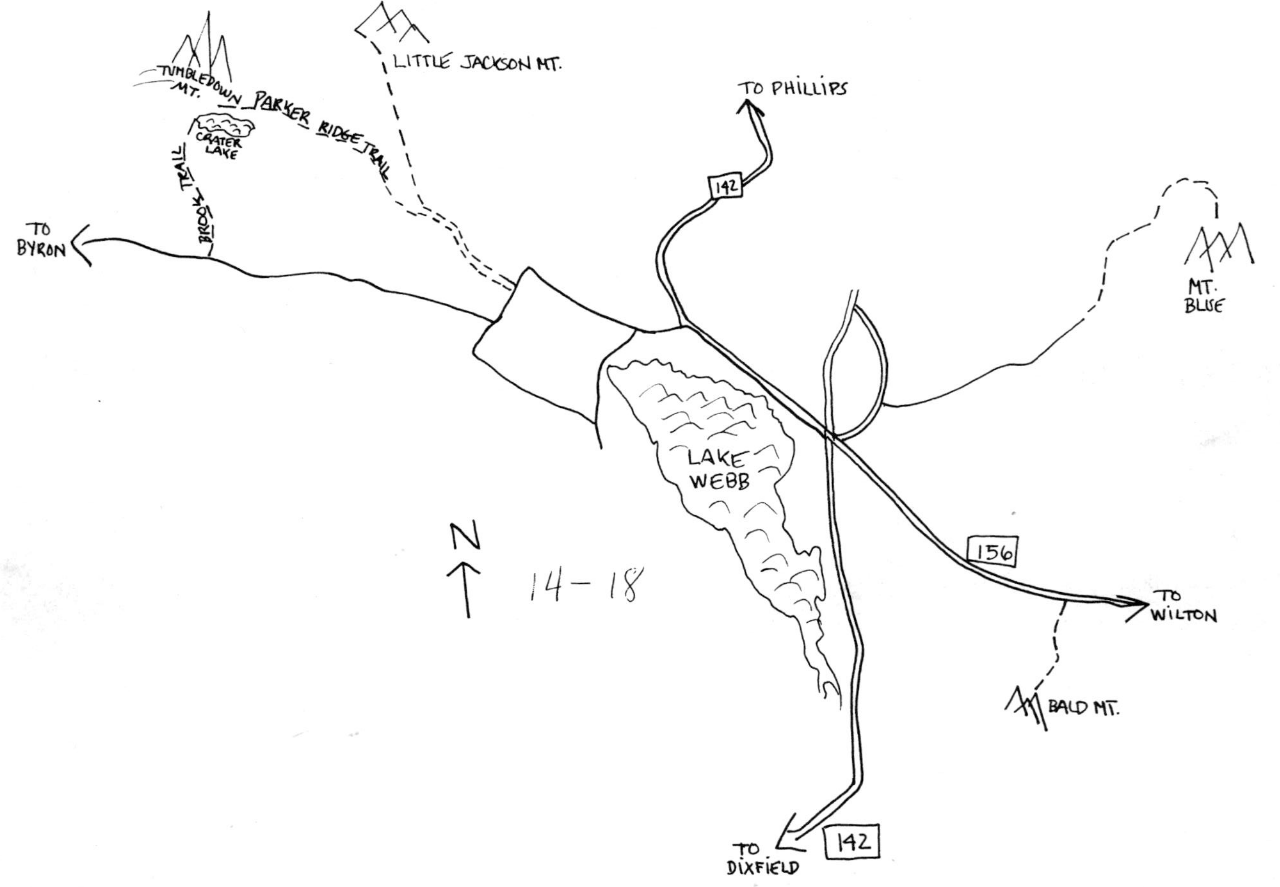

182

A "loop" trail can be devised by first going up the Little Jackson Trail (which traverses lots of lush, open areas) and then heading south along a rough trail from Little Jackson's bald rock summit (3,434 ft.). This trail crosses Parker's Ridge and eventually leads to Tumbledown Pond. From the pond, you can then return to your car by descending the Parker's Ridge Trail.

17. MOUNT BLUE

Mount Blue presents one of the most perfectly conical-shaped peaks in all of Maine. This 1.6 mile, straight-up climb never strays from a broad, well-cleared, easily navigated trail. Atop the summit is a steel firetower that affords *excellent views* of the surrounding countryside. (That expression "excellent views" is a classic Maine understatement. The views atop Mount Blue are supranormal.)

18. BALD MOUNTAIN

Like Fryeburg's *Jockey Cap* (trip #13), this is a hike that just about any well-preserved octogenarian can manage. It's a pleasant and easy climb of $7/8$ miles to the mountain's open ledges. The trail starts from a small parking area on the south side of Route 156 — which is only about 5 miles east of Weld.

Part of the White Mountain National Forest spills over from New Hampshire into western Maine. This easternmost end of the nationally protected woodlands is called the *Evans Notch-Chatham* region. And on the whole, the trails here are better marked than those in New Hampshire.

Heading north, just beyond the town of North Chatham, turn right onto Shell Pond Road (a narrow, dirt road). Follow the road (making sure to always bear right) until you see a green metal gate. Parking your car near this gate, continue walking along Shell Pond Road for about an additional ½ mile. The entrance to the Stone House Trail will then be clearly marked on your left hand side.

A flume — which is a deep gorge with cold, mountain water pouring through it — makes this trail particularly worthwhile. The Stone House Trail climbs to the top of Blueberry Mountain (1,820 ft.) and from there, to complete a "loop", you can return via the White Cairn Trail (see map).

20. RATTLESNAKE BROOK

Though this hike isn't even listed in the *Appalachian Mountain Club's Maine Trail Guide* (nor anywhere else for that matter), it's nevertheless one of the better day treks in the Evans Notch-Chatham region. Very simply, what you'll be doing here is following Rattlesnake Brook — hiking along the brook's meanderings from the beginning of the Stone House Trail right up to the rivulet's source, high atop Ames Mountain.

Besides this trail being a choice mushroom-hunting ground, you'll also intermittently be coming across deep mountain pools, many of them at the bottoms of tumbling cascades. And since you'll be far off the beaten path on this trek, I'd suggest taking a quick plunge into the icy waters.

A lot of this hike requires stone-stepping: you'll be jumping from rock to rock practically all the way up the brook. Make sure, therefore, that you have a pair of sturdy hiking boots. Your ankles will need the support.

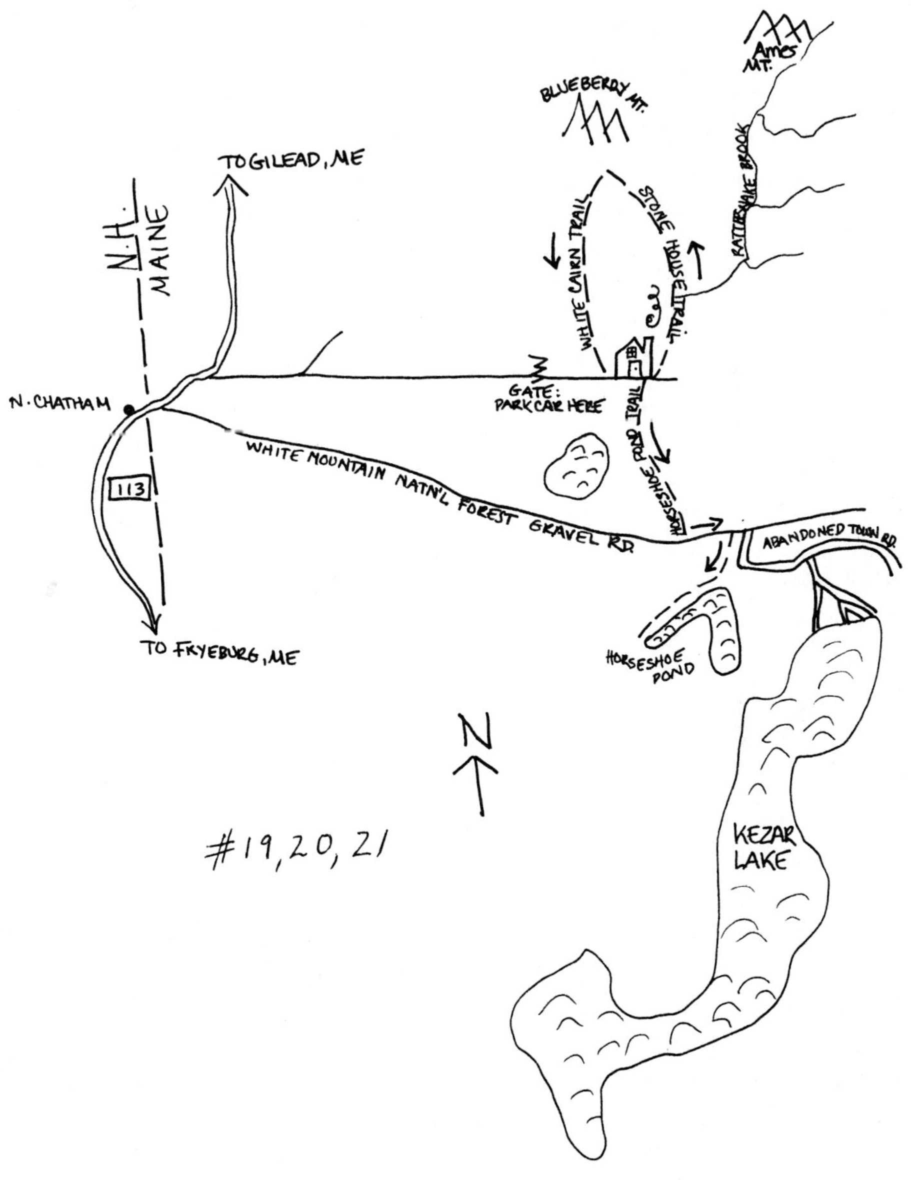

Ames MT.
BLUEBERRY MT.
RATTLESNAKE BROOK
TO GILEAD, ME
STONE HORSESHOE TRAIL
WHITE CAIRN TRAIL
N.H.
MAINE
GATE: PARK CAR HERE
N. CHATHAM
HORSESHOE POND TRAIL
113
WHITE MOUNTAIN NAT'N'L FOREST GRAVEL RD.
ABANDONED TOWN RD.
TO FRYEBURG, ME
HORSESHOE POND
N
#19, 20, 21
KEZAR LAKE

21. HORSESHOE POND TRAIL

To reach the beginning of the Horseshoe Trail follow the same directions that were given for trips #19 and #20. Horseshoe Pond Trail starts just beyond the stone house (marked by a sign). You'll be travelling southeast across level fields and woodlands until you'll gradually ascend to a White Mountain National Forest gravel road. By following this road eastwards (for a little more than a half-mile) and by then turning right onto a foot road, you'll soon reach the northwestern shores of Horseshoe Pond.

From Horseshoe Pond, you can reach the western shores of *Kezar Lake* by traversing a series of old and abandoned town roads (see map).

Kezar Lake (named for George Ebenezer Kezar — the first trapper and white settler on the lake's shores) has been called a "bit of Switzerland". Its beauty, in fact, back in the nineteen-thirties, attracted Rudy Vallee, the Maine-born star of stage, screen, and television. Vallee built a 300-acre estate on Kezar Lake and eccentrically named each of the rooms in his mansion after a song he popularized. Roguishly, Rudy named his own private bedroom — "Vagabond Lover".

22.   MOUNT KATAHDIN AND BAXTER STATE PARK

There are about seventy-five million people who live within driving distance of the Maine-New Hampshire-Vermont north woods. Fortunately, only a very small percentage of these people ever avail themselves of our northeastern wilderness. But *Baxter State Park*, located about eighty miles north of Bangor, near the town of Millinocket, is one of the region's most heavily used (some would even complain over-used) state parks. The park's beauty — being the home of Mount Katahdin, Maine's highest peak — no doubt accounts for the park's popularity.

I'd like to here offer a brief panegyric to Percival Baxter, the man whose visionary zeal both conceived of and materialized this more than 200,000 acre state park. Baxter was a former governor of Maine who, at a time when conserving wilderness areas was thought to be a ludicrous (if not a downright subversive-to-capitalism-and-free-ownership) idea, decided to preserve some of Maine's virgin lands. For thirty years, Baxter, using his own financial resources, accrued all the acreage surrounding Mount Katahdin. This monomaniacal project, which began in 1930 with the purchase of 6,700 alpine acres, finally ended in the early nineteen-sixties when the ex-governor bought his last parcel of land. Baxter died soon after, a man whose dream had come true.

Mount Katahdin is actually a series of four rugged peaks grouped around a Great Basin. This basin was once an ordinary mountain valley that thousands of years ago was carved by the movements of powerful glaciers into a vast bowl-shaped formation. Katahdin's four peaks are: Hamlin (4,751 feet) in the north, Pamola (4,902 feet) in the east, South Peak (5,240 feet) in the south, and Baxter (5,267 feet) in the west.

The park contains over *140* miles of hiking trails — all traversing the park's more than 46 mountainous peaks. For campground reservations (*and you'll need them in July and August*) write: Reservation Clerk, Baxter Park, Millinocket, Maine 04462.

23.   THE KNIFE-EDGE TRAIL

The Knife-Edge Trail is a 1.1 mile hike from Pamola to Baxter that crosses the edge of the Great Basin. It's a dangerous trail but one that's strongly recommended. "Knife Edge" is the name of a sharp ridge; so narrow, in fact, that it's possible to straddle it in certain places — with one foot on Katahdin's almost 2,000 foot vertical headwall and the other on the mountain's southern slope.

If either vertigo or acrophobia (fear of heights) assails you up here, it's all over. The trail has been called by the Appalachian Mountain Club's guidebook "the most spectacular mountain trail in the East."

NORTH BASIN
GREAT BASIN
CHIMNEY POND CAMPGROUND
S. BASIN
KNIFE-EDGE TRAIL
PAMOLA
KNIFE-EDGE
SOUTH PEAK
ABOL TRAIL
MILLINOCKET-GREENVILLE RD.
N
#23, 24
TO MILLINOCKET

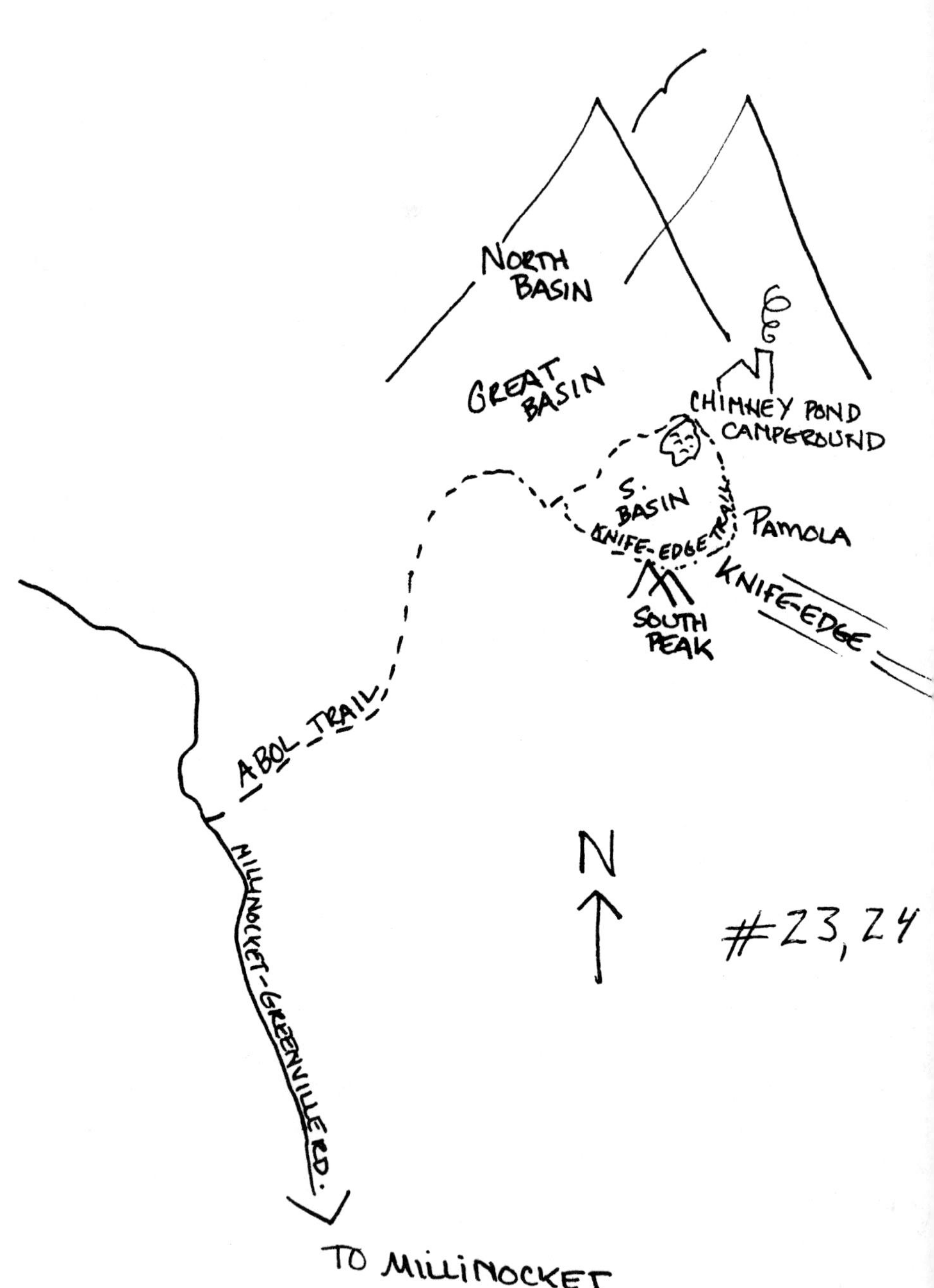

188

24. ABOL TRAIL

This is a 3.78 mile walk from the Millinocket-Greenville Road (which is 23½ miles northwest of Millinocket) to Katahdin's southwest summit. It's the path used by the region's first tourist — Henry David Thoreau.

Nature was here something savage and awful, though beautiful.
                    —Thoreau, from *THE MAINE WOODS*—

North and west of Baxter State Park is the *Allagash Wilderness Waterway* — an area consisting of streams, rivers, ponds, lakes, and falls. It was in this region that turn-of-the-century woodsmen — lumberjacks who worked for the various large timber companies — created their own larger-than-life Bunyanesque legends. It was incredulously reported, for instance, that these Allagash rivermen were so sure-footed that they could throw a bar of soap into a stream and then scramble across the bubbles to the other side. Or it was even mythically boasted that they could crash their cleated boots into any barroom's ceiling by simply doing a somersault and then hanging upside down.

The entire Allagash region is today a canoeist's paradise, with extended chains of interconnected rivers and lakes. And Eben Thomas' book — *NO HORNS BLOWING* — (Hallowell Printing Co., Hallowell, Maine) is a good guide to the region — including ten, very explicitly mapped-out canoe trips for the Allagash region.

Acadia, the only national park on the Atlantic coast, contains more than 30,000 acres of rocky seashore and rugged mountains. And ruefully, it also contains practically *three-quarters* of all Maine's publicly owned coast. One of John D. Rockefeller's sons, John, Jr., preserved for the public, part of this coastal gem of down-East Maine. (The Rockefellers kept one of their family's many vacation homes on the island, as did Joseph Pulitzer, the blind publisher. Pulitzer, in fact, ran his entire publishing empire from a sound-proofed room situated on some of Mount Desert's most lush acreage.)

Cadillac Mountain (originally called Green Mountain), the 1,520 foot mountain that rises from this coastal area, is one of the first spots in the continental U.S. to each morning receive the rays of the sun.

Unfortunately but understandably, Acadia is crowded in the summertime. More than 2.7 million people visited the park in 1975 alone. So I'd suggest visiting this lush island either in the spring, fall or winter. A trip to Acadia in the winter, in fact, is a very special experience. Standing atop Schoodic Point, an exposed rock promontory situated across Frenchman's Bay (see map), you can watch crashing grey-blue waves and an offbeat array of rare winter seabirds: eiders (which are really large ducks), American scoters, gannets, kumlein gulls, and alcids (being the generic name for the many northern-hemisphere equivalents of penguins — murres, puffins, aukes, guillemots, and dovekies.)

There are dozens of well-marked trails along Mount Desert Island. Vigorous mountain walks, seaside strolls, and walks along the island's no-cars-allowed carriage roads all offer the day hiker a versatile smorgasbord of topographies.

The Appalachian Mountain Club publishes a 32-page booklet describing nearly fifty hikes in this region. And the Acadia National Park Headquarters — on Maine 3 at Hulls Cove near Bar Harbor (see map) — is also a useful place for obtaining information about the area.

TO BUCKSPORT
1
ELLSWORTH
3
MAINE MAINLAND
BAR HARBOR
ACADIA NATN'L PARK
PENOBSCOT BAY
CAMDEN
JERICHO BAY
N
#25

VERMONT

Vermont's *Green Mountains* present a less rugged skyline than the White Mountains of New Hampshire. The topography is more level here, especially south of Rutland where the Green Mountains form a vast, unbroken plateau that extends southward to the Massachusetts border; a plateau that's as wide as 20 miles in the Stratton Mountain vicinity (see Trip #31).

North of Rutland, the Green Mountains begin to branch out into three distinct and parallel ranges. And it's here, in northern Vermont, where the state's highest peaks are located: Mt. Ellen, The Camel's Hump, Mt. Mansfield, Mt. Killington — all being slightly higher than 4,000 feet above sea level.

Compared to New Hampshire's White Mountains, the Green Mountains of Vermont annually host just about one-fifth the amount of hikers. As a result, Vermont's hiking trails are far less crowded, far less trampled, and usually, far less strewn with beer cans and candy wrappers.

Running along the entire crest of the Green Mountains — all the way from the Vermont-Massachusetts border right up into Canada — is the "Long Trail" — a 262-mile footpath that was built back in the early 1900's. All the hikes included in this Vermont section are hikes along segments of the Long Trail.

For additional information on this region write: THE GREEN MOUNTAIN CLUB, Inc., Post Office Box 94, Rutland, Vermont 05701.

As you walk on the Green Mountain's hiking trails keep in mind that this range of mountains are among the Northeast's oldest — their geological age having been estimated at 440 million years. Now admittedly, that figure doesn't mean much; such immense numbers often lose their meaning. But if we can just imagine that 440 million years ago these mountains were 6 miles higher than they are now, and that rushing waters during those millions of years actually carved away 6 full miles of tough, Green Mountain bedrock, then hopefully that 440 million figure will become more real to you.

* * * * *

Climb the mountains and get their good tidings. Nature's peace will flow into you as sunshine flows into trees. The winds will blow their own freshness into you and the storms their energy, while cares will drop off like autumn leaves.

—John Muir—

Every guidebook will tell you that the Bear Pond Trail, which ascends Mount Mansfield (4,393 feet above sea level, Vermont's highest peak), contains the steepest half-mile of trail in the entire state. It's a tough, tough climb — encumbered with tricky rock formations, precarious ledges, and just too much mud. The trail's beginning can easily be missed if you're relying on the directions of some of the region's older guidebooks. The trail begins a few hundred yards beyond the Smuggler's Notch Picnic Area (right off of Route 108). *It does not begin at the picnic site itself.*

* * * * *

As you climb any of the trails in the Northeast try to follow the designated trail. These trails are often marked by arrows that are painted on trees or by piles of rocks set on the ground (called cairns). And if you ever come across a fallen tree while you're hiking along some trail, chances are the tree wasn't put there by Mother Nature. Rather, park rangers and trail crews — to keep you on the marked trails — will often lay a tree across an old trail route or some cul de sac spur.

Failure to stay on the marked trails too often leads to bushwhacking nightmares. So pay attention when you're hiking, and don't stray too far from a marked trail.

* * * * *

My only reason for climbing the grueling Bear Pond Trail — Vermont's steepest — was to reach *Bear Pond* and the nearby *Lake of the Clouds*. Both bodies of water proved egregious fiascos. They were shallow pools — little more than stagnant water filled with way too much animal excreta.

The climb, though, gave me one of the soundest sleeps of my life . . . and for that reason alone I strongly recommend the Bear Pond Trail.

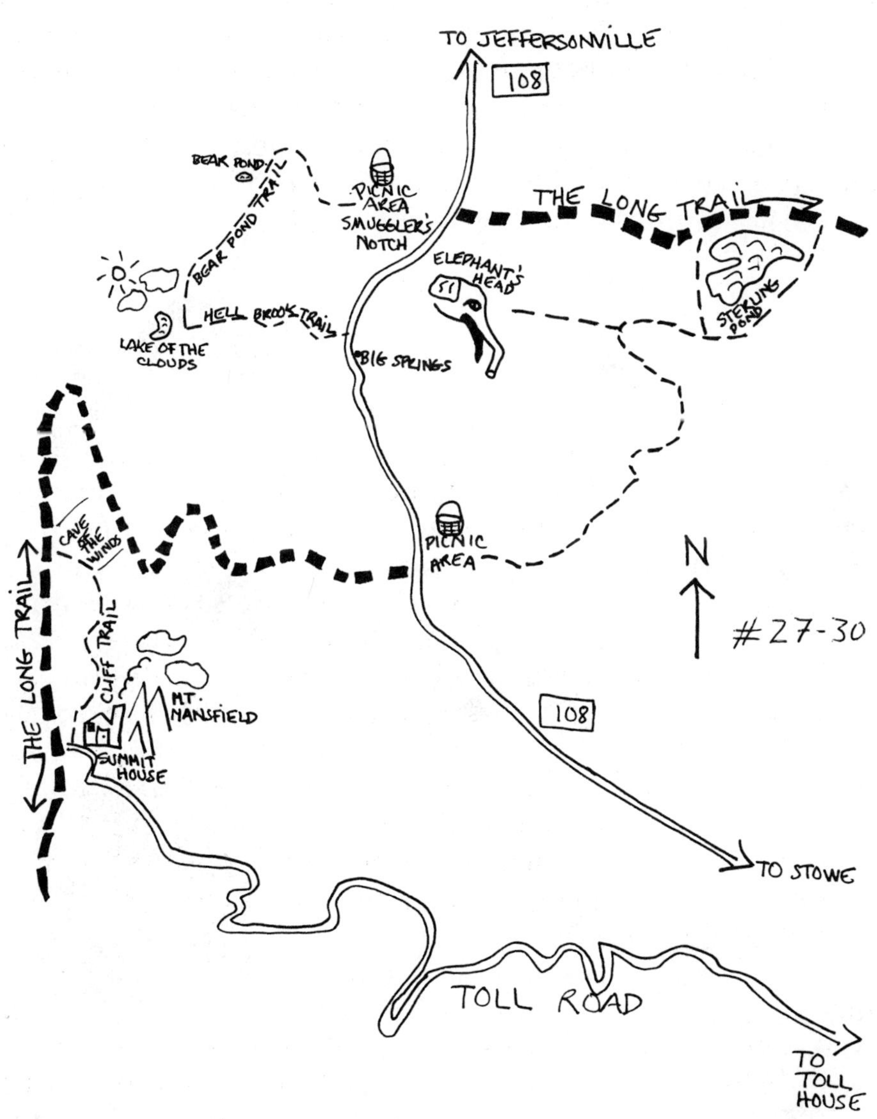

TO JEFFERSONVILLE
108
BEAR POND
BEAR POND TRAIL
PICNIC AREA
SMUGGLER'S NOTCH
THE LONG TRAIL
ELEPHANT'S HEAD
51
STERLING POND
HELL BROOKS TRAIL
LAKE OF THE CLOUDS
BIG SPRINGS
CAVE OF THE WINDS
PICNIC AREA
N
#27-30
THE LONG TRAIL
CLIFF TRAIL
MT. MANSFIELD
108
SUMMIT HOUSE
THE LONG TRAIL
TO STOWE
TOLL ROAD
TO TOLL HOUSE

This is a slightly more sane hike than the Bear Pond Trail. It starts at the south end of the Route 108 Smuggler's Notch State Picnic Area (on the opposite side of the road from the picnic tables). Elephant's Head — a huge cliff reached by this trail and located on the east side of Smuggler's Notch — affords many fine views of the Green Mountains. And after passing these cliff formations, you'll soon reach *Sterling Pond* — a *swimmable* and thankfully *excretaless* pond.

29. CLIFF TRAIL

To reach this trail's beginning take the Toll Road (which leaves from Route 108 near Stowe, Vermont) to the Summit Station of Mount Mansfield (approximately a four-mile drive). Here, on Mount Mansfield's summit, is the site of the once posh Mt. Mansfield Summit House — an inn that was in operation, until it was razed back in 1963, for over a hundred years.

Mount Mansfield has an interesting physiognomy. The Indians who used to live in this region thought the mountain resembled the head of a moose; and the white settlers, not surprisingly, saw the face of a long-lipped *injun* in the mountain's rocky contours. This toll road, regardless of whether you accept the visage of an indian or the head of a moose as being the most accurate description, will deliver you to the base of the "nose" of the mountain.

Just north of the Summit Station, where TV Road crosses the Long Trail, is the south end of the Cliff Trail — a trail that traverses the eastern slope of Mount Mansfield. And near the steeper northern end of the trail you'll spot a spur (on the left hand side of the trail) that leads 50 feet to the *Cave of the Winds*. This cave, even during the summer, has snow near its entrance.

A little beyond the cave spur you'll again find the Long Trail. This northern end of the Cliff Trail is tantamount to the "lower lip" of Mount Mansfield's face.

This is a steep trail (in Vermont, only the Bear Pond Trail is steeper). The trail begins across the road from the north end of the Big Spring Parking Area near Smuggler's Notch (reached by travelling north from Stowe, Vermont on Route 108).

By following the blue blazes up and up and up and up (and I almost want to repeat that sequence), you'll eventually, after 1.3 miles of **steep** climbing, reach the ridge. And as you're hiking and gasping for air, you'll all the time be watching the waters of the Hell Brook — effortlessly and almost mockingly — plunging beside you.

Protruding rock overhangs (which offer convenient shelters during unexpected rainstorms), waterfalls, alpine summits (that botanically speaking are swatches of Newfoundland), and high-altitude vistas (this being the "Chin" of Mount Mansfield) all add up to making this hike one of Vermont's most rewarding. From atop the summit, on a clear day, you can see Montreal's Mount Royal in the north, Lake Champlain to the west, and to the east — the White Mountains.

31.   STRATTON MOUNTAIN TRAIL

This trail, at the southern end of Vermont's *Long Trail*, begins along the Arlington-West Wardsboro Road. From Black Brook (see map) travel eastwards past the east branch of the Deerfield River and then past an historical marker (commemorating the site where Daniel Webster delivered an impassioned speech back in 1840 to more than 15,000 Whigs). Beyond this marker and bearing left, in approximately one mile you'll reach the Webster Shelter (a small bunk house). From this shelter it's then a steep ascent until you're atop the "South Peak" of Stratton Mountain (3,936 ft.). Here, a state fire tower, offering fine, unobscured views, is open to the public.

Finally, heading west beyond South Peak, you'll be steadily descending until you reach the eastern shores of Stratton Pond — the largest body of water on the entire *Long Trail*.

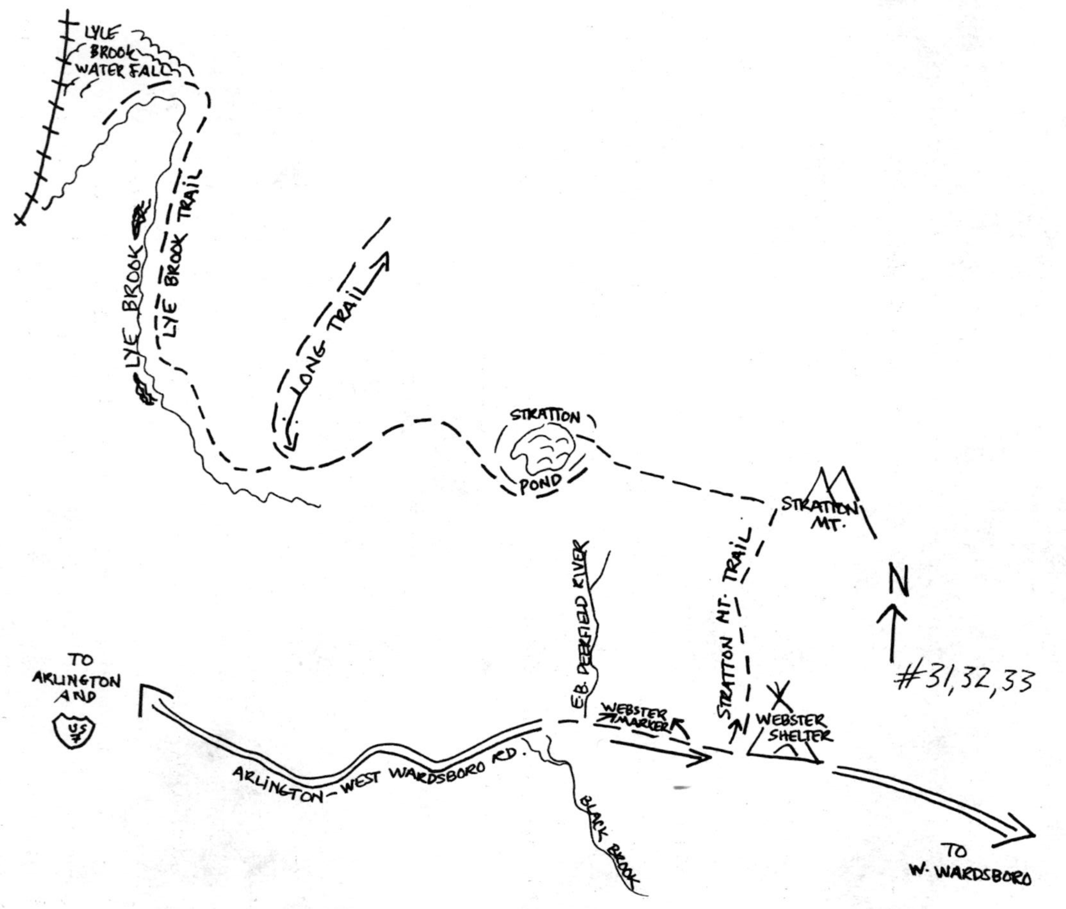

LYLE BROOK WATER FALL
LYE BROOK
LYE BROOK TRAIL
LONG TRAIL
STRATTON POND
STRATTON MT.
STRATTON MT. TRAIL
E.B. DEERFIELD RIVER
N
#31,32,33
TO ARLINGTON AND US7
WEBSTER MARKER
WEBSTER SHELTER
ARLINGTON—WEST WARDSBORO RD.
BLACK BROOK
TO W. WARDSBORO

32. LYE BROOK TRAIL

Lye Brook is a designated wilderness area containing 14,300 acres of woodland. *Before entering this area you must have a permit.* These permits are obtained, free-of-charge, from the U.S. Forest Service, Catamount National Bank Building, Manchester Center, VT 05255.

To reach the Lye Brook Trail take Route 11 east from Manchester Center and then turn right onto Richville Road. Approximately 1½ miles along Richville Road, Lye Brook Road will then appear. Turn left onto Lye Brook Road, travelling about two-tenths of a mile, and then park your car. The trail is blue-blazed and will start on your left hand side.

This is a long hike, about six miles until you reach the South Bourn Shelter. At the shelter (a small, wood framed lean-to) a Green Mountain Club caretaker will charge you a nominal fee for overnight use of the structure.

33. LYE BROOK TRAIL TO TRESTLE

If you hike from the beginning of the Lye Brook Trail (see Trip # 31) for about two miles, you'll run into an old railroad bed. Follow this diagonal bed to the right as it crosses the trail and then — (slightly less than a half mile beyond this point) — you'll see the Lyle Brook Waterfalls.

A deep gorge and the decaying remnants of an old train trestle can then be viewed from this site. A couple of decades ago trains filled with logs — spruces, pines, and hardwoods — used to cross this trestle on their way to the sawmills of the nearby Vermont towns.

MASSACHUSETTS

Maine, Vermont, and New Hampshire all have large wilderness areas. As we head south, however, into Connecticut, Massachusetts, and Rhode Island, these sort of expansive wilderness areas become much more scarce. Most of the trips, therefore, in this section on Massachusetts are short walks, many of them being well-marked trails through wildlife preserves and sanctuaries.

Massachusetts can conveniently be divided into four distinctive regions: the coastal lowlands (including Cape Cod and Boston); the eastern upland area (where the terrain is considerably less flat than it is in the coastal lowlands — the land here being low and rounded hills); the Connecticut Valley (consisting of rich, fertile farmlands abutting the Connecticut River); and finally, the western uplands (being the state's most rugged terrain, where the Berkshires, Taconic, and Hoosac mountain ranges all lie).

Furthermore, Audubon Society properties, as well as lands controlled by the Trustees of Reservation — another non-profit Massachusetts conservation organization — are also listed in this section.

Plum Island is roughly 30 miles north of Boston and 3 miles east of Newburyport, an old shipbuilding town in north-eastern Massachusetts. And the 6,000 acre *Parker River National Wildlife Refuge* occupies the southern three-quarters of the island. The refuge is positively the best coastal birding site in all of Massachusetts, with over 300 species of birds having been observed on the island. In the summer and fall, at the entrance to the refuge — off of Sunset Drive — make sure to ask the parking attendant for the refuge's bird, fish, and mammal lists — all compiled by the National Parks Service.

Thousands of Canadian geese, along with pintail ducks — their thin necks lined with white — and hundreds of green-winged teals (the smallest of our northern ducks) parade in flocks around the island.

Plum Island, in addition to its lush bird fauna, is probably the most perfect example of a *barrier beach* in the Northeast. Barrier beaches are simply beaches that over the centuries have been built offshore by sand-carrying waves and currents. These beaches are usually separated from the mainland by a series of marshes.

The rows of sand dunes at Plum Island are covered with beach-grass, beach goldenrod, beach pea, bayberry, and beach plums. These grape-sized plums, growing on small witchlike trees, are good for eating. Note, too, the various grasses that grow all over the island's marshy areas: *high-tide grass* which is reddish-brown and flat (used as hay for animals); *salt meadow grass* — buffy colored and soft; and *switch grass* — found where the water rises highest sometimes standing over two feet tall.

This two-mile trail (which is part of the Parker River National Wildlife Refuge) circles around a swamp that lies amidst a terrain of sand dunes. This is a fresh-water swamp created by man-made dikes. Purple Loosestrife, cattails, and reed grass are the swamp's dominant vegetation. (Cattails almost exclusively grow in fresh-water marshes.)

In addition to the fresh-water swamp, the Hellcat Swamp Nature Trail also abuts a salt water marsh. This marsh, like all salt water marshes, produces nutrients that are needed by both shellfish and finfish. At least 60 species of fish and shellfish, (including crab, clam larvae, flounder, striped bass, and menhaden) — all start their lives out in these marshes. Two-thirds of the commercial fish catch on the East Coast live part of their lives in marsh estuaries.

Salt marshes, bays, and wetlands produce more nutrients per acre than any of our nation's best wheat lands. One acre of cord grass salt marsh, for instance, produces an average of ten tons of nutrient material a year. (Cord grass is a plant capable of thriving in sea water. And while some marsh dwellers actually graze on the cord grass, more commonly it's the products of its decay that supply nutrients to fish and shellfish.)

Unfortunately, in recent years, these crucial life-supporting wetlands have been dwindling; and they've become the chosen sites for too many land developers' camelots. These wetlands — including both fresh and salt water marshes — because they feed fish, birds, and insects, must be preserved. If not, the delicate ecological balance of our environment will be destroyed.

LIFE AND DEATH OF THE SALT MARSH by John and Mildred Teal (an Audubon/Ballantine Book, 1969) is a clearly written paean to our nation's marshlands. The book nicely simplifies what could otherwise be a garbled conglomeration of overly technical biological data.

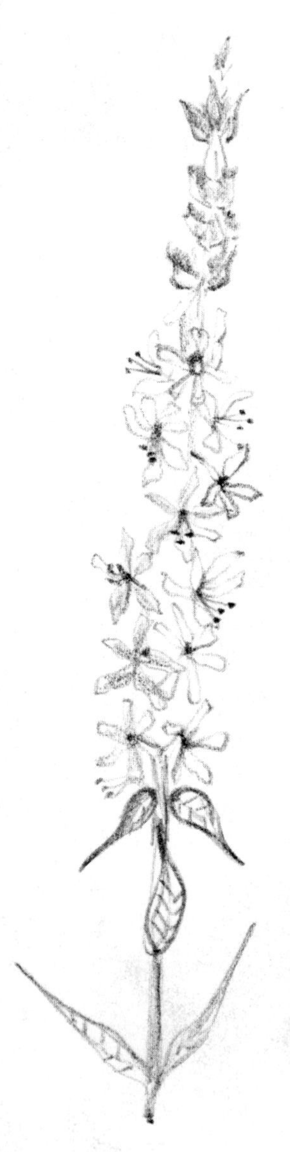

PURPLE LOOSESTRIFE

CORD GRASS

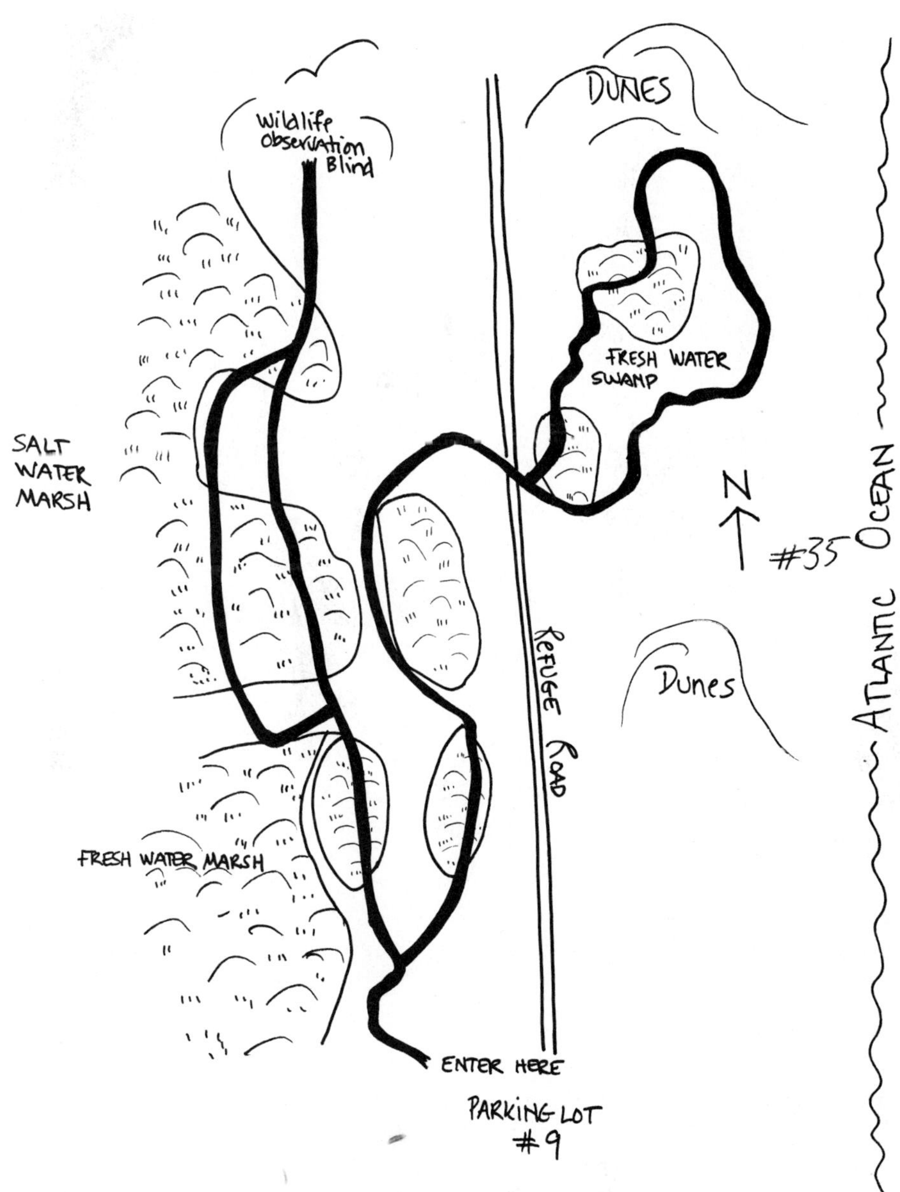

Wildlife Observation Blind
DUNES
SALT WATER MARSH
FRESH WATER SWAMP
N
#35
Refuge Road
Dunes
Atlantic Ocean
FRESH WATER MARSH
ENTER HERE
PARKING LOT #9

This 3,000 acre Audubon Society sponsored marsh, located off of Route 9 in Scarborough, Maine, is open from April to October (seven days a week). In the spring and fall the nature center is closed on Fridays and Saturdays.

Like all marshes, the Scarborough marsh is filled with birds: Canada geese, ducks, bitterns, red-winged blackbirds, snowy egrets, yellow-legs, belted kingfishers, and cormorants.

The center has continuous showings of nature-related films and slide shows (all for free!), as well as guided and self-guided field trips. For further information call 883-5100 or the Maine Audubon in Portland at 774-8281.

FOUR TRIPS TO CAPE COD

The northern Maine Coastline (see Trip #25) is rocky — the result of once high mountain peaks that were crushed and crunched by the advancing glacier during the Ice Age. From Maine all the way south to Cape Ann (which is just north of Boston), the Northeast's coast is rocky, consisting of boulders and cliffs of darkened granite. South of Boston, however, the coastline becomes much flatter with neither dunes nor rocks being visible. And here, between these two sorts of coastal extremes, is where Cape Cod lies.

Other than some purple splotches of cranberries (which grow in bogs or wet ground), most of the Cape is covered with pitch pine trees, along with some small, practically shrub-sized black oak and juniper trees. Pitch Pine trees, incidentally, will grow in a nearly totally sandy soil. And these trees like many of the hardwoods are capable of sending up new trunks after they've been reduced to stumps by either fire, wind, or man.

Back in 1961, the *Cape Cod National Seashore* was established. And the four trips included in the Cape section of this book all take you to these federally protected and managed areas.

Hint: When visiting the Cape, leave your hiking boots at home. Sneakers are the recommended footwear.

The Salt Pond Visitors Center, off of Route 6 in Eastham, Mass., offers a free ten-minute movie that artistically explains some of the geology and wildlife of the Cape. The movie serves as a useful introduction to this entire area.

Free self-guided, as well as guided nature tours, are also offered at the Visitors Center. These walks, which explore some salt ponds and two nearby beaches (Coast Guard Beach and Nauset Light Beach) are all worthwhile outings.

Throughout the summer, daytime and evening lecture programs are given free-of-charge at the Salt Pond Visitors Center. To obtain a list of these free, scheduled programs, you can write: Superintendent, c/o National Parks Service, U.S. Department of the Interior, South Wellfleet, Mass. 02683.

38. GREAT ISLAND

Great Island, really a peninsula that dangles into Cape Cod Bay (near Wellfleet, Massachusetts), has more than six miles of National Seashore trails. Some of the trails meander around a tidal inlet that's an exceptionally good birding site. In addition, a Park Department Ranger offers a lengthy and well-informed walking tour of Great Island. I'd recommend trying to schedule your visit to coincide with this tour. (Scheduling information for this tour can also be obtained by writing to the National Parks Service in South Wellfleet.)

* * * * *

Cape Cod's dunes, rhapsodized about in popular love songs, are actually waging a vicious war; a war that the lovers who stroll along them are no doubt totally unaware of. The Cape's sandy dunes, impelled by fierce sea-winds, are mercilessly trying to smother every flower or tree that come in their path. And the flowers and trees, meanwhile, their vanguard consisting of grasses and herbs and their sturdier rear flanks being composed of shrubs and small trees, are waging a strong counterattack; trying quite literally to hold their ground. Most of the Cape's beaches, then, are really battlegrounds where these two adversaries — the beaches vs. the forests — are ceaselessly vying for hegemony. A good place to observe this ongoing war is at:

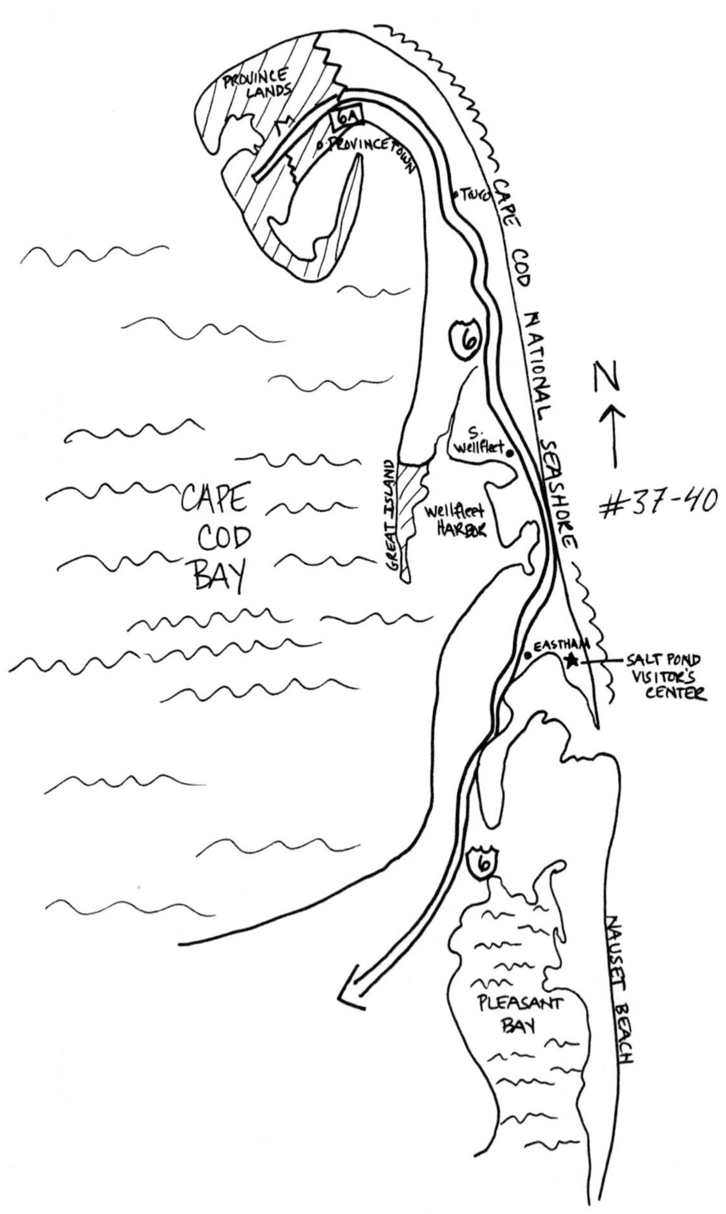

The Province Lands, consisting of 4,400 acres at the northernmost tip of the Cape (near Provincetown), offers the day hiker (there are no overnight camping facilities here) some of the Atlantic Coast's most spectacular sand dunes. A mile-long trail — *The Beech Forest Trail* (reached by turning right at the traffic light on Race Pond Road which is off of U.S. 6 near the Province Lands Visitors Center) — is an especially worthwhile walk. The trail, besides taking you through a forest that has over a half-a-dozen varieties of pine trees, also leads you to a populous growth of beech trees. Before all of the Cape's lands were either timbered, overgrazed, or ravaged by fires, the treescape here was varied, not just the hodgepodge of pitch pines and small oaks that you see today.

Our Pilgrim forefathers, it should be mentioned, had the foresight to preserve these same Province Lands. Back in 1620 they set aside all this land as a reservation.

The sand, interestingly enough, that accumulates on sand dunes is finer and lighter than the sand that's closer to the water's edge. This lighter sand is able to be pushed backwards into the dunes by the winds whereas the heavier sands remain closer to the shoreline.

40.   THE ATLANTIC WHITE CEDAR SWAMP TRAIL

By travelling north for 5.2 miles beyond the Salt Pond Visitors Center (see trip #37) and then turning right at the traffic light, you'll soon reach the Marconi Station parking lot. The start of the 1.25-mile *Atlantic White Cedar Swamp Trail* then leaves from this parking area.

This trail offers a wide variety of Cape flora: small bear oaks and pitch pine trees, bearberry, thorn lichen, sheep laurel, and the waxy green leaves of trailing arbutus (appropriately called *Mayflower* in Massachusetts). The trail finally leads to a swamp of Atlantic White Cedars. The stillness by the swamp, disturbed only by an occasional robin fluttering and then darting from a tree, is extraordinary.

41. IPSWICH RIVER NATURE CENTER AND WILDLIFE REFUGE

The 2,300-acre Ipswich River Wildlife Refuge is the largest Audubon Society refuge in the state. The sanctuary includes an arboretum with over 2,000 domestic and imported species, three man-made wildlife ponds, a wildflower garden, and a rock garden. Also included here are over 1,000 acres of the vast Wenham Swamp, five miles of the Ipswich River, two sections of an esker, a drumlin, a glacial pot hole, and many acres of undisturbed wildlife habitat.

The Agawam Nature Trail (named after the Agawam Indians who once lived in the valley of the Agawam — now the Ipswich River) is a self-guided nature trail that takes you through much of the refuge's unspoiled fields, forests, and marshlands.

Perkins Island, a small island on the refuge's land that's in the middle of the Ipswich River, is available for overnight camping. The cost is nominal (though you'll need a canoe to reach it). The Audubon Society restricts the usage of the island to fifty people per night. So if you plan to do some camping in this area, write the Ipswich Refuge for reservations. (Ipswich River Nature Center & Wildlife Refuge, Perkins Row, Topsfield, Mass. 01983. Telephone: 617-887-2241.)

The Massachusetts Audubon Society, the oldest Audubon Society in North America and the largest conservation organization in Massachusetts, was founded in 1896. Today the Society owns and operates more than 35 sanctuaries and open spaces in Massachusetts (about a third of these sanctuaries are staffed year round). All these non-profit Audubon sanctuaries charge nominal admission fees. The fees, however, defray just a small part of the Audubon Society's total operating costs. The majority of their money comes from voluntary donations.

210

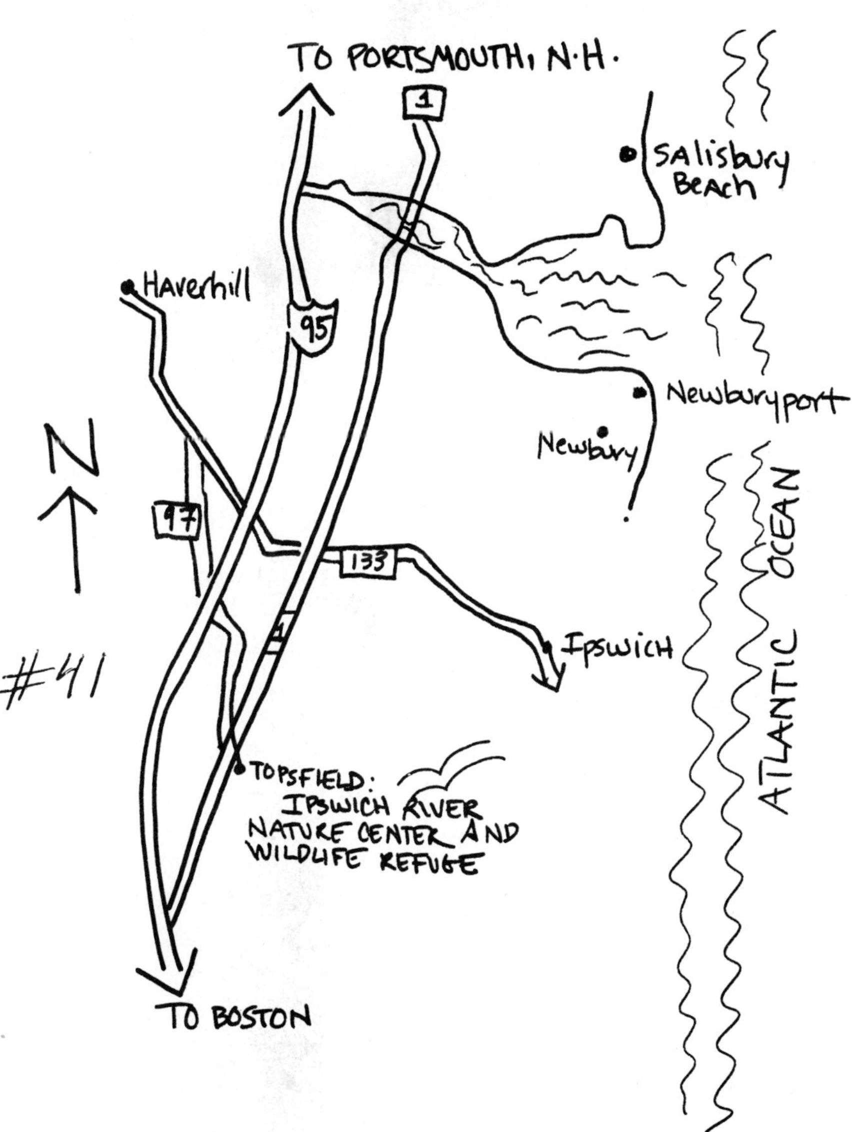

TO PORTSMOUTH, N.H.
1
SALISBURY Beach
Haverhill
95
Newburyport
Newbury
N
97
133
ATLANTIC OCEAN
Ipswich
#41
TOPSFIELD:
IPSWICH RIVER
NATURE CENTER AND
WILDLIFE REFUGE
TO BOSTON

A COMPLETE LISTING OF STAFFED AUDUBON SANCTUARIES IN MASSACHUSETTS
(each sanctuary makes an excellent day trip)

42. DRUMLIN FARM NATURE CENTER in Lincoln. A 220-acre farm which includes pasture, fields, woodland, ponds, and both domestic and wild animals. The Farm is on Route 117, 4.5 miles west of the 117 overpass over Route 128.

43. BROADMOOR/LITTLE POND WILDLIFE SANCTUARY in South Natick. This 538-acre sanctuary includes woodland, field, marsh, pond, frontage on the Charles River, marked trails, and the remains of both an old saw mill and grist mill. Directions: From the center of South Natick go west on Route 16. The sanctuary's entrance will be on the left 1.8 miles.

44. MOOSE HILL WILDLIFE SANCTUARY in Sharon. This 227-acre sanctuary is the Audubon Society's oldest refuge. Included here are acres of hilly woods, meadows, and marsh, a spring wildflower garden, several miles of trails, and some of the best high-altitude views of southeastern Massachusetts. Directions: From the intersection of Routes 1 and 27 turn east on Route 27, then take the first right (.2 miles) — Moose Hill St. — and the sanctuary will then be on your right in 1.5 miles.

45. STONY BROOK WILDLIFE SANCTUARY in Norfolk. This nature center and 101-acre sanctuary abuts the 200-acre Bristol-Blake State Reservation. Directions: From Norfolk Center follow Route 115 one mile south to North Street. The Sanctuary is then south on North Street.

46. BLUE HILLS TRAILSIDE MUSEUM in Milton. Trails, outdoor exhibits, and a museum. Directions: Located 1 mile north of the intersection of Routes 138 and 127.

47. WELLFLEET BAY WILDLIFE SANCTUARY in South Wellfleet. This 700-acre sanctuary includes a salt marsh, pine woods, field, brook, and a pond. Directions: The sanctuary's entrance is on the west side of Route 6, immediately north of the Eastham-Wellfleet town line.

48. FELIX NECK WILDLIFE SANCTUARY on Martha's Vineyard. More than 200 acres on one of Massachusetts' most scenic islands. Directions: From Woods Hole, Mass. take the ferry to Vineyard Haven. The sanctuary is then 4 miles southeast along Edgartown Road on the left side.

49. ASHUMET HOLLY RESERVATION in East Falmouth. This 45 acre reservation has 8 species and 65 varieties of holly, as well as a collection of heather, herbs, rhododendron, azaleas, and the unusual fall-flowering Franklinia. Directions: From the intersection of Route 28 and Route 151 in North Falmouth, follow Route 151 east for 4 miles. The sanctuary is on the north side of Route 151.

50. COOK'S CANYON in Barre. This 40-acre area includes upland woodlands, a pine plantation, pond, brook, and trails. Directions: From the Barre Common drive 0.5 miles south on South Street.

51. WACHUSETT MEADOW WILDLIFE SANCTUARY in Princeton. Includes 907 acres of upland meadow, pond, and brook. This sanctuary is the site of Crocker Maple, the fourth largest sugar maple in the United States. Directions: From Princeton center follow Route 62 West, 17 miles to Goodnow Road. The Sanctuary is then 1 mile on Goodnow Road.

52. ARCADIA WILDLIFE SANCTUARY in Easthampton. This 560-acre sanctuary (with woodland, meadow, and marsh) borders on an ancient oxbow of the Connecticut River. An observation tower overlooking the marsh makes this sanctuary an excellent birding area. Directions: From I-91 take Exit 18 South on Route 5, 1.3 miles to East Street (the first right across the oxbow) then 1.2 miles to Fort Hill Road. Then the first right leads to the sanctuary.

53. LAUGHING BROOK EDUCATION CENTER in Hampden. This is the former home of Thornton Burgess, the well-known children's author. The author's home, along with an animal center, a natural history museum, trails winding through the refuge's 84 acres, and an outdoor animal display are all included here. Directions: From the Massachusetts Turnpike take Exit 8, follow signs to Monson, and then turn sharply right at High Street. Follow this street for 6.7 miles to Hampden, bearing left as indicated.

54. PLEASANT VALLEY WILDLIFE SANCTUARY

in Lenox. This 680-acre sanctuary on the side and base of Lenox Mountain includes an alder swamp, a hemlock gorge, woodland, and meadows. An active beaver colony on the Yokun Brook is especially worth seeing. Directions: From the confluence of US Route 7 and 20 in Lenox, proceed 3 miles north to Dugway Road on the left (across from the Holiday Inn). Follow Dugway Road 1.6 miles to the sanctuary's entrance, bearing left at the fork.

(Be sure to contact the Audubon Societies in every state you plan on visiting. They all offer brochures and maps that are free-of-charge).

55. BARTHOLOMEW'S COBBLE

Located in Ashley Falls at the southern end of Berkshire County, and bordering the sinuous Housatonic River, is *Bartholomew's Cobble* — a 170-acre natural and wild rock garden. Two knolls (or rounded hillocks) of mingled marble and quartzite rise prominently — some 75 and 100 feet above the river — here. And it's these rocky crests (called cobbles) that give the sanctuary its name.

Nearly six miles of marked hiking trails traverse this extremely diverse wildlife habitat. The topography includes river meadows, swamps, ferny ledges, cedar outlooks, and deciduous and evergreen outlooks.

Over 700 species of plants have been catalogued here; about 500 of them being wildflowers, and the remainder being trees, shrubs, and vines. In addition, 49 species of ferns and well over 200 species of birds have all been seen at the reservation.

Bartholomew's Cobble (which includes a small but well-stocked natural history museum) is open daily from April 15 through October 15. The hours are 9 A.M. to 5 P.M. A small admission fee is charged.

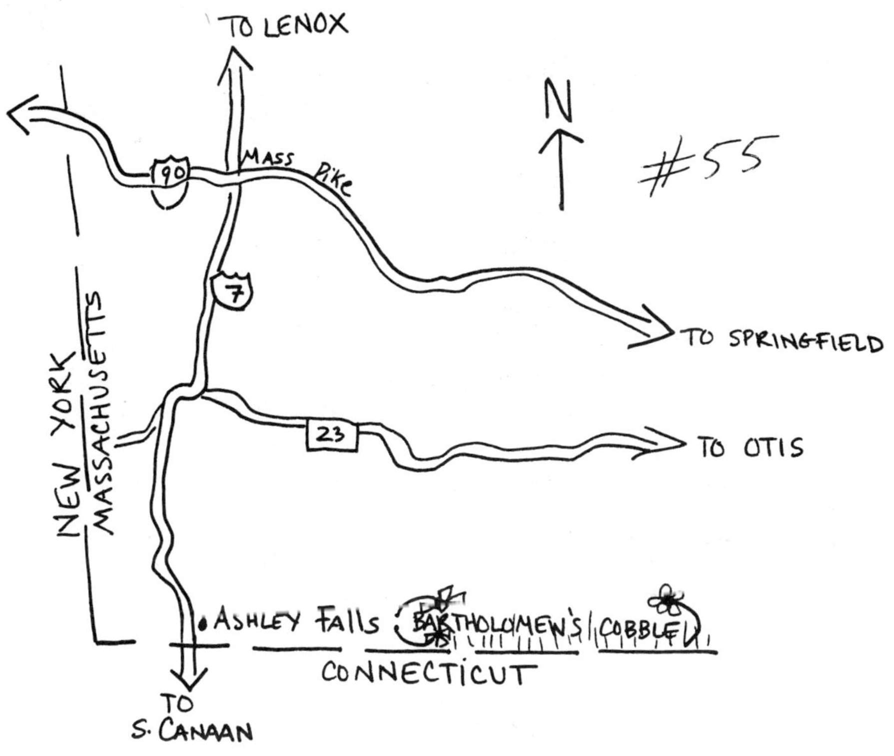

56. GARDEN IN THE WOODS

On just 48 acres of land (much of it being in the form of an esker), more than 4,000 species and varieties of native American plants are growing at GARDEN IN THE WOODS. Started in the early nineteen-thirties by Will C. Curtis and Howard O. Stiles, the Garden is today probably the best site in the entire Northeast for viewing wildflowers. Dry and acid woodland slopes are carpeted in May and June with early spring wildflowers; sunny bogs exhibit Pitcher Plants, Sundews, Calla Lilies and Yellow Western Skunk Cabbage; shady brooksides are filled with moisture-loving Ginseng; and sunny pond sides are rich in both the rare and colorful Cardinal Flower, as well as with Bottle Gentians.

The Garden, located on Hemenway Road in Framingham, Massachusetts, is open to the public daily except Sundays from 8:30 A.M. to 5:00 P.M. from April 1st to November 1st. A nominal admission fee is charged.

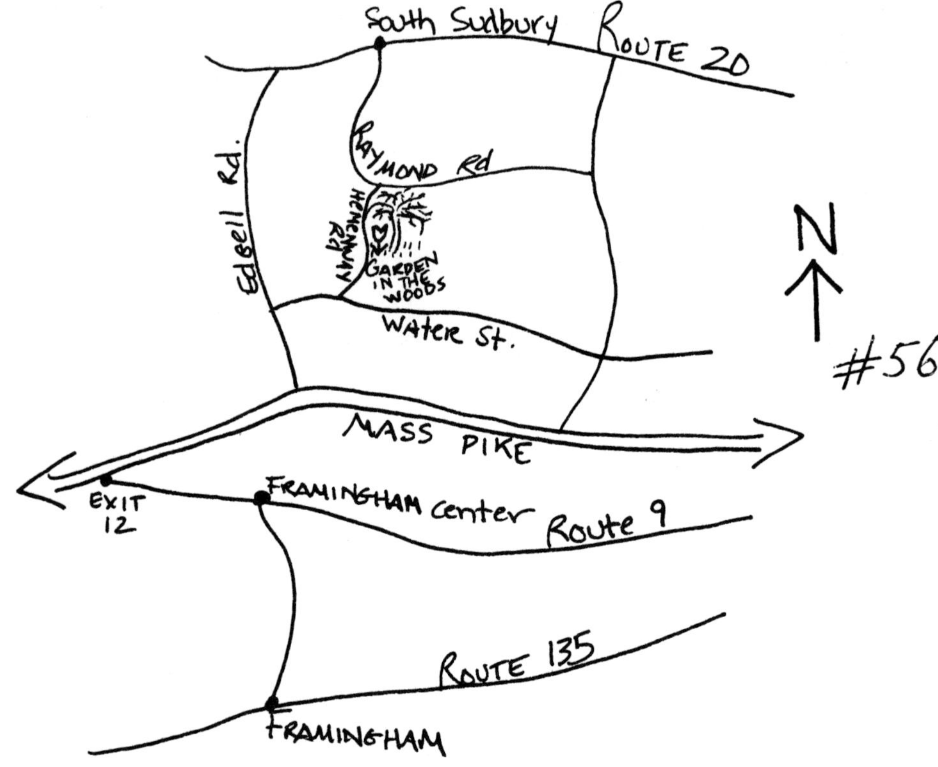

GARDEN IN THE WOODS is owned and operated by *THE NEW ENGLAND WILD FLOWER SOCIETY*, a non-profit conservation agency. The society's headquarters, along with its excellent library, is located at GARDEN IN THE WOODS. And in addition to GARDEN IN THE WOODS, the Society either owns or controls a number of other unique and worth-visiting wildlife locales:

57.   The largest stand of the Great Laurel (*Rhododendron maximum*) in the United States; Springvale, Maine.

58.   An extensive wild flower reservation with frontage on Merrimeeting Bay; Woolwich, Maine.

59.   A bog and woodland containing the northernmost stand of Atlantic white coast cedar; Bradford, New Hampshire.

60.   An extraordinary stand of luminous moss; Groton, New Hampshire. (This area is only open to special groups — including botanists and other specialists.)

216

61.   A hardwood slope and bank along the Connecticut River, notable for its great variety of wild flowers; Plainfield, New Hampshire.

62.   A bog and woodland filled with choice native orchids; Peacham, Vermont. (Presently under the jurisdiction of the University of Vermont. Only specialists are invited here because the area is so fragile.)

63.   A 22-acre suburban sanctuary with a good collection of native plants; Weston, Massachusetts.

64.   A wilderness tract and special sanctuary for trailing arbutus; Winchendon, Massachusetts.

Additional information about any of these sites can be obtained directly from THE NEW ENGLAND WILD FLOWER SOCIETY, Inc., Hemenway Road, Framingham, Massachusetts 01701. Telephone: 877-6574; 237-4924.

65.   NOTCHVIEW RESERVATION

Owned and operated by the Trustees of Reservation, a privately administered, non-profit organization (founded back in 1891 for conservation purposes), the Notchview Reservation contains more than 3,000 acres. Just east of Windsor Center on Massachusetts' Route 9, the land here is mostly rolling woodland and old pasture land. At the Budd Visitor Center, a heated building on the reservation, you can picnic, rest, or wax your skis in the Visitor Center's basement waxing room. Cross country skiing is encouraged at the reservation.

To obtain a complete listing of the more than 11,000 acres controlled by the Trustees of Reservation, write: TRUSTEES OF RESERVATION, 224 Adams Street, Milton, Massachusetts.

66.   MASSACHUSETTS WILDLIFE MANAGEMENT AREAS

Throughout Massachusetts, the Massachusetts Division of Fisheries and Game has established a system of wildlife management areas to insure sportsmen a place to hunt. These areas, when not being used by hunters, make more-than-worthwhile hiking and picnicking areas. Maps of these Wildlife Management Areas can be obtained from the Massachusetts Division of Fisheries and Game, Information and Education Section, Westboro, Mass. 01581

67. DOROTHY FRANCES RICE SANCTUARY

Located on South Road, about one mile south of Mass. 143 in Peru, this sanctuary offers several color-coded nature walks through its 273 acres of woodland. Because the trails are well-marked and easy to follow, and because all varieties of wildlife abound here, this sanctuary is an excellent place to bring young children.

68. MASSACHUSETTS STATE PARKS, FORESTS, AND RESERVATIONS

There are more than twenty state parks in Massachusetts, more than twenty-five state forests, and over sixty unimproved forests. Information about these areas can be obtained from: THE MASSACHUSETTS DEPARTMENT OF NATURAL RESOURCES. (Skinner State Park in South Hadley and Wendell State Park in Wendell, are two of my favorite parks. Both are excellent mushroom-hunting fields.)

218

69.   MOUNT GREYLOCK

Mount Greylock, the highest point in Massachusetts (3,491 feet) is located in the town of North Adams. The 10,000-acre Mount Greylock Reservation (which is situated right off of Route 2 West) has three automobile roads and dozens of trails leading straight to the mountain's summit. Atop Mount Greylock a somewhat extraterrestrial-looking war memorial tower affords excellent views of the surrounding countryside.

70.   PURGATORY CHASM

Purgatory Chasm (located twelve miles south of Worcester, Mass., just off of Route 146) is a half-mile fissure in solid rock with granite walls rising upward from 70 feet. Geologically, the area is really a deep slit in the earth; this dark, chilly chasm being the work of the Continental Glacier.

71.   QUABBIN RESERVOIR

The 'Windsor Dam Entrance' to this huge man-made reservoir is right off of Route 9 in Belchertown. And the entire Quabbin Reservation covers an area larger than 128 square miles.

The reservoir was built back in the 1930's by Boston's Metropolitan District Commission. And in its construction, four towns — Enfield, Dana, Greenwich, and Prescott — all had to be flooded out of existence.

Near the 'Windsor Dam Entrance' to the reservoir, the Metropolitan District Commission has its headquarters. You can pick up trail guides to the reservation here, along with interesting historical and geographical pamphlets. There are six nature trails located in the southern section of the reservoir, and each one is well-marked on the trail guides.

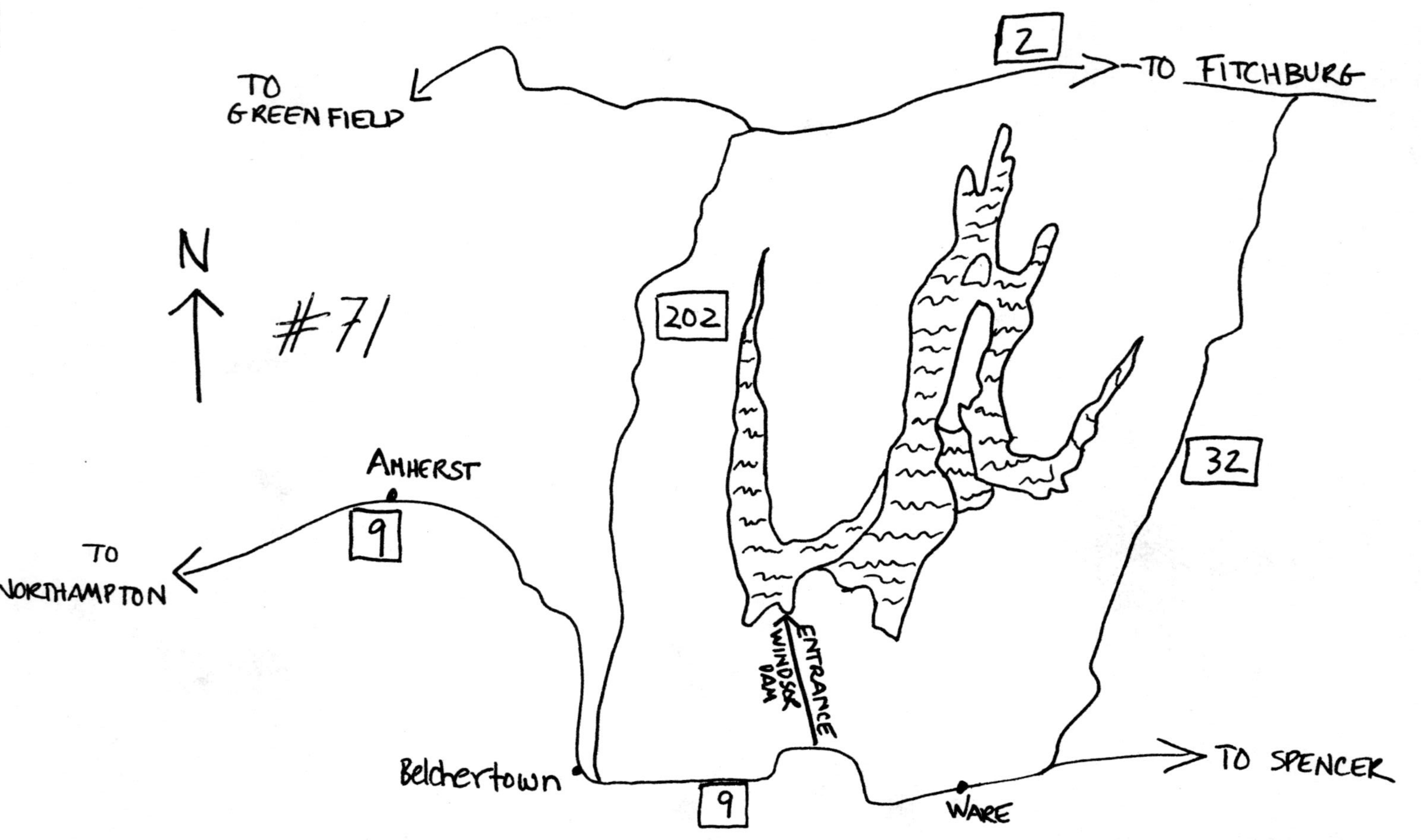

220
TO GREENFIELD
2
TO FITCHBURG
N
#71
202
32
AMHERST
9
TO NORTHAMPTON
ENTRANCE
WINDSOR DAM
Belchertown
9
WARE
TO SPENCER

72. METACOMET-MONADNOCK TRAIL

This is the longest continuous trail in Massachusetts (98 miles). Originating in northern Connecticut (southeast of Springfield, Mass.), the trail stretches north through the Connecticut Valley in Massachusetts, eventually crossing the Connecticut River between Mount Tom and Mount Holyoke. The trail then climbs Mount Grace (which is in the northern end of the state) and finally ends on Mount Monadnock in New Hampshire.

THE GUIDE TO THE METACOMET-MONADNOCK TRAIL, published by the Berkshire Chapter of the Appalachian Mountain Club, describes this trail in detail. The book is available from the Appalachian Mountain Club, 5 Joy Street, Boston, Mass. 02108.

73. HOLYOKE RANGE TRAILS

Owned by the Amherst Conservation Commission, this 141-acre tract of land offers a network of six hiking trails — each of them being less than a mile long. The trails are reached by turning east off of Mass. 116 onto Bay Road. Then, 1.3 miles after you've turned onto Bay Road, you'll see a sign on your right-hand-side for the conservation area.

In the fall, the colors here are spectacular. And the all-year-round views afforded of the Connecticut Valley from the summits of these mountains are unsurpassed.

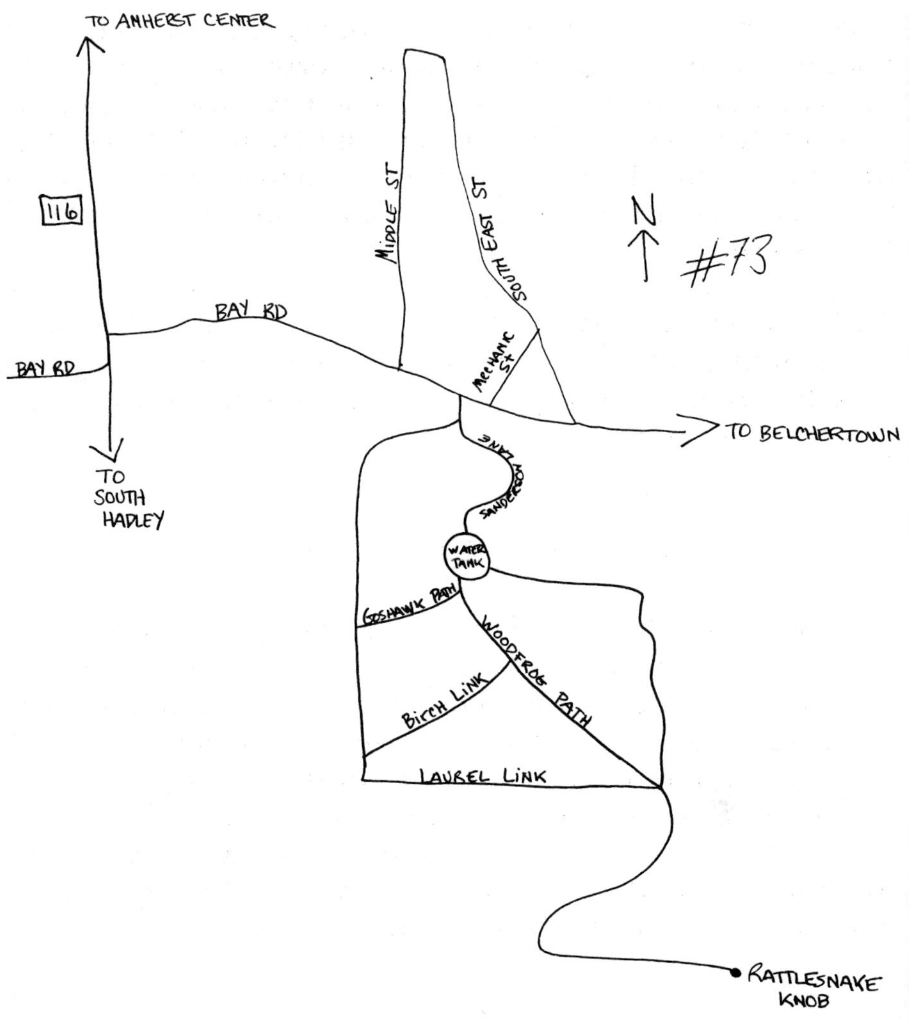

TO AMHERST CENTER
116
BAY RD
BAY RD
TO SOUTH HADLEY
MIDDLE ST
SOUTH EAST ST
MECHANIC ST
N
#73
TO BELCHERTOWN
SANDERSON LANE
WATER TANK
GOSHAWK PATH
WOODFROG PATH
BIRCH LINK
LAUREL LINK
RATTLESNAKE KNOB

CONNECTICUT AND RHODE ISLAND

Connecticut's 5,009 square miles, compared to Rhode Island's 1,234 square miles, offers a fairly extensive network of hiking trails. And while there are no dramatic peaks in the state (Bear Mountain, at only 2,316 feet, is the state's highest point), Connecticut still manages to offer the day hiker a unique topography. Her rolling hills, waterfalls, covered bridges, and colonial manses all make the state a worthwhile area for amateur naturalists.

(*A NATURALIST BUYS A FARM* by the Pulitzer Prize winning writer/photographer Edwin Teale serves as an excellent introduction to Connecticut's flora and fauna.)

Rhode Island, being the smallest of our fifty states, offers just a few worthwhile hiking areas. The four trips included here for Rhode Island, however, are probably the state's most unique wildlife areas.

CONNECTICUT

74. BARTLETT ARBORETUM

Supervised by the University of Connecticut's College of Agriculture and Natural Resources, the Bartlett Arboretum (on the west side of State Highway Route 137 in North Stamford, Connecticut) is filled with oak, maple and hickory trees, as well as a few scattered ash, birch, beech, and yellow poplar.

In addition, there are nature trails, a dwarf conifer garden, a bog walk, and hundreds of varieties of flowering shrubs. The trails here are easily travelled; little more than leisurely strolls in the woods.

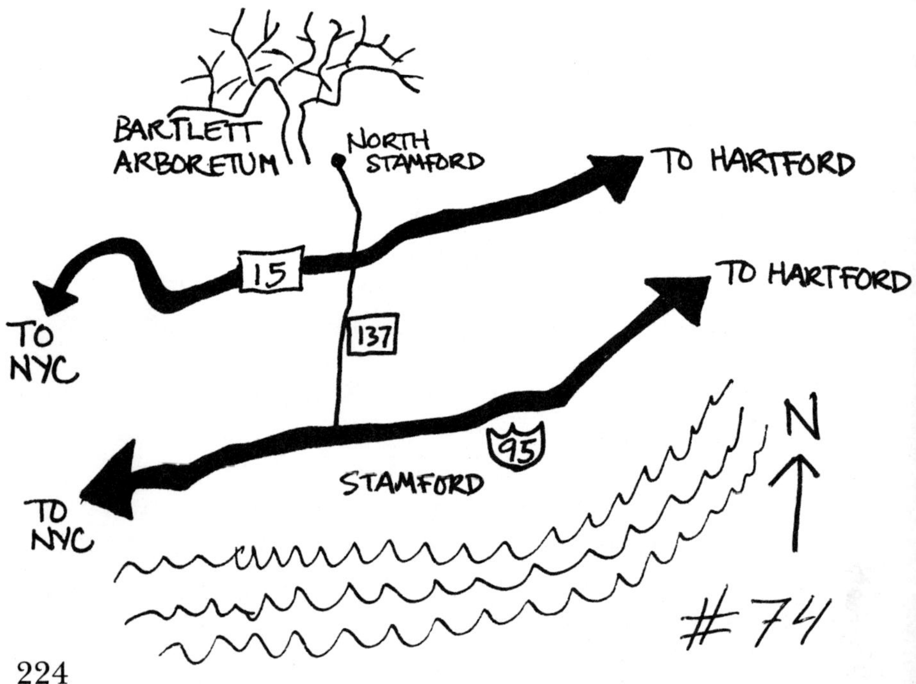

75. INDIAN LOOKOUT

In the spring and early summer, Indian Lookout presents a colorful display of both rare and native varieties of mountain laurel. To reach this site take Route 4 West (North Elm Street) out of Torrington, Conn. Then, drive only a few miles, and directly after the Yamaha Motorcycle Dealer take a right turn. The laurel fields are then on your right-hand-side at the top of the hill.

76. PACHAUG STATE FOREST
(north of Voluntown, Conn.)

This is the largest state forest in Connecticut. Ruefully, the 24,000 acres that comprise the forest were among the most thoughtlessly lumbered in the entire Northeast. Vast virgin stands of evergreens and hardwoods were greedily toppled here. Today, as a result of skillful forestry management, hemlock, white pine and coastal white cedar have been reestablished. A rhododendron sanctuary that's in full bloom on the fourth of July makes this state forest additionally alluring.

The park contains two short trails — the Castle Trail (1.5 miles) and the Canonicus Trail (2.5 miles).

77. BURR POND STATE PARK

To reach this state park and its 88-acre pond (a walking path encircles the pond) head north on Route 8 from Torrington, Conn. until you arrive at the center of Burrville. At the blinking light in Burrville's center, turn left and the state park will then be just a few miles along this road. More than 1,000 acres of state-owned forest surrounds Burr Pond.

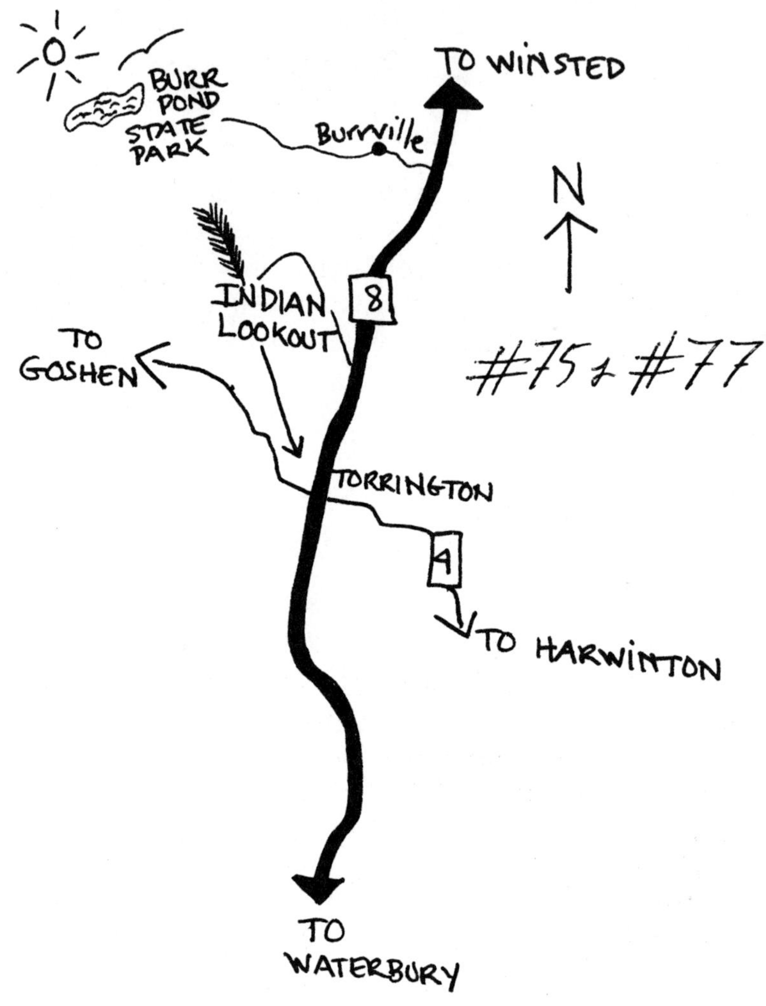

78. THE WHITE MEMORIAL FOUNDATION

This is among the best nature centers and small natural history museums in the entire New England area. Just outside of the center of Litchfield, Conn. (off of Route 25), this preserve includes over 4,000 acres of woodland, field, lakes, and streams. The Foundation's museum (open 9-5:00 P.M., Tues. thru Saturday) has a well-maintained collection of regional minerals, butterflies, birds, and mammals.

On Saturdays at 2:00 P.M., a free guided nature tour of the sanctuary is offered. And in April and May, when congries of migrating birds are returning to the Northeast, free birding tours are offered. Call the Foundation for the dates and times of these walks.

79. NATCHAUG STATE FOREST

This state forest in Eastford, Connecticut is a favorite springtime haunt of mine. I've seen more wild violets growing here than anywhere else in Connecticut.

The Natchaug Trail — which travels through both the Southern and Northern Natchaug Forests — is this area's most interesting trail. Its 11.6 miles includes a scenic trek past rivers, brooks, and streams.

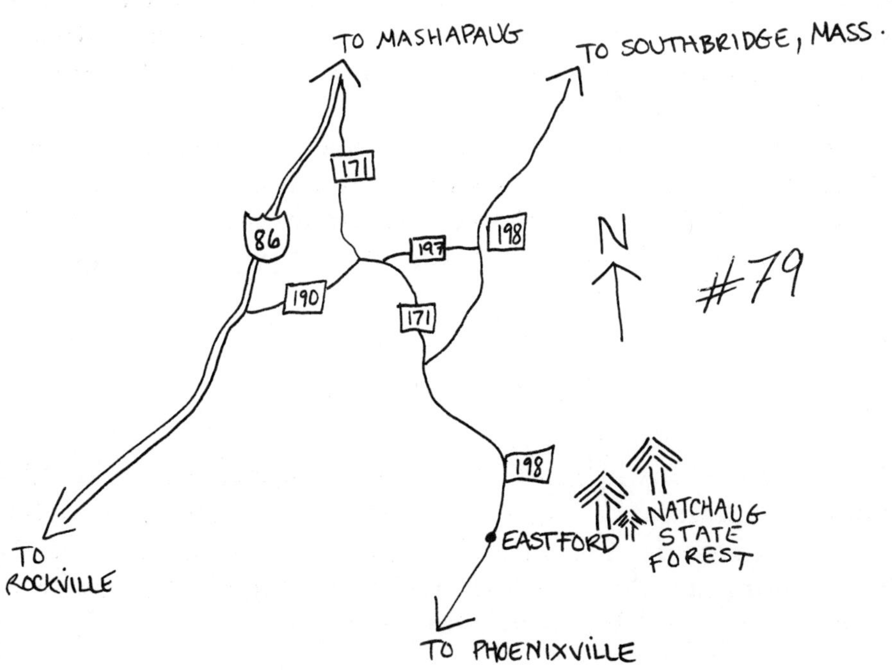

80. THE ROY AND MARGOT LARSEN WILDLIFE SANCTUARY
OF THE CONNECTICUT AUDUBON SOCIETY

This sanctuary (at 2325 Burr Street, in Fairfield, Conn.) contains more than six miles of walking trails. Woods, meadows, a marsh, a pond, and a swamp are all part of the preserve.

81. COCKAPONSET STATE PARK

To reach Cockaponset State Park take Jail Hill Road out of the town of Haddam, Conn. and turn onto Turkey Hill Road. Then, off of Turkey Hill Road turn onto Filley Road. The park's entrance is then just a short drive from this intersection.

The Cockaponset Trail, a 7.3 mile hike that meanders through the state park — passing woodlands, several brooks, and Pataconk Reservoir — begins 2.6 miles east of Route 81 at the intersection of Route 148 and Filley Road.

82. DEVIL'S HOPYARD STATE PARK

Devil's Hopyard State Park, off of Route 82 near Millington, Connecticut has more than 15 miles of hiking trails. The park includes Chapman Falls, a number of unique glacial formations, and a waterfall that's the Eight Mile River's steepest and most dramatic plunge.

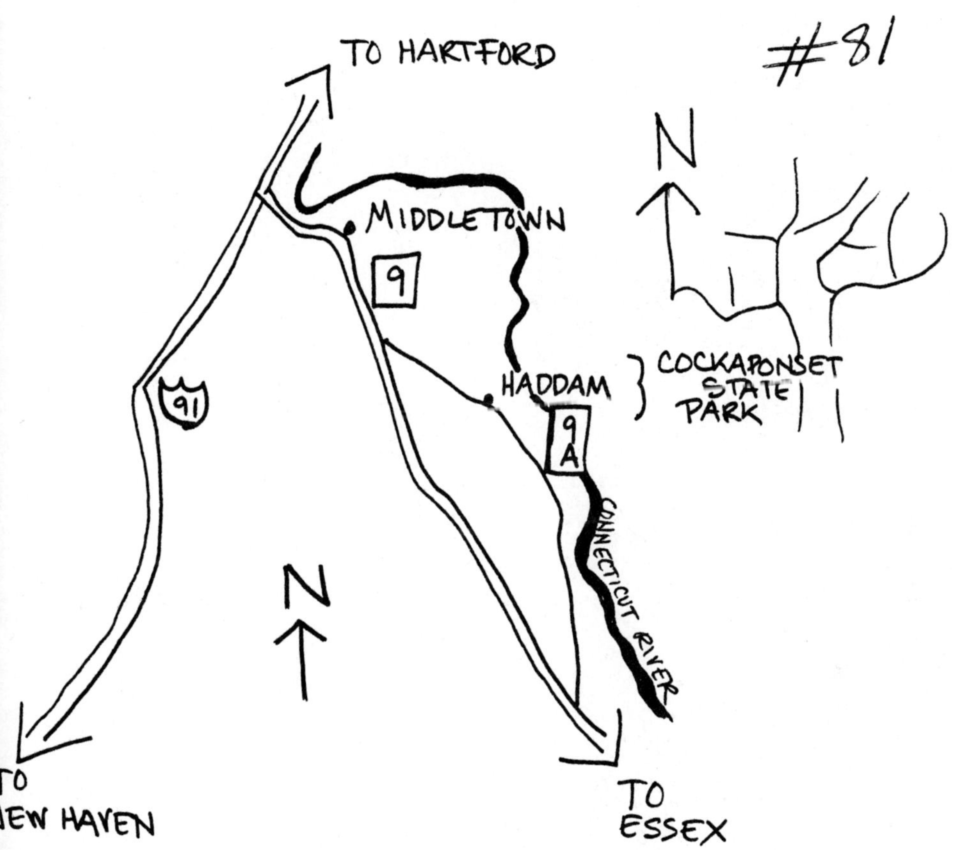

TO HARTFORD
#81
N
MIDDLETOWN
9
N
91
HADDAM
9A
COCKAPONSET STATE PARK
CONNECTICUT RIVER
TO NEW HAVEN
TO ESSEX

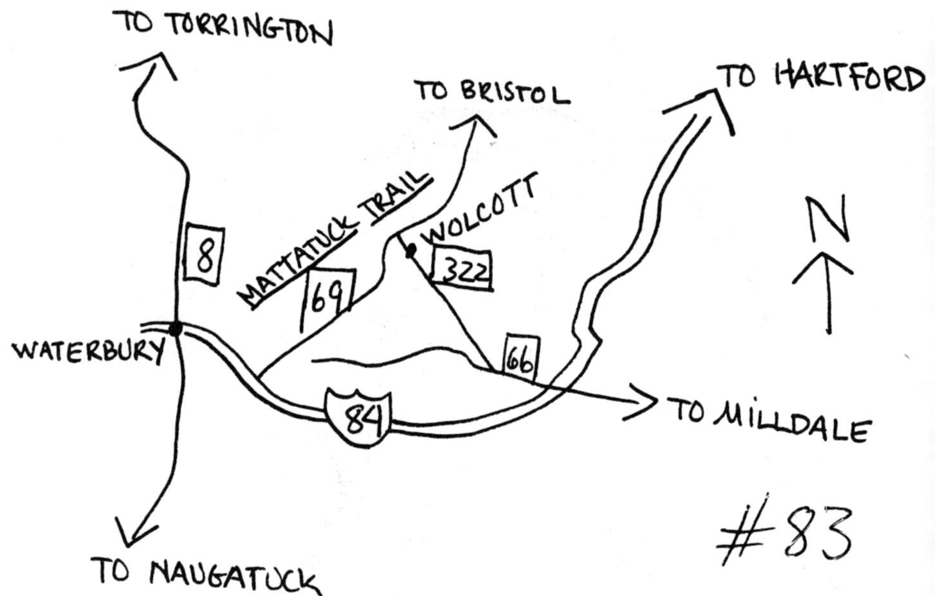

83.   MATTATUCK TRAIL

This is a 35 mile trail in western Connecticut. (Mad River Road on Route 69 in Wolcott, Conn. is where the trail begins.) Lakes, brooks, waterfalls, two mountains — Mohawk and Mount Prospect — a sewage plant, and two state parks — Black Rock State Park and Mattatuck State Forest — are all traversed by the trail. From Wolcott the trail follows a northwesterly direction, finally ending at the Appalachian Trail — which is just beyond Mohawk Mountain.

To reach this 2.5 mile scenic trail (a trail affording excellent views of the Housatonic River) drive 1.1 miles south on U.S. 7 from the Cornwall Bridge. Then, at the nearby parking lot on the west side of U.S. 7, the trail begins. The trail winds its way through both the Housatonic Meadows State Park and the Housatonic State Forest.

A useful book describing trails and hikes in Connecticut is *THE CONNECTICUT WALK BOOK,* published by the Connecticut Forest And Park Association. Their address: 1010 Main Street, East Hartford, Conn. 06108.

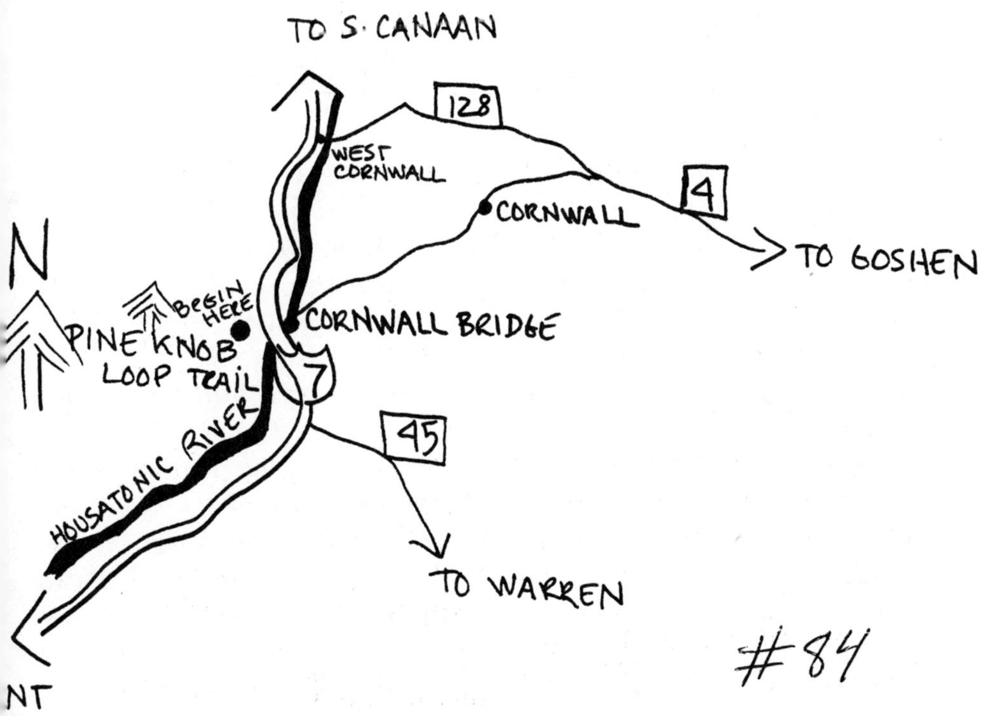

RHODE ISLAND

85.   GREAT SWAMP MANAGEMENT AREA

The Great Swamp Management Area is easily reached from Kingston, Rhode Island by travelling six miles on Route 138 West until Route 138 intersects with Route 2. At this intersection turn left and drive one mile until you see a sign for the park area. Turning left at the sign (Liberty Lane), continue for two miles until you pass the first set of railroad tracks. Then, directly after these tracks, make a sharp right and the park's entrance is right down this road.

The Great Swamp Management Area is one of those spots that somehow manages to go unnoticed by travellers. Its 3,000 acres (most of them swampy) afford a genuinely singular experience. The area's water impoundment, surrounded by an elaborate dike system, attracts a variety of water birds — green herons, ospreys, Canadian geese, quail, ducks and dozens of other species. There's a small catwalk, too, going across the impoundment that's safe to walk on, and it makes an excellent site to see some of these water birds close-up. (Because hunters dominate the area from September 22nd through the last day of February, I'd recommend not visiting until the early spring or summer.)

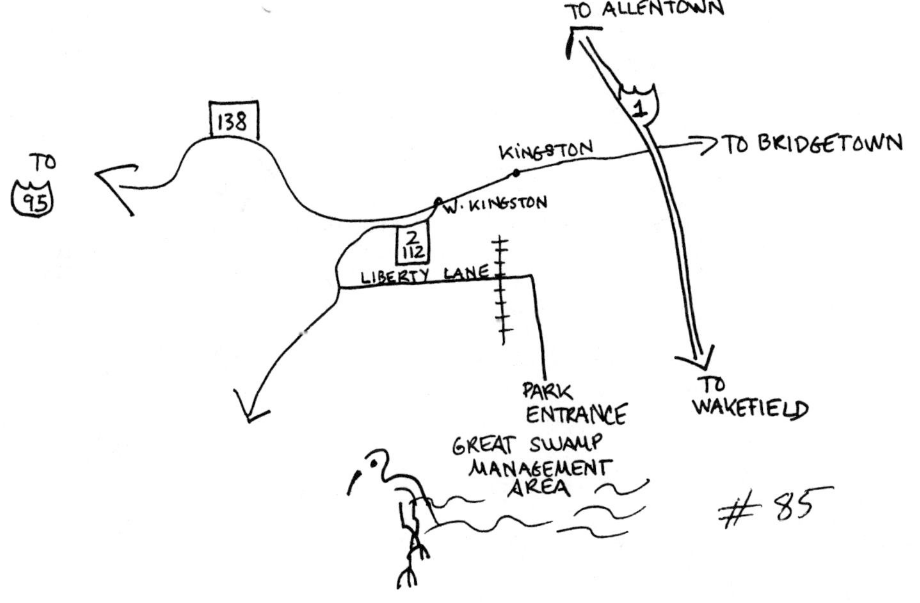

86.   RUECKER WILDLIFE AREA

Heading south from Tiverton, Rhode Island along Route 77, you'll reach Sapowet Avenue. To reach the Ruecker Wildlife Area turn right at Sapowet Avenue and after driving a mile you'll see the sanctuary's entrance. The sanctuary's salt marshes, which attract all species of water fowl, make this area a worthwhile birding site.

TO ROCKVILLE
TO PROVIDENCE
TO NOOSENECK
138
3
ARCADIA MANAGEMENT AREA
138 TO KINGSTON
HOPE VALLEY
95
N
3
TO HOPKINTON
TO NEW LONDON
#87A

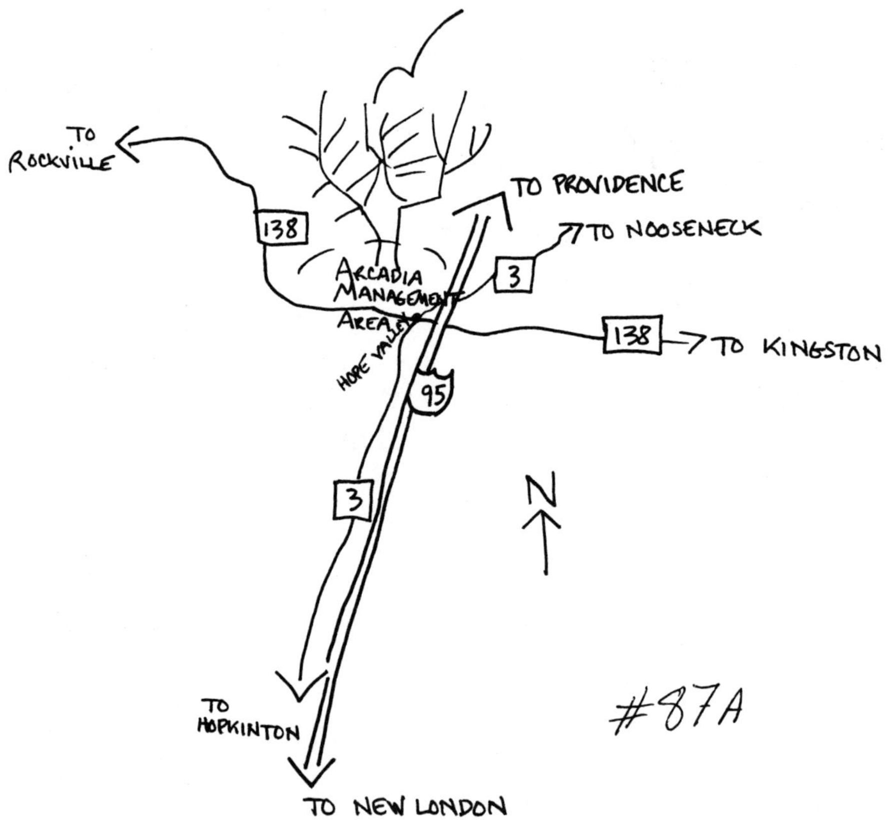

234

This is an 11,000-acre complex in southwestern Rhode Island. Travelling west from Kingston, Rhode Island along Route 138 turn right where Route 3 North intersects with Route 138. Then simply follow the signs to the management area.

A good walking trail here is the Tippecansett Trail which starts at the Steppingstone Falls Picnic Area off Escoheag Hill Rd. just about 2.5 miles north of RI 165. (See additional map below.) This trail is marked with yellow painted blazes.

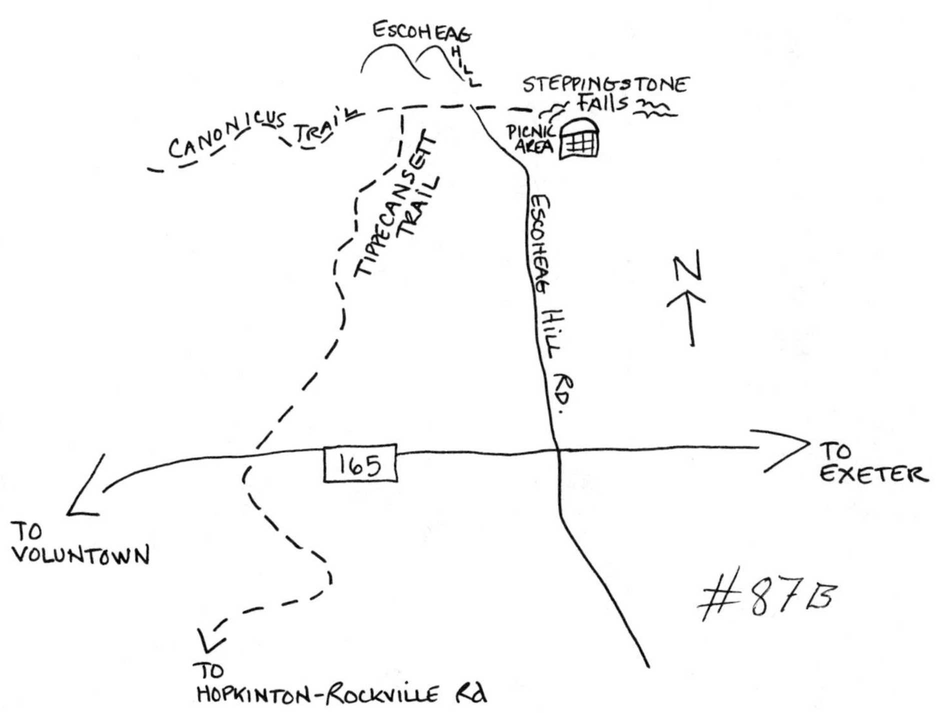

Located in the George Washington Management Area on the north side of U.S. 44 (two miles east of the Connecticut-Rhode Island state line), is this 8-mile trail. The trail is a "loop" trail, starting and ending at a small picnic area. The picnic area is situated at the second fork on the left hand side after entering the George Washington Management Area. The Walkabout Trail is marked with white rings.

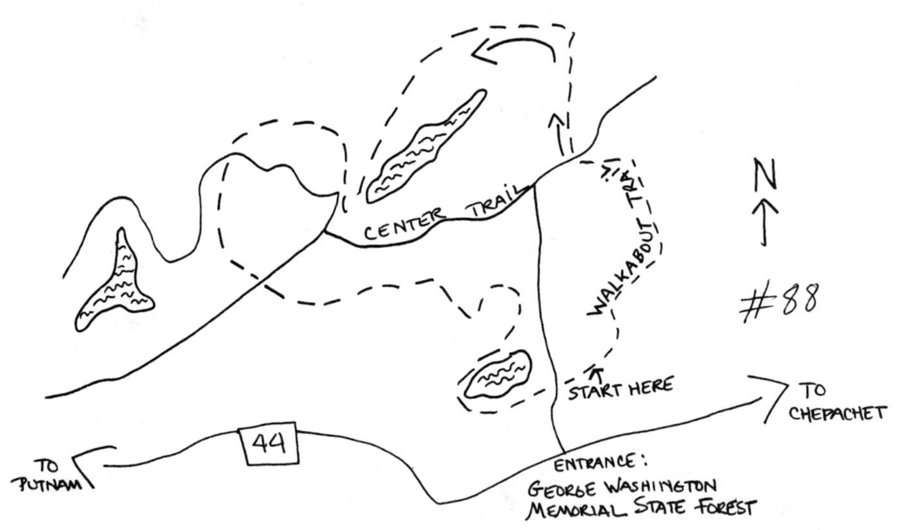

NEW YORK

One of the wildest wilderness areas in the entire Northeast is the Adirondack Park, in upstate New York. The Adirondack State Park (6,032,000 acres) includes an area comparable in size to the Grand Canyon, Yellowstone, Glacier, Yosemite, and Olympic National Parks combined (these all total approximately 5,150,000 acres). The Park, created by an act of the New York State Legislature back in 1892, today contains a combination of state-owned and privately-owned lands. Indeed, nearly 60 per cent of the Park's acreage is privately owned. As a result, it sometimes feels strange to come across towns — complete with elementary schools, fire houses, and dime stores — in the middle of this vast park.

Other than *THE ADIRONDACK MOUNTAIN CLUB'S GUIDE* to the area (published by the Adirondack Mountain Club, 172 Ridge Street, Glens Falls, New York 12801), another worthwhile guide for this region is *HIKING TRAILS OF THE NORTHEAST* by Thomas A. Henley and Neesa Sweet (Great Lakes Living Press).

New York State's wildlife habitats, however, aren't just limited to the Adirondack State Park. There's also the Rip Van Winkle country of the Catskill Mountains, filled with maple and oak trees, as well as the too often neglected western and central parts of the state. And there's even (hard to believe) New York City — which surprisingly has a number of worthwhile natural locales.

The Jamaica Bay Wildlife Refuge is in New York City — really in Queens, one of New York's five boroughs. The sanctuary can be reached by travelling along Cross Bay Boulevard. The refuge's eastern boundary, in fact, abuts the John F. Kennedy Airport.

Amidst what can only be called "urban blight" — old, darkened trains that rumble across a delapidated causeway and planes from the nearby airport that constantly spew their noxious fumes — this sanctuary, (with New York's steel skyline always in view), is about the only oasis for ornithophiles in the entire city.

In the fall, a few years back, *The New York Times* reported that some snow geese, a blue goose, a white pelican, and even a flamingo were sited at the refuge. Black ducks, scamp ducks (these two being very common in Long Island's bays and ponds), and buffleheads (or buffalo-heads, so-called because the males of these little ducks have puffy feathered heads) are almost always spotted at this refuge.

90.   SAPSUCKER WOODS

About three miles northeast of the Cornell University campus in Ithaca, New York is the Cornell Laboratory of Ornithology. Commonly known as Sapsucker Woods, this 180-acre sanctuary is named after the yellow-bellied sapsucker — a common species of American woodpecker. Over 4 miles of walking trails wind through the sanctuary.

A ten-acre pond that attracts a wide variety of waterfowl can be viewed from behind a huge picture window in the Lyman K. Stuart Observatory — the sanctuary's headquarters. You will find photographic exhibits, a modest reference library, and a sound laboratory.

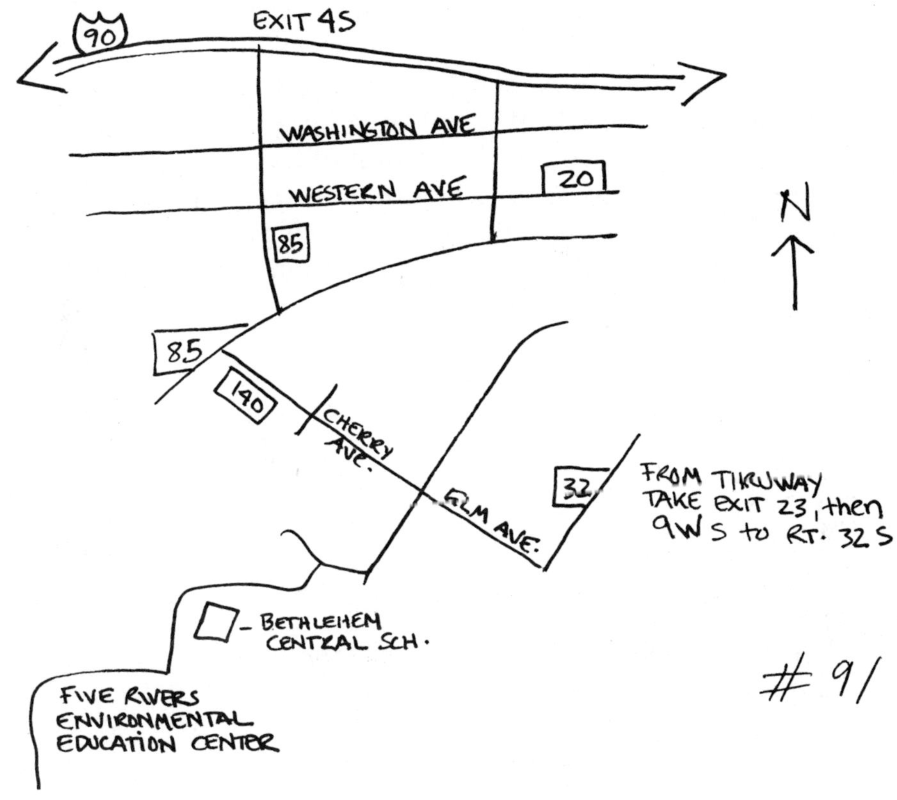

91. FIVE RIVERS ENVIRONMENTAL EDUCATION CENTER

This 260 acre nature center includes ponds, streams, mature forests, and an old field. Four especially well-planned guided nature walks — The Beaver Tree Trail, The Old Field Trail, The Vlomankill Trail (a *kill* is a small stream), and The North Loop Trail — all make worthwhile, informative walks.

To reach the Center, take the New York State Thruway to Exit 23. From this exit, pick up Route 9W South into Route 32 South. Then, at Elm Street, turn right off of 32 South and finally, turn left after the Bethlehem Central School in Delmar. Signs to the Nature Center are then visible.

This 480-acre nature center in Sherburne, New York offers 10 short hikes, each of them traversing a diverse terrain: ponds, marshes, swamps, and a section of the Chenango River. A natural history museum (with 350 mounted bird specimens), along with a 3,500 volume library are also on the grounds.

The Center is right off of Route 80, just a short distance (1 mile) west of the town of Sherburne.

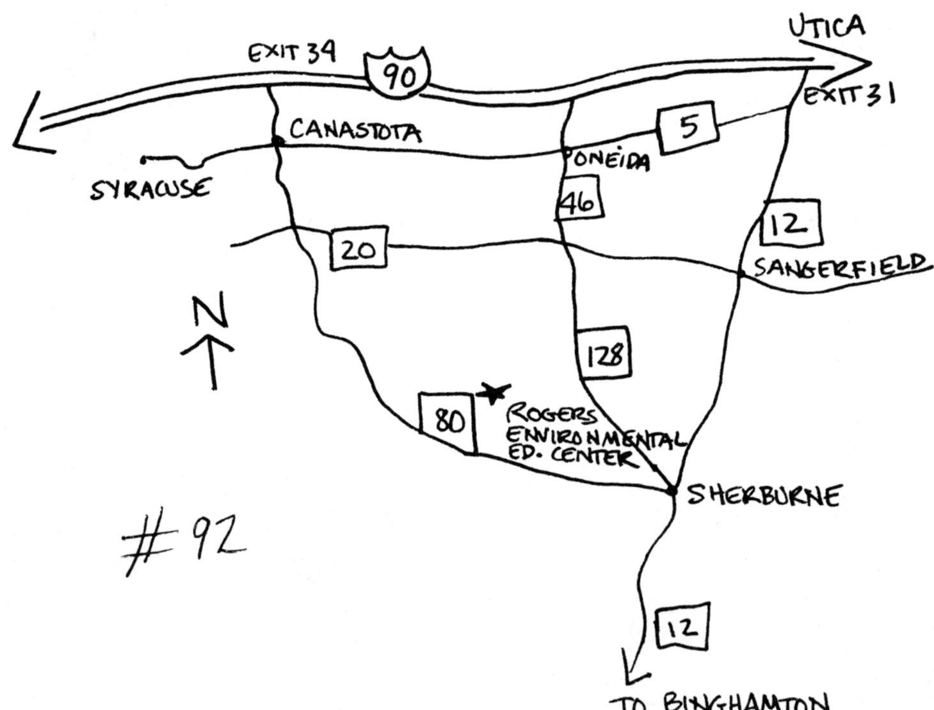

93.   BROOKFIELD STATE PARK

Thousands of acres of pine trees, planted back in the 1930's by the Civilian's Conservation Corp (CCC) comprise this not-well-known state park. Atop Moscow Hill, tucked deep in the state forest, is an old firetower. (The mountains surrounding the park are a low-lying peripheral range of Pennsylvania's Alleghenies.)

94.   ALBANY'S NEW YORK STATE MUSEUM &
NEW YORK CITY'S MUSEUM OF NATURAL HISTORY

I don't usually recommend museums to nature lovers. If you want to see nature then see her first hand — not in some gloomy, cavernous building. But New York State does have two museums that shouldn't be missed: New York City's Museum of Natural History located on 79th Street and Central Park West and the New York State Museum in Albany.

The State Museum (mailing address: New York State Museum, Cultural Education Center, State Education Department, Albany, New York 11230) is worth visiting before you do any serious hiking in the Adirondacks. One of the museum's permanent exhibits — 'The Adirondack Wilderness' — includes dioramas, short films, and mounted flora and fauna specimens. The exhibit serves as a useful orientation to the entire Upstate Region of New York State.

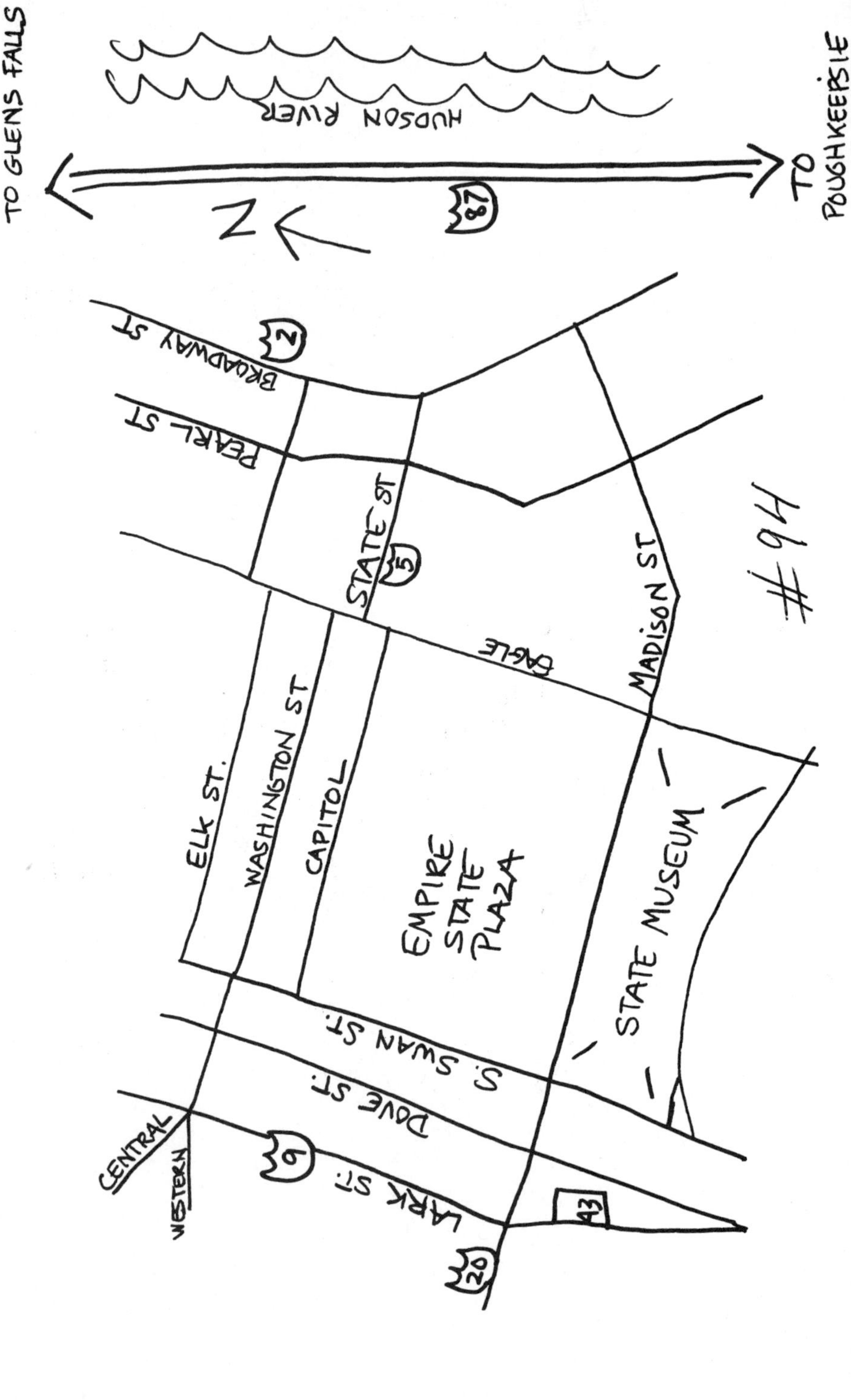

TO GLENS FALLS

TO POUGHKEEPSIE

HUDSON RIVER

87

N

BROADWAY ST

PEARL ST

STATE ST

5

EAGLE

MADISON ST

#94

ELK ST.

WASHINGTON ST

CAPITOL

EMPIRE STATE PLAZA

STATE MUSEUM

S. SWAN ST.

DOVE ST.

CENTRAL

WESTERN

LARK ST.

9

20

43

95. SARATOGA SPRINGS MINERAL BATHS &
THE SHARON SPRINGS SULPHUR BATHS

About an hour's car-ride north of Albany is Saratoga Springs — where, years ago, the 'Beautiful People' would summer; spending their mornings soaking in revitalizing mineral baths and their afternoons gambling at the town's racetrack. Today, at three state-run spas — the Washington Spa, the Roosevelt Spa, and the Lincoln Spa — you can enjoy these same warm baths, leisurely soaking in Saratoga's mineral-rich, naturally-carbonated water. The price for a bath is $4.00 — which includes a towel, a warm sheet, and a private room for resting. Telephone: (518)584-2010. Call 24 hours in advance for reservations.

Heading west from Saratoga is Sharon Springs, another town famous for its healing waters. Sulphur is here the principal property in the water; and a hot (body temperature) sulphur bath is said to heal everything from arthritis to impotency.

(Water is among our most precious natural resources. And enjoying both its relaxing and healing properties is a much as part of appreciating nature as either hiking or bird watching.)

96. THE HUDSON RIVER

Probably because I was born in New York City, where the Hudson River is a polluted nightmare, I feel compelled to include this trip. Really, the trip is little more than a swim in an unpolluted section of the Hudson. But the swim might prove a symbolic leap into this great river's clean and unpolluted past.

To reach this *swimmable* section of the Hudson first drive to the town of North Creek, New York. There, pick up Route 28N off of Route 28. Then, just over a small bridge in the town (at a sign that says "Hudson River"), you'll spot a narrow footpath. Follow this path as it descends a quarter-of-a-mile to the river. And anywhere from this rocky shore is a good place to plunge into the Hudson.

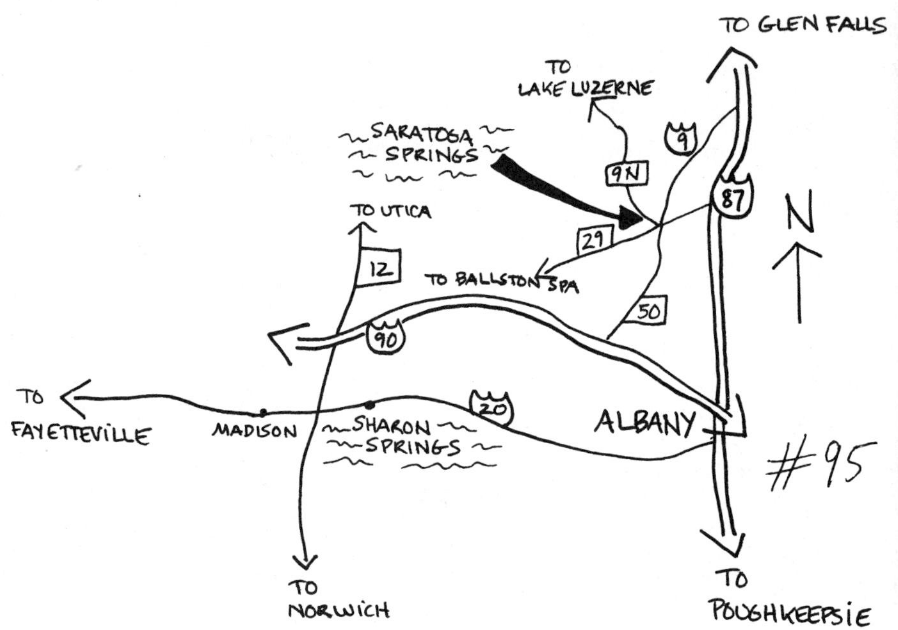

97.   MONTEZUMA NATIONAL WILDLIFE REFUGE

Located at the northern tip of Lake Cayuga is the 5,300 acre Montezuma Wildlife Refuge. Here, over 5 miles of interpretive nature trails wind around a practically unspoiled marshland. All species of waterfowl are attracted in droves to the area.

244

(Try to obtain a copy of the *DIRECTORY OF NATURE CENTERS, OUTDOOR STUDY AREAS AND ENVIRONMENTAL EDUCATION CENTERS IN NEW YORK STATE* published by the New York State Department of Environmental Conservation, Publications — Room 107, Albany, New York 12233. It's an extensive listing of practically all the wildlife refuges in the state. And in addition, a number of useful pamphlets for hikers and campers can be obtained by writing to THE NEW YORK STATE DEPARTMENT OF COMMERCE, 99 Washington Avenue, Albany, New York 12245.)

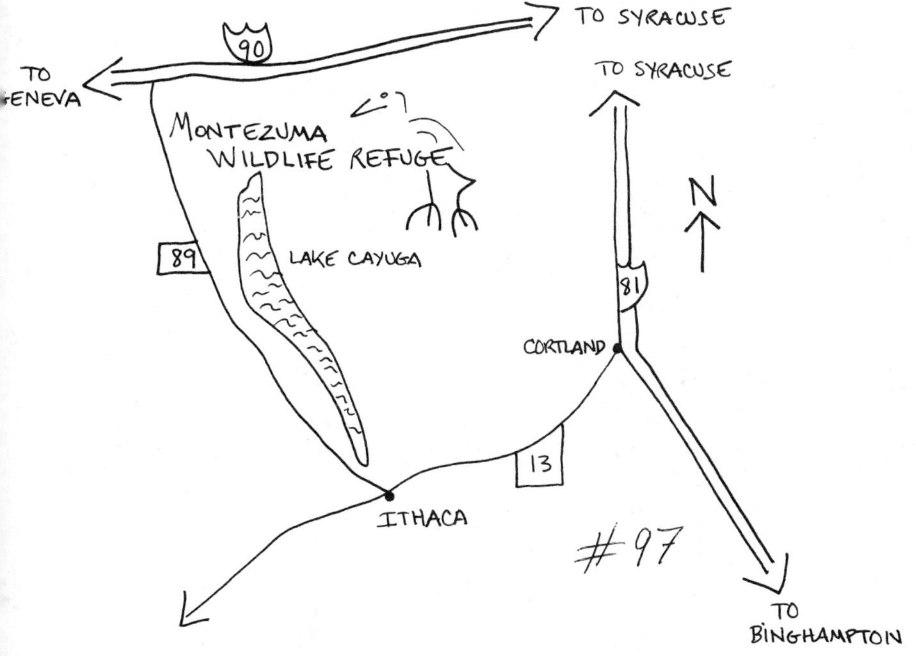

SOME TRIPS IN THE ADIRONDACK STATE PARK

98.   AMPERSAND MOUNTAIN

This 3,352 foot peak is a moderately strenuous 2.71 mile hike. To reach the trail's beginning drive about 8 miles southwest of the traffic light at the bridge in Saranac Lake Village along Route 3. You'll then see a parking area on the right hand side of the road. The trail starts directly across the road from this parking area. A New York State Department of Environmental Conservation sign marks the trail.

The ascent is at first gradual, traversing a practically level hardwood forest. But as you climb (passing several brooks, a swamp, and a hemlock grove) the ascent steepens.

Atop the mountain's bare granite summit (decorated with all species of graffiti — from prosaic, romantic drivel like "Patty & Bobby, '73" to slightly more profound scribblings — "Hello God, I made it") you'll have a superb view. To the south is tiny Ampersand Lake and to the southwest are lots of high, jutting peaks. And to both the north and northwest lie the Saranac ponds and numerous ponds beyond.

The trail ascending Ampersand is clearly marked.

99.   MIDDLE SARANAC LAKE

A neglected area (hence, one that's also relatively private) that's close to the beginning of the Ampersand Mountain Trail is Middle Saranac Lake. To reach the lake's shores (and a nearby lean-to) just follow a .5 mile trail that begins at the parking area directly across from that start of the Ampersand Trail (on Route 3). The lake is large and swimmable.

This less than a mile climb (.89 miles) up Baker Mountain (2,452 feet) affords the most spectacular views of the Adirondacks for the least amount of climbing. From its wooded summit, you can see Moose and McKenzie Mountains, the MacIntyre Range, the Sewards, and the entire lake country that's to the southwest of the Saranac ponds.

The trail begins at the north end of Moody Pond just east of Saranac Lake Village (see map).

101.   WARD BROOK TRAIL

This approximately 10-mile trail is the western approach to the High Peaks Regions. This High Peaks Region is where the more than forty well-known, over-4,000-foot-high-peaks of the MacIntyre Mountain Range are located. The majority of these towering peaks are situated south of Lake Placid; with Mount Marcy (5,344 feet) at the center.

The trail begins at a Department of Environmental Conservation parking lot that's near the south end of Upper Saranac Lake (see map). This trail ends at the Duck Hole Ranger Station where two lean-tos are available for overnight camping.

At the north end of Mountain Pond (about 8.80 miles from the Ward Brook Trail's start) this red-marked trail intersects with the blue-marked Northville-Placid Trail. And 3.65 miles down this Northville-Placid Trail on the shores of the Cold River is the old hermitage of Noah John Rondeau.

Noah Rondeau was perhaps the most celebrated hermit of the Adirondacks. He lived in the Cold River section of the Adirondack State Park (which is about 12 miles, as the crow flies, south of Little Saranac Lake). Rondeau — "the Mayor of Cold River" (population 1) — was formerly a barber who became disenchanted with society because of "the sharp practices of businessmen." He took flight to the woods as a young man and never again returned to civilization. For more than 30 years (until his death in 1967), he lived happily in the mountains.

Rondeau was a true hermit. Unlike Thoreau, whose mother and sister used to bring him baked goods every week, Rondeau would sometimes go years without ever seeing another human being. He wore deerskins for clothes, used bear grease for cooking, and built wooden tepees for shelter. These wooden tepees where Rondeau lived were really his extensive woodpiles; they were the wood he actually used in wintertime for heating and cooking. So each year Rondeau would essentially 'burn his house down', eventually being left shelterless by the time spring arrived. In the warmer months he slept outdoors.

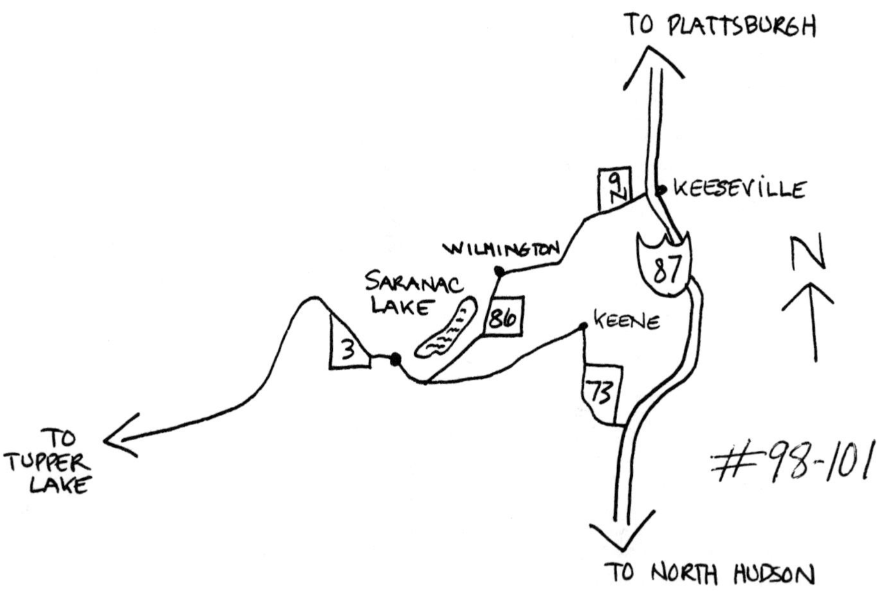

There are about ten trails that ascend Mount Marcy, the highest peak in the Adirondack State Park. The most popular and shortest of these is the Van Hoevenberg Trail, a 7.46 trek that begins at The Adirondak Loj. This Loj, operated by the Adirondack Mountain Club (located 9 miles south of Lake Placid off Route 73 at the end of the Adirondak Log Road) has both sleeping and eating facilities. For a rate schedule write: Adirondak Loj, Box 867, Lake Placid, New York 12946. Telephone: (518)523-3441. The Loj isn't cheap, though, so plan to save money by camping out.

The 10.11-mile Upper Works Trail is an easy trail up Marcy. It ascends the mountain from the southwest. The trail is reached by taking NY 28N for 9.1 miles east of Newcomb, then turning right, then right again at the first fork (passing the Sanford Lake bridge and a huge titanium open pit mine on the right) and finally continuing on this road up to a small parking area. The trail then follows the meanderings of the Calamity Brook and passes both Calamity Pond and Lake Colden. The trail starts in what amounts to a ghost town — a town formerly known as *Tahawus*. (Tahawus was the Indian name for Mount Marcy, meaning 'cloud-splitter'.) Iron mines previously populated this area.

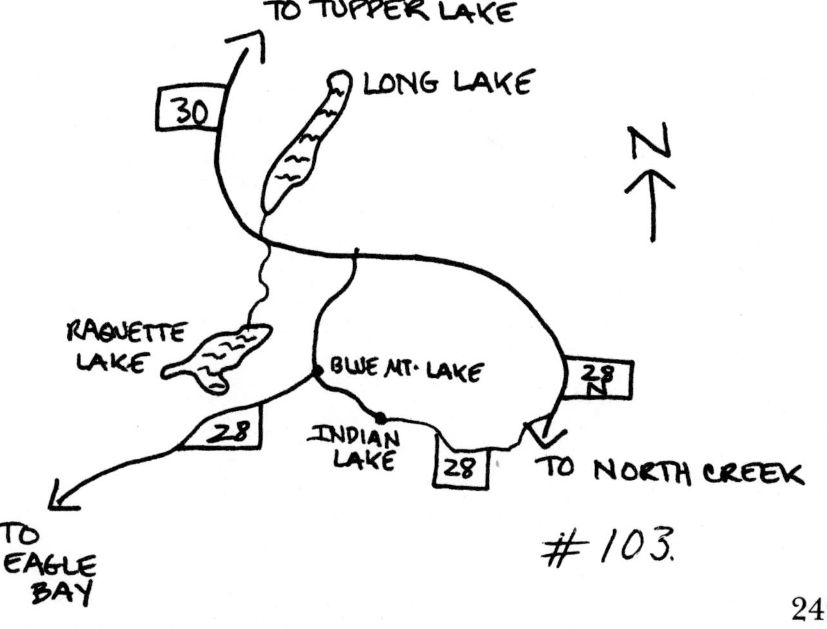

The entire Adirondack Region, with its lakes, streams, and ponds, is ideal for canoeists. An easy trip with only a few portages includes "putting in" at Long Lake, paddling down the Raquette River, and finally crossing the Raquette Lake (see map).

An excellent canoe guide describing over 700 miles of canoe trails in the St. Lawrence River and Lake Champlain drainage basins is published by the Adirondack Mountain Club (172 Ridge Street, Glen Falls, New York 12801). And a free list of canoe liveries can be obtained from the New York State Department of Environmental Conservation, 50 Wolf Road, Albany, New York 12205.

PENNSYLVANIA

Hikers can conveniently divide Pennsylvania into three sections: western Pennsylvania, central Pennsylvania, and eastern Pennsylvania. And each of these areas contains dozens of short walks and longer treks.

In western Pennsylvania the Allegheny National Forest offers an extensive network of hiking trails. In central Pennsylvania a 200-mile continuous footpath is available. And in eastern Pennsylvania it's game lands, state parks, and the banks of the Delaware Canal that supply the amateur naturalist with ample terrain for hiking.

Maps of Pennsylvania can be obtained from: the U.S. GEOLOGICAL SURVEY, Distribution Section, 1200 So. Eads Street, Arlington, Virginia 22202. Request their free Pennsylvania Index.

Also, road and trail maps of Pennsylvania's state forests are free from: the Pennsylvania Department of Environmental Resources, Harrisburg, Pa. 17120. The Department of Environmental Resources also supples a current *Pennsylvania Official Transportation Map* which shows all the state parks, forests, and game lands, as well as the Appalachian, Baker, Black Forest, Loyalsock, Susquehannock, Traders Path, and Warrior trails.

Pennsylvania's Game Commission (Box 1567, Harrisburg, Pa. 17120) will send on request a list of their available maps.

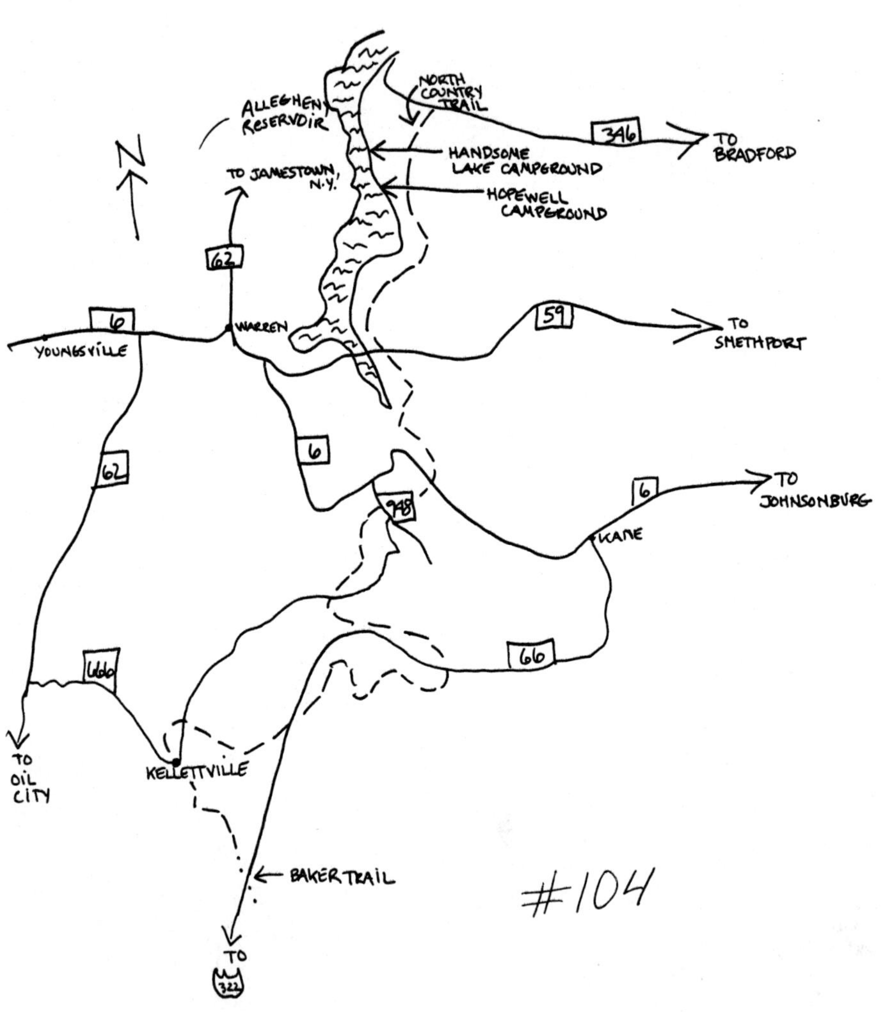

N
ALLEGHENY RESERVOIR
NORTH COUNTRY TRAIL
346
TO BRADFORD
HANDSOME LAKE CAMPGROUND
HOPEWELL CAMPGROUND
TO JAMESTOWN, N.Y.
62
6
YOUNGSVILLE
WARREN
59
TO SMETHPORT
62
6
6
TO JOHNSONBURG
948
KANE
466
66
TO OIL CITY
KELLETTVILLE
BAKER TRAIL
#104
TO 322

104. NORTH COUNTRY TRAIL

This more than 30-mile trail winds its way through the Allegheny Naional Forest. The northern part of the trail begins a mile south of the New York State Line and then follows the eastern shore of the Allegheny Reservoir for seven miles. Camping facilities are available at both Handsome Lake and the Hopewell Boat Access campgrounds. The trail then heads south through the Tionesta Scenic Area for 28 miles to a point 3 miles south of Kellettville.

From there, a road passes the Musette Fire Tower and Route 22 and connects with the Baker Trail into Cook Forest State Park.

105. BAKER TRAIL

The Pittsburgh Council of the American Youth Hostels established this trail in 1950. The trail crosses farmland and woodland, passing through Crooked Creek State Park, the Mahonig Creek Reservoir area, and Cook Forest.

There are eleven lean-to shelters along the trail.

For a complete guide to this 140-mile trail write: Pittsburgh Council, American Youth Hostels, Inc., 6300 Fifth Avenue, Pittsburgh, Pa. 15232.

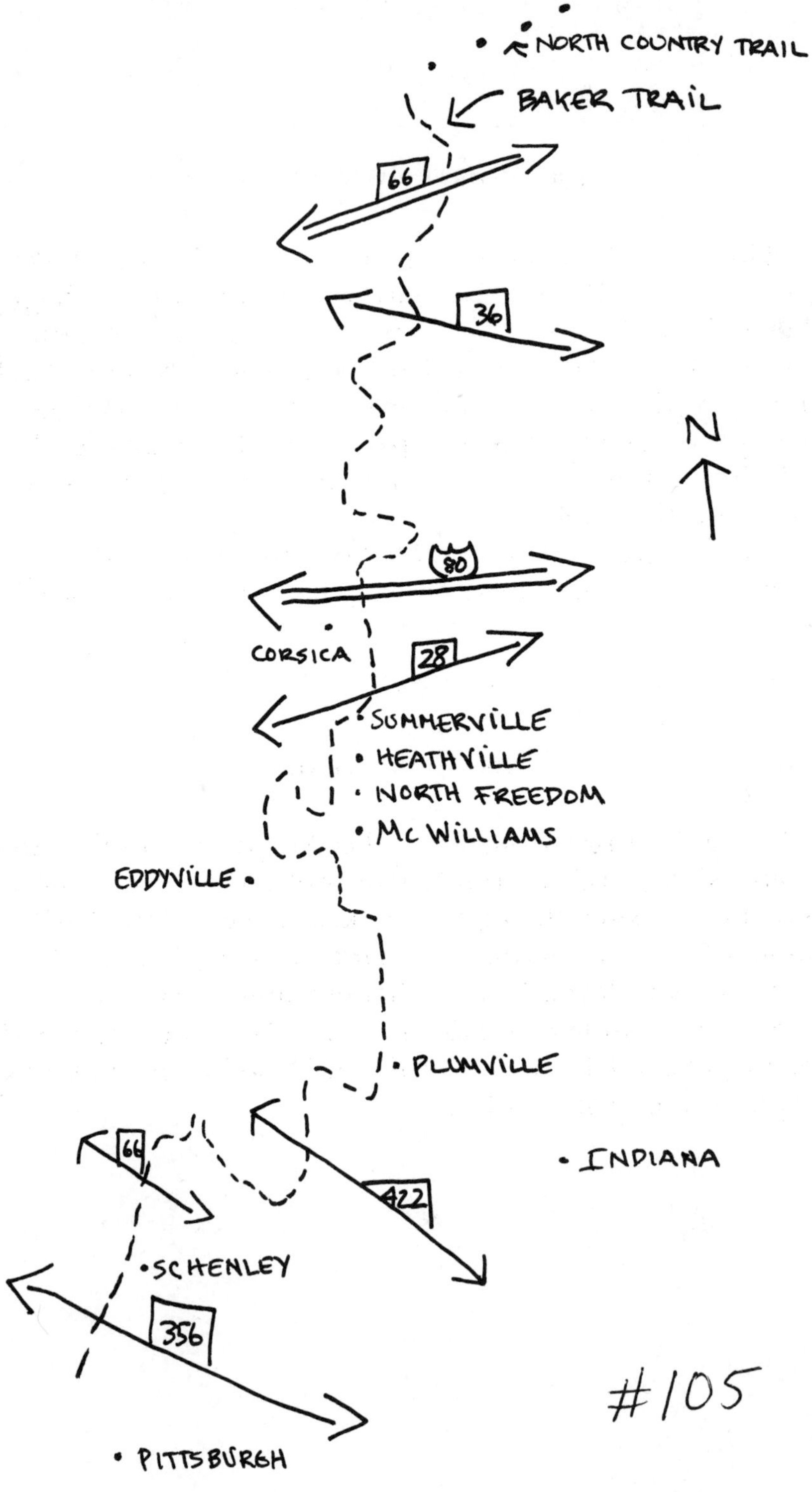
NORTH COUNTRY TRAIL
BAKER TRAIL
66
36
N
80
CORSICA
28
SUMMERVILLE
HEATHVILLE
NORTH FREEDOM
McWILLIAMS
EDDYVILLE
PLUMVILLE
66
INDIANA
422
SCHENLEY
356
PITTSBURGH
#105

106. TRADERS PATH

This is a 33-mile trail, formerly an Indian trail that criss-crosses through southwestern Pennsylvania. During the French and Indian War this trail provided an undetected route for two colonial emissaries.

The western terminus of the trail is the Allegheny River at Edgecliff (just south of Freeport, Pa.) and the eastern terminus is on U.S. 422 at Shelocta (just west of Indiana, Pa.). And near the trail's Idaho Shelter is a link with the Baker Trail.

A 23-page brochure, supplying the trail's extensive history as well as some of the region's other eighteenth-century Indian trails, is offered by the: Moraine Trails Council, Boy Scouts of America, 830 Morton Avenue Extension, Butler, Pa. 16001.

107. WARRIOR TRAIL

This 67-mile trail begins at Greensboro on the Monongahela River and extends westward to Cameron, West Virginia on U.S. 250. The trail is well-marked — (rounded posts with WARRIOR TRAIL carved into them dot the trail).

108. LAUREL HIGHLANDS HIKING TRAIL

Starting at Ohiopyle and running northeasterly along the mountainous ridges between Fayette, Somerset, and Westmoreland counties, the Laurel Highlands Hiking Trail passes Ohiopyle State Park, Laurel Ridge State Park, and Kooser State Park.

A leaflet about the trail can be obtained by writing: The Park Superintendent, Laurel Ridge State Park, R.D. 3, Rockwood, Pennsylvania.

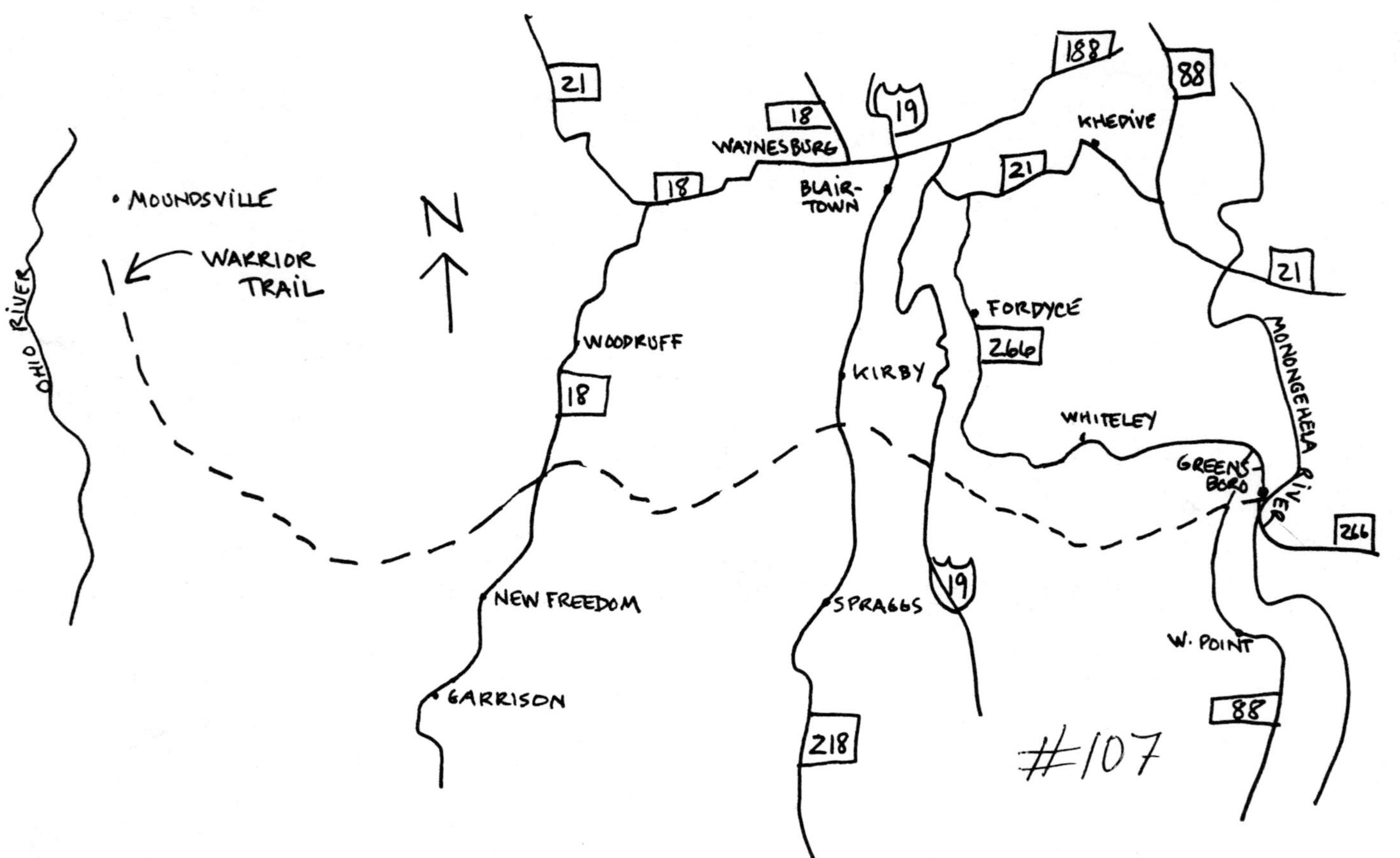

WARRIOR TRAIL
N
MOUNDSVILLE
OHIO RIVER
21
188
88
18
19
KHEDIVE
WAYNESBURG
BLAIRTOWN
21
21
FORDYCE
266
WOODRUFF
18
KIRBY
MONONGEHELA RIVER
WHITELEY
GREENSBORO
266
19
NEW FREEDOM
SPRAGGS
W. POINT
GARRISON
218
88
#107

109. SUSQUEHANNOCK TRAIL SYSTEM

This is an 85-mile loop trail in north-central Pennsylvania (situated approximately 10 miles east of Coudersport). The trail connects many old Civilian Conservation Corps (CCC) fire trails, old logging roads, and railroad grades.

A detailed guidebook describing the trail can be obtained from: Potter County Recreation, Inc. P.O. 245, Coudersport, Pa. 16915.

110. BLACK FOREST TRAIL

This 42-mile loop trail traverses some of the finest mountain country in Pennsylvania. The trail's name was derived from all the dense, dark virgin conifer forests that populate the area.

This trail starts and ends in a pine plantation that's .8 miles from the village of Slate Run, which is 27 miles north of Jersey Shore.

A complete guide to the trail (price: $1.00) can be obtained by writing: Tiadraghton Fire Fighters Association, Bureau of Forestry, 423 E. Central Avenue, South Williamsport, Pa. 17701.

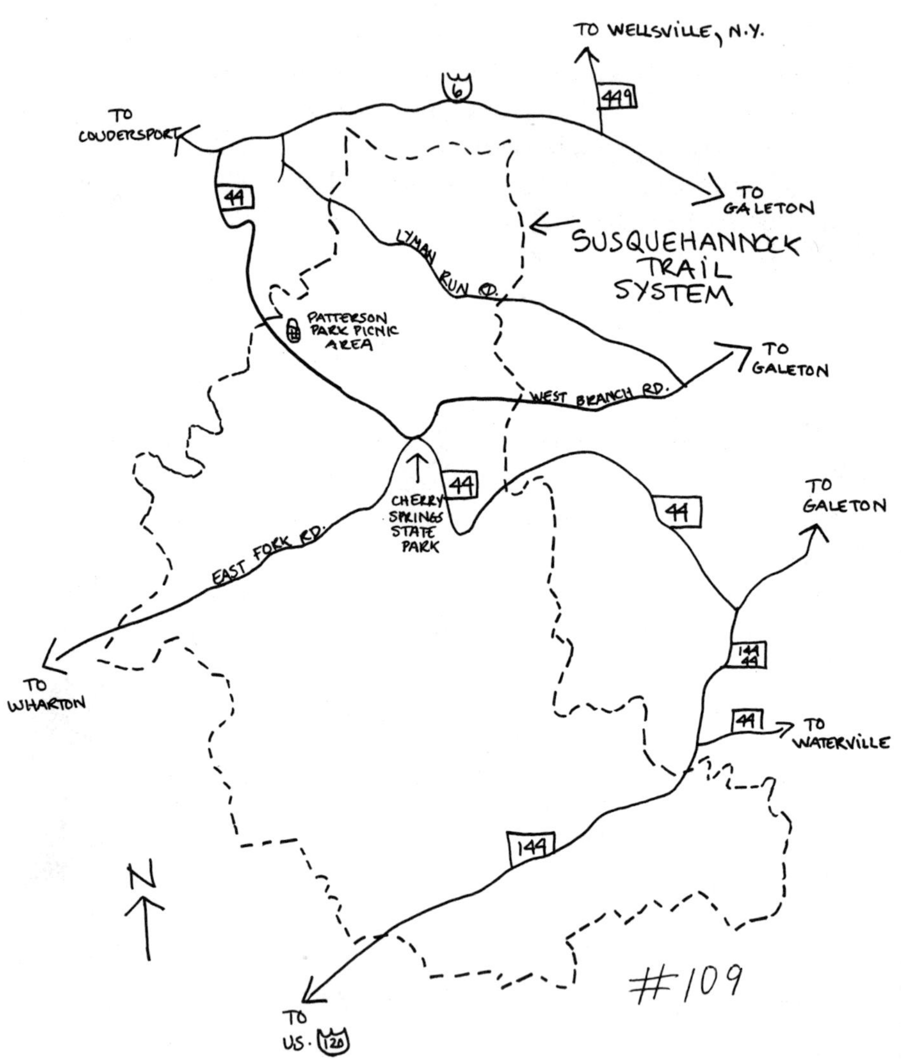

TO WELLSVILLE, N.Y.
6
449
TO COUDERSPORT
TO GALETON
44
SUSQUEHANNOCK TRAIL SYSTEM
LYMAN RUN RD.
PATTERSON PARK PICNIC AREA
TO GALETON
WEST BRANCH RD.
44
TO GALETON
44
CHERRY SPRINGS STATE PARK
EAST FORK RD.
144 44
TO WHARTON
44
TO WATERVILLE
144
N
#109
TO US. 120

111.   LOYALSOCK TRAIL

This 57.1-mile trail, maintained by the Williamsport Alpine Club, crosses some of Pennsylvania's most beautiful wilderness. The trail runs from Route 87 at a point 10.1 miles north of Montoursville to U.S. Route 220 at Ringdale, Pa. The trail is marked with metal markets that are painted red with a yellow LT.

A trail guide can be obtained from: The Loyalsock Trail Chairman, c/o The Williamsport Alpine Club, P.O. Box 501, Williamsport, Pa. 17701.

112.   TUSCARORA TRAIL

This 105-mile trail (which connects into the 100-mile Big Blue Trail in Maryland, West Virginia, and Virginia) has its northern terminus at the Appalachian Trail in Deans Gap, and its southern terminus in the Shenandoah National Park (near the Mathews Arm Campground in Virginia). The trail crosses the Potomac River at Hancock, Maryland.

For further information write: Keystone Trails Association, R.D. 2, Coopersburg, Pa. 18036.

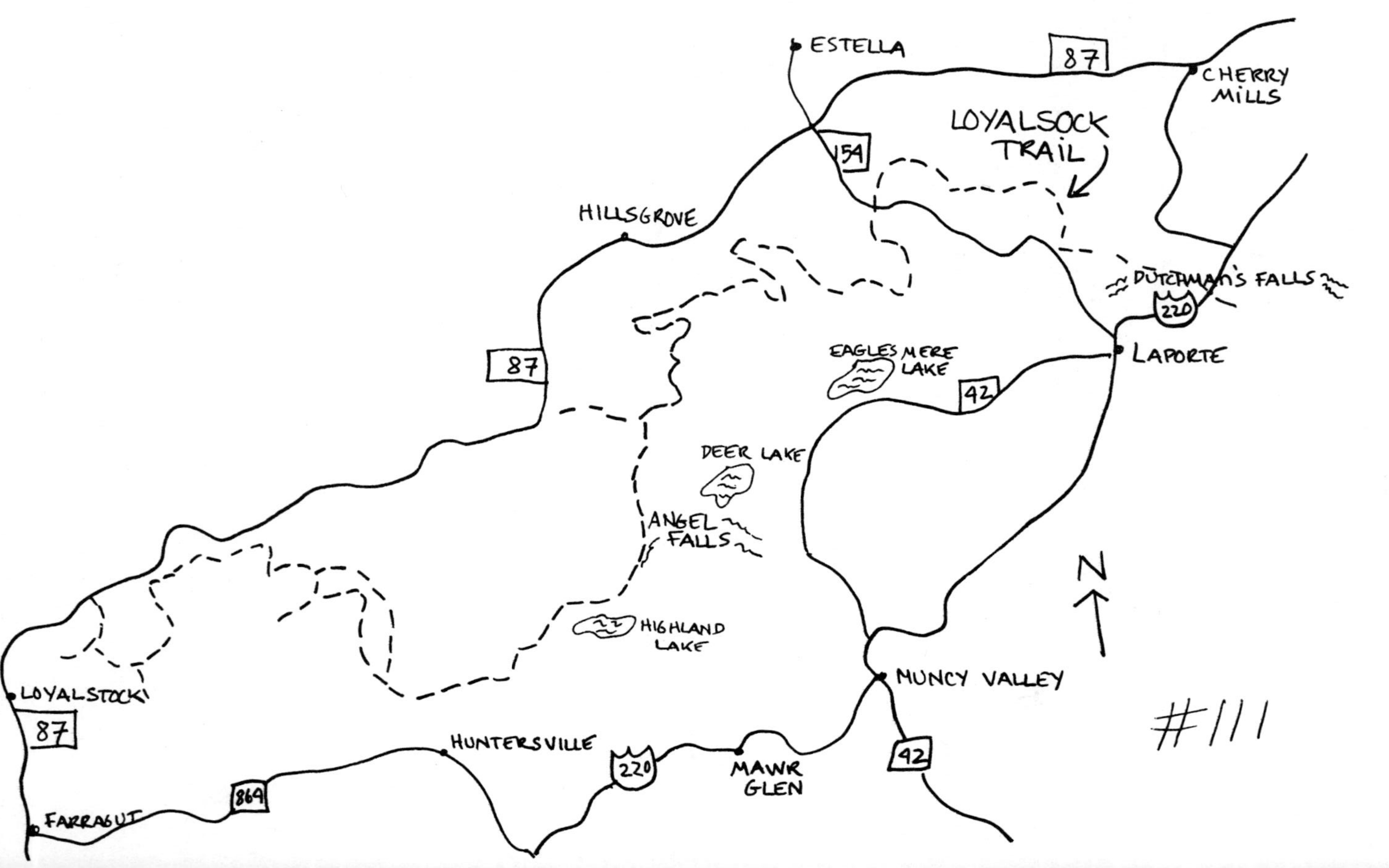

ESTELLA
87
CHERRY MILLS
LOYALSOCK TRAIL
154
HILLSGROVE
DUTCHMAN'S FALLS
220
LAPORTE
EAGLES MERE LAKE
42
87
DEER LAKE
ANGEL FALLS
N
HIGHLAND LAKE
MUNCY VALLEY
LOYALSTOCK
87
HUNTERSVILLE
220
MAWR GLEN
42
#III
869
FARRAGUT

113.   SOUTHERN YORK COUNTY
(Near The Otter Creek Recreation Area of the
Pennsylvania Power & Light Company)

This is one of the best hiking areas in the region of the Susquehanna River. Reached by Route 425, the northern sections of this area (owned by the Glatfelter Paper Company Tree Farms) afford excellent views of the Susquehanna River especially from a point called *Urey Lookout.* The remains of the locks of the Old Susquehanna & Tidewater Canal (active in the nineteenth-century), a museum filled with Indian artifacts and Indian Maiden Falls all make this area particularly worthwhile.

114.   MIDDLE CREEK WILDLIFE AREA

These 5,000 acres, set aside by the Pennsylvania Game Commission, are located north of Lititz and the Pennsylvania Turnpike, east of Route 501, and south of Kleinfeltersville.

In migrating season, Canada geese, ducks, and swans are always sighted here.

Hiking trails, along with an excellent Visitor Center (complete with wildlife exhibits and films) make this wildlife area a good place to bring kids. For additional information write: Resident Manager, Middle Creek Wildlife Management Area, R.D. 1, Newmanstown, Pa. 17073.

115.   HORSE-SHOE TRAIL

This 120-mile trail (used by both hikers and horsemen) begins at Routes 23 and 252 in the Valley Forge State Park and runs westward to its junction with the Appalachian Trail on the crest of Stony Mountain (12 miles north of Hershey). The trail is marked with yellow paint blazes.

TO KLEINFELTERSVILLE
OFFICE
N
VISITORS CENTER
WOODCOCK DRIVE
FAWN HOLLOW RD.
ELDERS RUN SHELTER
LAUREL DRIVE
SEGLOCH RUN
1 MI. to Youth Hostel on Fox Rd.
MIDDLE CREEK
TO HOPELAND
DAM
WHITE OAK PICNIC AREA
MILLSTONE RD.
VISTA
MILLSTONE TRAIL
#114

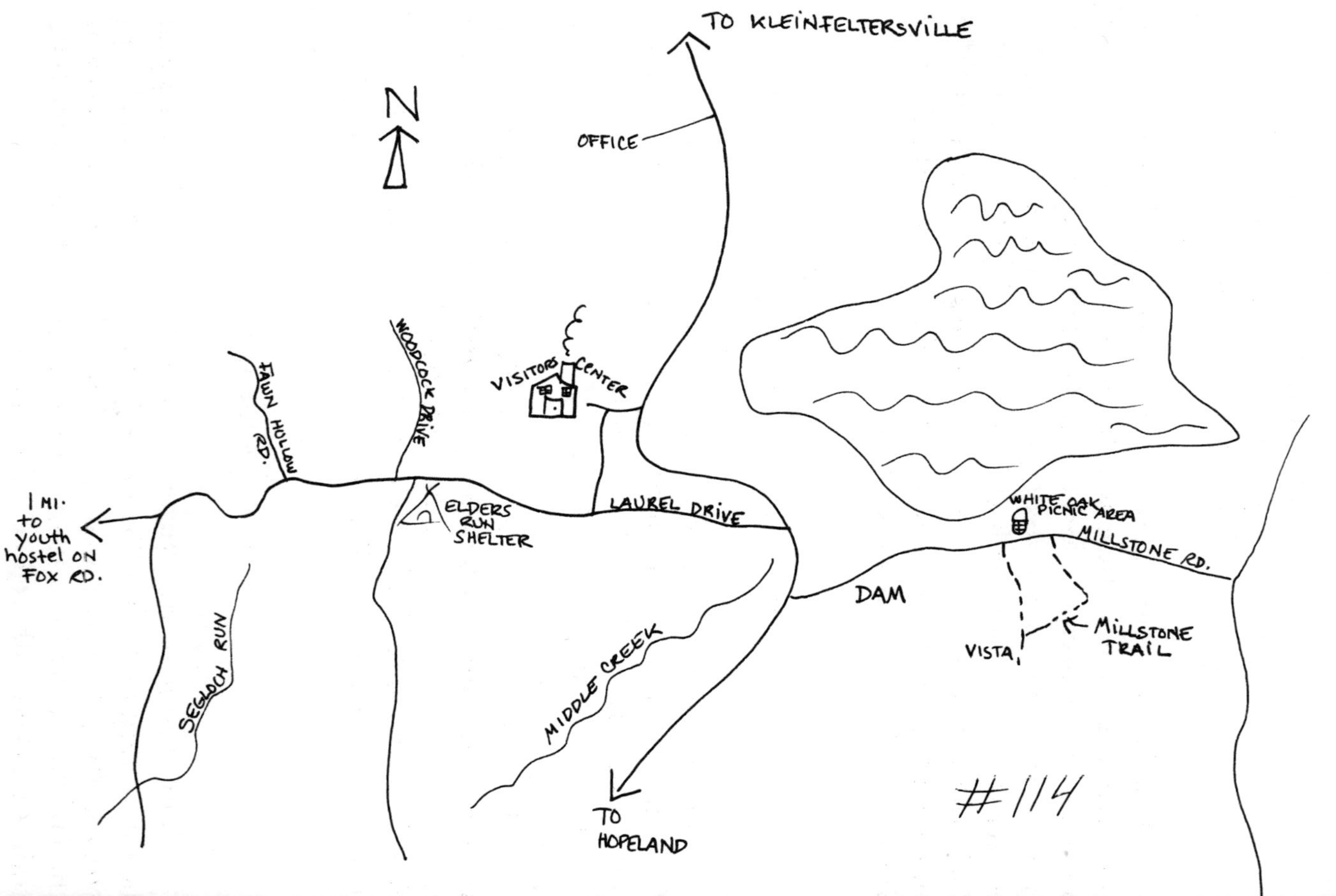

262

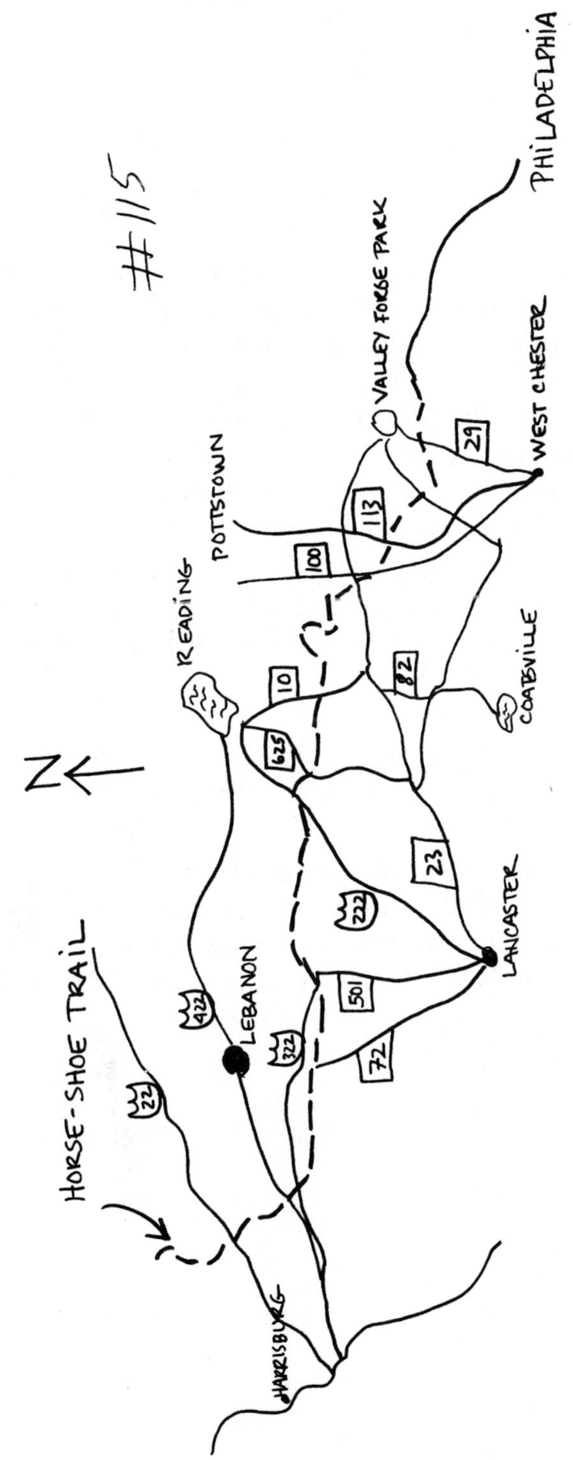

#115
N
HORSE-SHOE TRAIL
PHILADELPHIA
VALLEY FORGE PARK
WEST CHESTER
POTTSTOWN
READING
COATSVILLE
LANCASTER
LEBANON
HARRISBURG
29
113
100
82
10
625
23
222
501
72
422
322
22

116. THE DELAWARE & LEHIGH CANAL TOWPATH TRAIL
(Between Bristol and Easton)

Back in the 1830's, the Delaware Canal — running 60-miles in Bucks County — was constructed. The canal, chiefly used for transporting coal, connected into the Lehigh Canal at Easton. In 1931, however, the canal was closed — leaving waterways for canoeists and a towpath for hikers.

The southern stretch of the canal, because it passes the heavily industrialized sections of Bristol, Morrisville, and Yardley, should be avoided.

For either a free mimeographed sheet with an elaborate map, or a more extensive guidebook to the canal region write: Hugh Moore Parkway, c/o Canal Museum, P.O. Box 877, Easton, Pa. 18042.

117. WISSAHICKON GORGE TRAIL

This is a six-mile trail within the city limits of Philadelphia's 3,000-acre Fairmount Park. The actual gorge area can be reached from U.S. 422 (Germantown Avenue) down either side of Cresheim Creek. Parking space is available in the park.

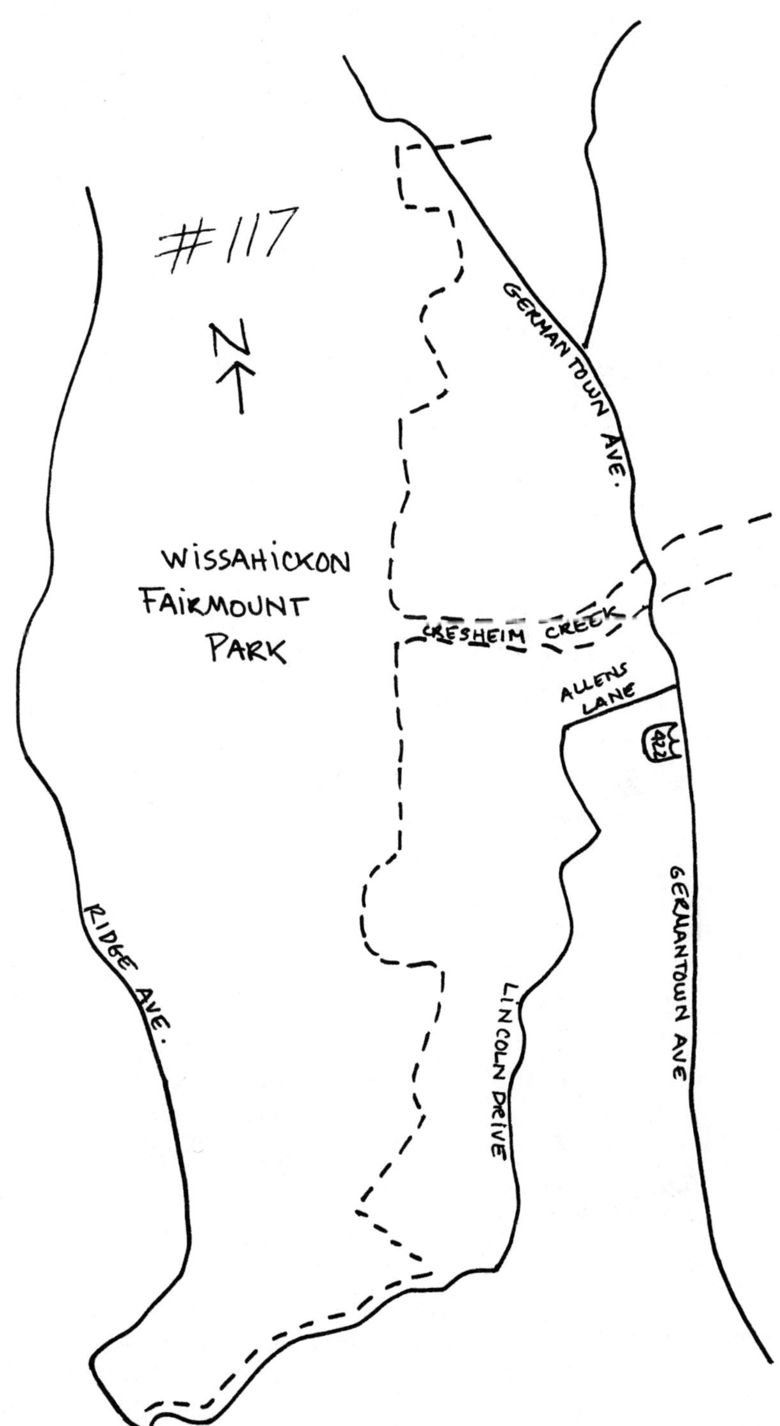

#117
N
WISSAHICKON FAIRMOUNT PARK
GERMANTOWN AVE.
CRESHEIM CREEK
ALLENS LANE
LINCOLN DRIVE
GERMANTOWN AVE.
RIDGE AVE.

APPALACHIAN TRAIL

"The ultimate purpose of the Appalachian Trail is to walk, to see, and to see what you see."

—Benton MacKaye — founder
of the Appalachian Trail—

The Appalachian Trail is the only National Scenic Trail in the Northeast. Back in 1968, with the passage by congress of "The National Trails System Act", the trail became the first federally-protected footpath in the U.S. Today, The Appalachian Trail runs as one continuous footpath all the way from Maine's Mount Katahdin to Springer Mountain in Georgia (a total distance of 2,025 miles). In the Northeast, New Hampshire, Maine, Vermont, Massachusetts, Connecticut, New York, and Pennsylvania all have segments of the trail traversing their lands. It's possible to map-out one extended walking tour that would cross practically all the northeastern states.

For information about the Appalachian Trail and a listing of the several guidebooks that specifically deal with its topography, write: The Appalachian Trail Conference, P. O. Box 236, Harper's Ferry, West Virginia 25425.

Fact: Branley Owen, of Knoxville, Tennessee, after his release from the paratroopers, traversed the Appalachian Trail (the entire 2,025 miles) in an incredible seventy days. Though he probably zoomed by all the flora and fauna, his feet's feat certainly rivals the heroic tales of Daniel Boone, Davy Crockett, and Paul Bunyan.

EPILOGUE

THERE ARE NO SHORT CUTS

*Understanding — even partial understanding — grows almost
as slowly in the mind as a tree in the woods.*
            —William A. Breyfogle—

Knowing and seeing nature is not an overnight project.
You don't all of a sudden become a sensitive naturalist. As with
everything else in nature, knowing her — really knowing her
— is a slow process, the result of years and years of walking
and observing. And needless to say, reading a book such as this
one, while useful, should never be confused with actually
going out into the woods and observing nature first-hand.

Initially, you'll probably carry into the woods a bandoleer
of field guides. Your curiosity will be such that you'll want to
know the names, habits, and uses of everything you see. Hopefully this stage will last just a few months; ultimately giving way
to a less compulsive and more enjoyable approach to appreciating the outdoors.

Throughout your lifelong romance with nature, you'll inevitably be running across people whose eyes are more finely
tuned to her subtleties than your own. These people are to be
your teachers, your *gurus*. Don't allow pride, that deadly sin
born and maintained by our egos, to interfere with your learning from these often anxious-to-share teachers. Be humble,
pay attention, and absorb all you can.

When you finally start to feel at home in the outdoors —
when you can begin to feel a familiarity with the wildflowers,
birds, and trees — then almost imperceptibly you'll also begin
to feel more 'centered', more at ease with yourself. Simply by
knowing a little about nature you'll be able to feel a bit more
anchored to the earth. And consequently, you'll always feel less
a stranger wherever you are.

268

And remember: There is no final goal to be reached. You don't one day get up and say "Ah. I no longer have to go walking in the woods. I now know everything there is to know." The point of it all — maybe what nature is really trying to tell us — is that there are no ends, only beginnings; and that each moment, if we really know how to see it, is always new and deserving of our attention.

FURTHER READING

The list of books that follows is by no means exhaustive. I merely tried to include here certain books that, for me, never lose their potency.

The following few books are all imbued with a very strong magic; a sense of wonder that stretches our thoughts into the cosmos and then returns us to earth slightly more appreciative.

THE LIVES OF A CELL . . . NOTES OF A BIOLOGY WATCHER by Lewis Thomas, Bantam Books.

THE SEA AROUND US, SILENT SPRING by Rachel Carson, Signet Science Library.

KING SOLOMON'S RING by Konrad Lorenz, Signet Non-Fiction.

WILDLIFE IN AMERICA by Peter Mathiessen, Viking.

A SAND COUNTY ALMANAC by Aldo Leopold, New York: Oxford, 1949.

AUTUMN ACROSS AMERICA, JOURNEY INTO SUMMER, WANDERING THROUGH WINTER, NORTH WITH THE SPRING by Edwin Way Teale.

THE BIRDS OF JOHN BURROUGHS . . . KEEPING A SHARP LOOKOUT by John Burroughs, Hawthorn Books.

ANIMAL ARCHITECTURE by Karl Von Frisch, Harcourt Brace Jovanovich.

THOREAU — his writings, edited by Edwin Teale.

THE WINTER BEACH by Charlton Ogburn, Jr., William Morrow & Company, Inc.

THE IMMENSE JOURNEY by Loren Eiseley, Vintage Books.

PILGRIM AT TINKER CREEK by Annie Dillard.

THE OUTERMOST HOUSE by Henry Beston.

The photography of Ansel Adams, Edward Weston, and Minor White.

Less suffused with magic but nevertheless useful are:

HOW TO TALK TO BIRDS AND OTHER UNCOMMON WAYS OF ENJOYING NATURE THE YEAR ROUND by Richard C. Davis, Alfred A. Knopf, 1972.

THE GREAT BEACH by John Hay.

A NATURAL HISTORY OF NEW YORK CITY by John Kieran, American Museum Science Book.

LIFE AND DEATH OF THE SALT MARSH by John and Mildred Teal, Ballantine.

SNOW CRYSTALS by W. A. Bentley and W.J. Humphreys, Dover Publications. (This book has 2,453 photos of snow crystals. A beautiful book.)

HOW TO ATTRACT, HOUSE, AND FEED BIRDS by Walter E. Schutz, Collier Books

INSECTS — THEIR WAYS AND MEANS OF LIVING by Robert Evans Snodgrass, Dover Publications, Inc.

WILD PETS by Clifford B. Moore.

STALKING THE WILD ASPARAGUS, STALKING THE BLUE-EYED SCALLOP, STALKING THE HEALTHFUL HERBS, STALKING THE GOOD LIFE by Euell Gibbons, David McKay Company, Inc.

The writings of Edward Hoagland, John McPhee, and Hal Borland.

LET THEM LIVE — A WORLDWIDE SURVEY OF ANIMALS THREATENED WITH EXTINCTION by Kai Curry-Lindahl, Morrow Paperbacks Editions.

LOOK AT THE SKY AND TELL THE WEATHER by Eric Sloane, Funk & Wagnalls, New York.

THE OUTER LANDS by Dorothy Sterling, Anchor Press/ Doubleday, 1974. (A natural history guide to Cape Cod, Martha's Vineyard, Nantucket, Block Island, and Long Island.)

All the *Peterson Series Field Guides* published by Houghton Mifflin Company, Boston. (Guides to birds, bird songs, shells, butterflies, mammals, rocks and minerals, animal tracks, ferns, trees and shrubs, reptiles, wildflowers, stars and planets, and insects.)

THE NEW ENGLAND LANDSCAPE by N. Jorgenson, Barre Publishing.

KNOWING THE OUTDOORS IN THE DARK by Vinson Brown, Stackpole Books.

MY WILDERNESS — EAST TO KATAHDIN by William O. Douglas.

All the writings of John Muir.

ANIMALS IN MIGRATION by Robert T. Orr, Macmillan Company.

BORNE ON THE WIND — THE EXTRAORDINARY WORLD OF INSECTS IN FLIGHT by Stephen Dalton, Reader's Digest Press, 1975.

THINGS TO DO

The seventh day should be a day of work, for sweat and toil; the remaining six days man should be free to feed his soul with "sublime revelations of nature".

—Henry David Thoreau—

'What do you want to do today' are the seven words of the weekend/vacation/holiday litany. Like a droning mantra, the words are uttered by all of us. To once-and-for-all obliterate those seven words from our vocabulaties, I decided in the final few pages of *THE NORTHEASTERN OUTDOORS* . . . to include . . .

. . . AN EXHAUSTIVE LIST OF 'EVERYTHING YOU CAN DO TODAY' . . . (being a compilation of all the life-respecting and free activities that have already been mentioned in this book).

So —

"What do you want to do today?"

"Why don't we . . . . .

. . . . . pick blueberries, walk in the woods, bird watch, gaze at the constellations, predict the weather, take a canoe trip, swim in either the ocean or a secluded mountain pool, forage for wild foods and then prepare a wild food supper, feed some birds, sketch some birds or wildflowers, snow-shoe across the Maine woods one night when the moon is full, cross-country ski, visit a natural history museum or an arboretum, read Thoreau's journals, pan for gold, stroll along a beach, dive into Maine's highest mountain lake, sip some dandelion wine, lie beneath a pine tree at dawn and watch the sun's rays filtering through the needles, collect beach shells, rocks and minerals, mushrooms, or different types of sands, take a night walk in a forest, meditate on the complex geometric patterns of a sunflower, look at a human being and appreciate the thousands of years of evolutionary activity that went into their present form, climb some mountain (all the while remembering the continental glacier that sculpted it ten thousand years ago), or sometimes simply allow yourself to just be awed by it all.

And if all these activities fail to engage you, then spend some quiet afternoon by yourself, dealing with what must be a truly prodigious apathy.

USEFUL ADDRESSES

The following addresses are good sources for maps and other travel-related information:

AMERICAN AUTOMOBILE ASSOCIATION (AAA), Washington DC 20006

ALLSTATE MOTOR CLUB, 2882 Sandhill Road, Menlo Park, California 94025

GULF TRAVEL CLUB, Box 4852, Chicago, Illinois 60680

NATIONAL AUTOMOBILE CLUB, 65 Battery Street, San Francisco, California

CHEVRON TRAVEL SERVICE, 555 Market Street, San Francisco, California 94120

GULF TOURGUIDE BUREAU, 7th & Grant Streets, Pittsburgh, PA 15219

MOBIL TRAVEL ROUTING SERVICE, Box 265, New York, NY 10011

TEXACO TRAVEL SERVICE OFFICE, 135 E. 42nd Street, New York, N.Y. 10017

For tourist information (including museums, state forests and parks, and camping facilities) write:

CONNECTICUT DEVELOPMENT COMMISSION, Box 865, Hartford, Conn.

DEPARTMENT OF ECONOMIC DEVELOPMENT, State House, Augusta, Maine 04330

DEPARTMENT OF COMMERCE AND DEVELOPMENT, 100 Cambridge Street, Boston, Mass. 02202

DIVISION OF ECONOMIC DEVELOPMENT, Box 856, Concord, New Hampshire 03301

STATE DEPARTMENT OF COMMERCE, 112 State Street, Albany, N.Y. 12207

BUREAU OF TRAVEL DEVELOPMENT, Pennsylvania Department of Commerce, Harrisburg, PA 17120

RHODE ISLAND DEVELOPMENT COUNCIL, 207 Roger Williams Building, Providence, R.I. 02908

TRAVEL DEVELOPMENT, 61 Elm Street, Montpelier, Vermont 05602

WILDERNESS AND ENVIRONMENTAL ORGANIZATIONS

NATIONAL AUDUBON SOCIETY, 1130 Fifth Avenue, New York, N.Y. 10028
   (Write to the Audubon Society's main offices for information about their local chapters.)

NATIONAL PARKS ASSOCIATION, 1701 Eighteenth Street NW, Washington, DC 20009

NATIONAL WILDLIFE FEDERATION, 1412-16th Street, Washington DC

NATURE CONSERVANCY, 215 Market Street, San Francisco, California 94105
   (Write to them for a listing of all the lands they either own or control.)

NEW ENGLAND WILD FLOWER SOCIETY, Hemenway Road, Framingham, Massachusetts 01701

THE GREEN MOUNTAIN CLUB, 63 Center Street, Rutland, Vermont

APPALACHIAN TRAIL CONFERENCE, 1916 Sunderland Place NW, Washington DC

APPALACHIAN MOUNTAIN CLUB, 5 Joy Street, Boston, Massachusetts 02108

ADIRONDACK MOUNTAIN CLUB, 172 Ridge Street, Glens Falls, New York 12801

AMERICAN YOUTH HOSTELS, 6300 Fifth Avenue, Pittsburgh, Pa. 15232

US GOVERNMENT PRINTING OFFICE, Washington, DC 20402
   (Here is where thousands of useful pamphlets are available. The subject matter of these publications range from "Winter Activities in National Parks" to a directory of all the national wildlife refuges. Send for the Printing Office's catalog. It's an invaluable research tool.)

US GEOLOGICAL SURVEY, Washington DC 20242
(Send for the US GEOLOGICAL SURVEY's map brochure.)

THE NATIONAL CAMPERS AND HIKERS ASSOCIATION, 7172 Transit Road, Buffalo, NY 14221

THE WILDERNESS SOCIETY, 729-15th Street NW, Washington, DC 20005
(This organization actually organizes hiking expeditions.)

INTERNATIONAL BACKPACKERS ASSOCIATION, Box 85, Lincoln Center, Maine 04458

*I believe a leaf of grass is no less than the journeywork of
the stars.*
*And the pismire [ant] is equally perfect, and a grain of sand,
and the egg of the wren.*
And the tree-toad is a chef-d'oeuvre for the highest,
And the running blackberry would adorn the parlors of heaven,
*And the narrowest hinge in my hand puts to scorn all
machinery,*
*And the cow crunching with depress'd head surpasses any
statue.*
*And a mouse is miracle enough to stagger sextillions of
infidels!*

—Walt Whitman—

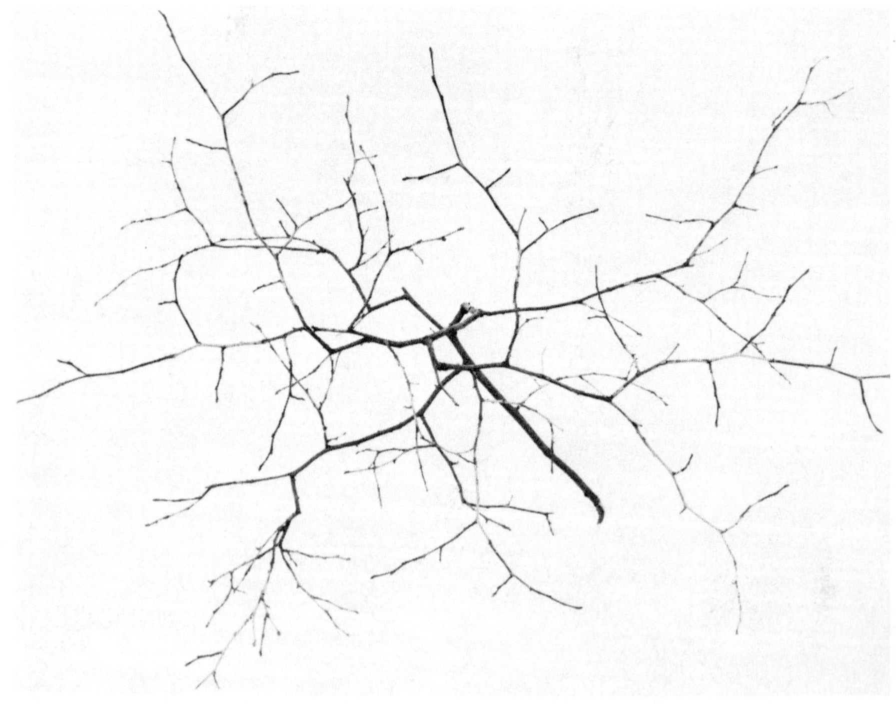

INDEX

Cape Ann, 202
Cape Cod, 71, 116, 201
Cape Cod National Seashore, 206
Caps Ridge Trail, 175
cardinal flower, 215
carrion flower, 30
Carter-Moriah Range, 161
Cassiopeia, 145
Castle Trail, 225
caterpillars, 48
cattails, 107, 203
Cave of the Winds, 196
Cavis Major, 146
cedar, 71, 216
Cepheus, 145
Chicory, 52
chlorophyll, 81
chrysallis, 48
cirques, 114
cirrus clouds, 124
citronella, 152
Clintonia, 72
clover, 52
clubmosses, 62
Coast Guard Beach, 209
Cockaponset State Park, 228
columbine, 13
conifers, 68–73
Connecticut, 223–231
Connecticut Valley, 201, 221
constellations, 145
Cook's Canyon, 213
Cook Forest State Park, 253
cordgrass, 203, 204
cormorants, 206
cowbird, 34
cottontails, 88
cranberries, 206
Cree Indians, 40
crickets, 50
Crooked Creek State Park, 253
cross-country skiing, 177
crow, 39
cumulus clouds, 124

Daddy-long-legs, 49
daisies, 52, 58
Dalton, Stephen, 45
damesflies, 50
Dana, James Dwight, 118
dandelion, 52, 107
dandelion wine, 108
Darwin, Charles, 122, 132
daylily, 104
deciduous trees, 68, 74–79
deer, 97
Deerfield River 197
Delaware Canal, 251, 264

Devil's Hopyard State Park, 228
dogwood, 72, 81
dolomite, 120

Dorothy Francis Rice Sanctuary, 218
dragonfly, 50
drumlin, 118
Drumlin Farm Nature Center, 212
Dryad Fall Trail, 174
Duck Hole Ranger Station, 247
dulse, 132
dunes, 138, 207
Dutchman's Breeches, 75

edible plants, 101–110
eiders, 190
Elephant's Head Trail, 196
endangered species, 41–42
English sparrow, 34
esker, 116
Evans Notch-Chatham Region, 184
evergreens, 67

fairy rings, 25
Falling Waters Trail, 164
false hellebore, 13
feldspar, 119
Felix Neck Wildlife Sanctuary, 213
ferns, 62–64, 72, 214
fireflies, 20
Five Rivers Environmental Center, 239
flume, 184
fox, 95
Franconias, 164, 166

Garden-In-The-Woods, 215
garden spider, 49
garnet, 119
garnet gneisses, 120
garnet schist, 120
geodisic dome, 30
George Washington Management Area, 236
giant otter, 41
Gibbons, Euell, 103
ginseng, 215
glacial striations, 114
glacier, 114–118
goldenrod, 52, 60
grackle, 34
granite, 119, 131, 206
grasses, 202
Great Blue Heron, 39
Great Blue Whale, 41
Great Gulf Wilderness, 161
Great Island, 207
Great Presidentials, 161
Great Swamp Management Area, 232
Greenleaf Trail, 164
Green Mountains, 192
Griscom, Ludlow, 32

Halfway Brook, 162
hawkweed, 30, 52
Heath family, 84
Hell Brook Trail, 197
Hellcat Swamp Nature Trail, 203

284

The White Leopard

The White Leopard

Poems

by

R. Vincent Razor

VERNOX Publishing, Quee 11415

Library of Congress Cataloging-in-Publication Data
1988, 1989, 1990, The White Leopard

ISBN-13: 978-0-9786682-0-4
ISBN-10: 0-9786682-0-0

VERNOX
PO Box 150308
Kew Gardens
New York 11415-0308

contents

                    the fox and the twister

trapped!
chasing 'round a whirlwind track
a tracking unrecorded history blinds
chasing --
the coat is ashen red
this link is fox
the hunter is prey--

in fox eyes volcanic fierce
inside morning's breaking towering twist
perpetuity's first beck' is plead
spinning a tragic fantastic feast
upon this carcass nature's lightning slash
truth with chase,severed free
this uncaptured dignity ruptures
eternity twists and furies
resounds unshackled,free!

in the eye of storm breeds eternity's nature
wicked,sorrowed -attuned
creation fur-bristled royal heart
pumping faster running bate
the game is hunt is either
skill or thrusting currents 'volved
from lower depths this fox is cunning
tripping through this twister eased
into centuries upon vulgar centuries
unclassed,then uproariously gathered
into linked and polished silver
strike! outbreak this eternal 'cane!
redwood rooted,hurried!

rainbowed fur,
of fox and destiny's versi-bloodied coat
combat's unresolve is caustic link
'round all colored sanguined hue
dripping misting venge on brow
ancient slavers wooded flesh
splintering even greater splits
into history's darkest pass
clash! the fox is dead!
mourning piercing hunter's soul

ragged,unrepaired but linked
to time and fated paradise's whitened
unrepentent nature strides
unwhitened,reded,joined,foxed

                          farmer

the farmer hoes and hoes
his field is summered dust
he hoes

turning his look,all destinies featured
on hand in palm he is written
clear,turning over and over and over
the hoe is raised
the dust is lift
a command is forth'
          yield!

wintered questioned tainted fall
angel bluey skies let fly
tears and tresses tumble low
sweep this dried and crusted menu
there is pause --

spirits and wets,evils and goods --settle
deep these seeds of nectar sleep
between the juices and life's ephemeral breathing
remain immortality and passion
now leap out over once barren fields
locking horns of revolution
a rainbow's arc of gold and dust
there is thunder --

now deep these furrows
planted seeds all futures married
ancient rooted suckling thoughts
nurtured naked tears are tremor
pause,yet another moment projects a block
lightning --
there is birth!

cause these sleeping seeds turn and wake
and rise new armies uncatastrophic acts
employed but softer vices,visions conjur
upon all wraths each memory distant
pasts voted,denied,altered --
a cancer probing

of stars and hues and destiny's things
a prism pose a century's gallant lust
refract a revolutionary's reaper,grim
riding through these fields unrape
burrowed genius,random growing
out-stitch and grasp all winged dreams
take sight and soar
mighty glimmered futured wait
take flight!

how far past these fields and skies
is destiny's rigid count
beyond time and light's disparate juncture
chaotic patterns resound affirm
a chain of rows and seeds
where all returns and departures utter
one phrase, eternity's measure

                    flowers and stone

on gods and immortality
fire and sage scar eternity green
here all nature and time
devise and settle --
there is magic!

surrounding mountains pause -
a whisper! a forest! a giant!
there must be a clearing!

mystery!
a young man strolling
through a forest,darkly strolling
deeper into blackness burning
'tensely blue lumen bloss'
deeper darker strolling
'till a clearing -

upon this open clearing
oddly dark,still burning
eminating from this awesome pitch
-- a note!

a musical thought,strange is fluted
riding a dawn's old beam this note
is majestic,sovereign,imperial

eternal laws ------------------------ emerge!

ancient scribe!
bodyfull beard of snow and gold
history's long blinding glimmer woven
deep into every tuck and weave
is destiny's unyielding measure
projects!

omni-shadowed futured frame
bluesey opaque
silhouette's a sculpted marbled visage
sagacious fossiled luminous sheath
lined as ancient mariners faces often shipped
souled with pearl blacks perceive

reflective universe viewed
ocean's determined
gently floating guide and course
approach!

nature still,cool,rivered
unshadowed grace
wisdom becomes the dawning treat
sharp on perpetuity's windless edge
wings knowledge discoursed on every plain
let undiscovered dimensions fly
and settle-float eternity's incautious peril

blowing seasons mercy course
upon this youth
upon time's immortal stat'
unknowing measured anticipation
all glories unbound
there is season!

donning morning's blazing guise
tricks what magic stars possess
explode upon majestic schemes
brightness robed bursts when touched
genius textured awe
inspired,unguised --toned
aged,incisive,extraordinaire

multiplicity's shadows unlift
complexity's becomes the calm
all matter has come and moved
on spring's bouquet is flush is ever
waking,sleeping,singing,dreaming
of unplummeted lakes
and wintered shallowed ponds
of crashing falls and ageless trees
on mossy banks of rivers breeding
more lines written than written
upon his reading face
at peace,yearning

here youth and peril come to try
each adversarial composition
sketched from old composite force
reverenced,determined,challenged

age of ages,dire curious wonder
seeking illusion's options search
out all rainbows pre-sensed land wing and shoulder
here unburdened,daring,noble,exposed
raw each nerve,burst and singed
each new pattern comes a universe
consternation,disputation -victory!

                    the white leopard

an open window
a candle flickers,
light, contagious, perennial

cool, this heated wind dispels
time and history leap and fall
upon this record
hangs life and immortality's precarious balance
achieved —

in one, glorious, 'spended pose
a nation breed a mourn its genius
civilation's cradle-pause
weeping passionate rainbows storm
one monumental tearing prowl
arc of soul —
kinetic, pured, struck;
thunder nature's winterest freeze
burning collect illusions
born deep this century's leaping
profundit cat is ripping
quantum mystery aspirations growl
linking wailing tormented dreams
igniting perpetuity's rounded bend
full circle stars refined,
reconstruct a paradox!
a humming bird stilled!
a heartbeat stopped!
this perpetual motion — perceived!
captured for all measured purpose
posterity's hold, momentary sublime —
the white leopard —
exists! Ten billion centuries of dreams and death
blaze across eternity's shatter
of wars and winnings and destiny's s'lect
a trillion grieving stars propose
survive these spirits defeat and conquer
universe — stand part!
triumph and sorrow flayed as equals
catastrophy at ease with principled decay
celebration to the ends of striking beams
are sweetly comforting, reliant
at last a face — seen and understood

gentle comfort — destiny's evil ply
comprise!

kiss all eternity lithe and sorrowed
spitting back illusion's kindred souls
sweetly pictured history locking
last breath of a master's grasp
drinking, gasping sucking out
all minerals a universe proffers
within earth's bosomy clays and oils
passionate cut through stone to heart
deep eternity's womb a bonding
all centuries and nations now come to revel
harmoniously joined, silenced and goaled
empires and jewels heaped at footing
cannot engulf this tempest creates
one soldier emblazoned greatly
all memory of minds constructs
a time, a place, a thought
without bonds, perpetually searching —

sweet agony of succession
'spire none the art
for art's sake the universe rails
for all trial and capture — there is thunder
mighty nature peaks and shallows
the immodest leopard growls and postures
a heart, a leaf, nature's prettiest matter
while lakes and volcanoes volunteer equal
footing at bbase soul most profound
nestles goodness and evil's betrayal wise
comes not in time, but maturity's shorter breath
on moments of fire and comedy relived again
perceived and paused for one last gasp
onto this threshold eternity bears
the white leopard

                         last soldier

shivered -

winter's last full moon
is birth-marred,ashen,alone

under this perpetual loom
her ancient skies undress
honored angeled souls up-glint
battled-raw,pured,transcend

so history's unparagoned snow-god bleeds
bloody fallen ash is born
whispering halls,eternity shaken
exists a century's crowded lust
transcendent nations born full,manifest
all come upon one soldier ridding
battle-single-quantum
too numerous mention!
there is burden blinding war
peace abounds without constrict
danger time unbends
this soldier's horse will not carry
ultimatums pressed against a universe violins
the drum,the continuum,
the axis ---alone!

align universe!
weepy fatalities -silhouette!
abandon old stars,awesome unused
the universe abounds each touch
spectered marbled palaces glimmer
full design,stars reflect!
wisdom's patriarch forsakes its dead!
pieces stars new born advise
off showery dusty boots and swords
eternity airs its calm and storm
gone lightning,hero brief
each expanded draw is scorch!
there is birth -
new destinies appeal!

from country laws,brief respect

perpetuity's soul is scarred
through this universal gene comes scratch
tender,tender tissue torn
all the fabric memory scrapped
a universe!

all battles are printed bloody mirror
a trillion light years of dust designs
stilled new prophets counter shed
ragged armies specters mount
bursting shoots across a universe dream
rides a satin soldier's willowy spin
whipping into culmination
futures and fortunes bunched and dropped
onto legions of spiders eternity hurdling
toward one more destiny clash
illumination flesh-human-war-prescribe
dutifully exact,meritorious,transcend

listen!

a commanding note!

an angel's tear will fall on grounds un'sired
its beat will mortal flesh
fall far from cling and rot
and hang across earth's darkest soil
distant,scattered,unpoised

but on a horse,a soldier's journey,complete
it will take wing and fly?
another begins!

                    where lions sleep

one crest alone
pre-dawn ascent -
a luminous mane is ride and cast
over towering mountains,stoic
nobility's supreme
this emperor's stand
is blood,fierce,unpoached

below this guard,a gather
his watchful gaze,benign
for the moment
a gentle wind is spat
they sleep

the dawn is broke
glory sun in prided lust
reveals all animals calmly denned
dreaming 'mong the butchered fam'
of aspirations dripping plea and cop
a century's ravaged corpse is 'fest
is prey to beasties time unlent
quick pounce,possess and 'file
'voured 'for sleepness,nightish edge
serrated-incarnate respite sleep
a morning star is brandished,scarred - risin!

frags-
of pieces civilizations lost or buried
here center den,studied,uncared
rests all secrets boned
bared their inclinations shallow
morning questions risen dawn
collecting fleshes all assemble
a soldier's heart to beat,brain to matter
this warrior will not ride again
stripping back all gain and flesh
this bloodied memory falls a pathos
deep through ancient 'ternals core
forever tombed decimate,lost,opposed
these placid creatures yawn,unmattered
nightish close their peacy loyal
listing blankets 'llusions mellow
into deserts quiet,order struck

their is sleep

conjur!
one last volume spirit
destiny outlast!
among the stars,their infinite poses
catastrophic disease
lay here amidst,ruin and 'cover
lofty conquerors fortress clawed
civilization's dancing fruits and pennies
spinning destiny's passions
mightily roared,tailor-suited terrors
extant! timidity cries out!
history's ferocity is lion's mock
bolders juggled and tumble back
courtly lastly fanged unseen pervade
simplicity's master joke
is calm,inconspicuous -dense

a tawny bleedy sleepy 'morrow
is denned here passions once chaste breath
for life and future and futility's ride
drips winds on shaggy manes unruffed
'gainst the drawn sandy desty's
of passing times unsouled,uncount
here exists nature's royalty's fatest
sated,pleased,unmoved
they sleep --

                    storm and silence

(death of an emperor)

its bloody eyes
turn silken white

here,beside nature
rests its head
cowled of body-cloaked in black
its iris' peers eternity's gather
of mourning
of peoples
        -of nations!

of lilies and war and smoke and thunder
of majesties once throned of gods
born beyond sign and discover
all is read in tender-violent visions
of tears in tea sipped pre-dawn
by an ancient scribe versed by time
indoctrinated centuried coursed
directed,ancient,dire,enlightened;
awaken harlequin sacred dawn -
dispense all colors impassioned
brightly hibered turned and loosed
on rousing wisdom-tears
beams a soul
of nations and war and sovereignty
inhabits the whole of nature
deep her loins,her storm,her calm
her seasons affect -
here,embodied magic culm's the mortal
above lover and taker,peering out -eternity incarnate!

storm and silence
majestic perch -
from this dust of pyred ash
swings eternity's lush design
inspired,wicked -ambitious

supreme!
a bold of destiny strikes
showering bouquets of gold and thunder
raining perpetuity's glitter parade

consummate marching orchids -
be born!

of sinewy human morsels
blossomy flowers pain the burden
weeping lustily immortality human
becomes the wet and grassy forum
imbued with nature's seething quiet
subtle - complex - devious

mocking destiny rages
on all wars won and lost
through all centuries totaled
futility grapples fits of dreams and death
leaping off mountainous souls undaunted
twisting time and history's
ticking roses budding,blushing,falling
unfill,neatly fractured pieces
once again mistily blooming
ragged torch,inspired,uncommon,
comes thrive

here -- gathered farthest corners all oblivion
sources pleased and unpleased
is core --

smoked and savored
each victory wetly kissed
sweetly succulent enveloped lips
devour all notions of greatness
dreamed impassioned,caused - effect
majestic contemplation -
seeds austerity fired
all souls whispering,burning
on all tragedies engendered ripe --
assume the posture of genius!

assemblage among the gods
transmuted - unfleshed
danger history's twisted visage
risen impervious blackest night
filled with stars,unconquered, 'spired
birthing evolutions yet conceived
of greeness and pleasure yet unfelt
of distances unreached
of greatness unattained still waiting

in wings of popularity's cloudy resolve
full blooming spirits soar
recanting nothing
obliquity reserves its nations
giant,unassuming,driven
-- and the eyes turn and become!

22

                    house of book

centuried mystic
lettered giant
bounding 'bove the fields, a house
risen tragic nobled mists
brilliant out layered scores
here among simplicity's march and splendor
settling upon the olive trees
surrounding, mastered

here soul and flesh encumber
eternity's boundless depths, unlisting
'scriptive genius, unpioused plural 'plicity light
shedding new favor upon the core
undead, naked spread out all eternity's nervy thrive
is twisted destiny unfurled
shattered, rebuilt history's torn reprise
commanding, loyal, undead -

here,new sleepy frontiers awaken
century's sorrowed uncouth misfits
uncultured,untutored towering
in this book sleeps greatness
from this book wakes a century
from these pages all nations rapture
terms volumed,prospered,gained

weeping mistress' revenged and pitied
surround destiny's bottomless pit
drawn genius summoned gods
from this well inspires torch
upon torch lifted,raised in questioned triumph
extinguished not 'till service rendered
nature-symphony's master conduct

to sustain the flow of blossomed nation
dancing spirits parade
shows of erudition and lust
passionate knowledge bleeding back
countless corpse millennium
shrill-pitch whistle darkness illuminates
all these souls conspire
dreaming eternity's new found wealth
abundant,profuse,majestic

one book
lone source filled and luminous
pulling all these celebrants center court
commanding best and worst designs
to bow and scrape where all parts significant
loosed blazing borning thoughts
manifest kingdoms nations dine and savor
then rest!

                              a city

over cast -
from behind a shadow
lifts a sun
blazing -

she stands the entrance,centered
hooded,greyed,mourning
she has seen one thousand years
and now she is burning

here vision a nation cured and fated
under tax of kings and paupers
the soul of fable and history mix
stealing the spirit in destiny's sting
the heart of civilization's peril
bleeds errant! step by youthing step
foot by less wrinkled foot
she is stepping backwards
deeper into her city,lines soften,weaken
and all structures do so in unison
younger now,she blossoms -

once upon a morning star
illumination filled events with prosper
a city whole of everything,trembled
each structure wind a beating heart
breathing into society sails by wealth
breathing out sighs of unearthly excess
a desert posture retained
now a city vincible -

out light!
mistress towers morning light
continuous motion hued,vibrant struggles
a city thrives here life contingent
best suited dine and sport
celebrations ad continuum play
endless portraits dance,storm to shadowed
to ignored profound,momentum must
implore these bustlings,maintain
standards rose but one pictured time
the lady continues flower,a city dream

here eyes and age blink and fathom
history's greater conquests lie
beneath a troubled yet pervasive strive
en perpetuity's strident posing
what form of motion sets this court
as a city rendered,so she youths
her face now softens a middle tone,if found
but the city weakens,peering precipitously lost
one memory,possibly more forever
our hosting mistress continues momentum
backwards - time and destiny always center

and on this horizon,a chase of buckets of gold
slowly rising dawn,setting eternity's whim
on the edge of civilization's port and carry
these ancient gods patiently imbibe
time's tribulations,eternity seeking stretch
expanding universe,forever expanding
dreaming out to its last detail
clean imprint upon each citizen soul
the embark,the harvest,the rain
all pursuits manifest in gardens
perplexed yet cultivated,
nourished on time's ephemeral promise
our maiden now pleasures her skin in youth
her soft tresses now bask noon's incautious flood
as rain is wash upon these gardens
fresh! alive with promise,holding

silent tenor of genius,broaching morning's sullen 'vide
between the lines of civilization's proving wake
every other petal turns -wilting
flowers coarse and gentle touch
propose! one nation of absolutes!
one destiny of purpose,
the nonexistent rainbow thrive!
persists decently dogging
born wisdom grandure manifest
shedding minds of terror extract
this city pursues
neglect and harvest so aptly combined
join harmony's beckoned saunter
here the center mistress 'bliges
younger still youth first destiny blossoms
she 'members this core -awaken!

now her infancy cries historic foul
screams the infinite bounce,dark without light
voidness falls with bricks and stones
this city's soul recants oblivion,again
and this baby growing smaller and smaller
reduction by time's insist
reaches out from all this change
to grasp
yet the fettered fingers one by one
let loose eternity's pattern sorrow
once released
exists no more!

                        wind and ash

a half moon has yielded
dawn's ferocity,crimson rise
        unkillable!

its broken angry venge
of bloody rays
is shed over a valley-field
        divided!

one side north   --   the other south
nature tunes its curiosity
        faced off!

on one clearing its passion is pure,unbroken
white smoke and light settle ease
here sits wisdom cowled,sated

on the other side,scorched,begging
where thunder strikes its parch
sits a warrior scarred,groomed,centuried

on southern plains
shackles of war and sulfur scatter destinies
highly skilled more highly potentialed
unbloomed possibilities
eat the dust of eternity's promise
what stars ungained propose -
let all proportions rise and vary
from smokey fields of battles
fresh of ruddy pleading ecstasy
of ideologies fired ashen
black-simper and drift
into wails of humans passion bloody
then unbloody all the sorrows medaled in honor
all the conflicts given lift to honor
defeat! and conquer the simple grace of solitude
neglected!

what prize of trades undawned
unsurpassed a blind and deaf man's counter punch
bullies a cooing bird from perch
a speckled heart furiously pounding
unable to match the specs,

emotion willing -
unwinged,this bird takes flight
paying the ultimate price
of history's ungallant squandor
time's noble march is again well defined

on this northern sit,
nature beams of gold and reticence
angels and plague-hobblers wisk
wear a century's wardrobe
elementally wizened less,wiser greater
keenly clinging onto coattails
of aspiration's rosy glower
of some things best left a curiosity
warriors stars reprise!
what jackets are lined with history's weakest thread
a civilization's salient wonder in check
romantically more eternal than soil
tattered remnants,grapple and beg
hanging onto history's merciless threads
move over! tired countries lose
their equanimity nobled,praised,grandiloquent strife!
time's nagging insincerity wonders-

this century has been too damned noisy!
destiny's rude awake is teethed a calm
a tenacious misty seeping calm
forging a new sun brings red dance,ferocious calm
deep the soul plotting unscarred
but flowers again
bloom full again,unbent

no pyre of blood will cast
its shadow unmercied,catastrophic portent
gracious history locks nature's appalling front
with gentle ease of course and circumstance
becomes a timorus cast
against history's ungracious alliance,
metered folly,characteristic dispassionate discourse
with the stinging resound of harmony's willful censure
tunes the cold hearted folly of genius
cautiously-
ever so gently
toward eternity whispering
thoughtfully whispering
where all points converge as one-

                    the wall

a tongue of fire whispers
of blue and greatness
atop a monumental wall of ice
eternity's air of memory and celebration
whips and trembles

of nations and genius
and civilization's born remind
there casts a wicked dance
souled of pirouettes flip scrape and cut
graffiti deep this icy bleed remembers
melting,melting,holding back
all attempted tides of spikeless will
and soldiered honor
crash into dawn's unkindly burden
of revelation and dismay

before the tragic fleshless rise
of whimpering dawn's boney fade
there is cause

encased! ten centuries fevered peering
out from this ephemeral womb of ice
eternity's teary night is measured
back! reaching back one thousand years
into these innumerable faces luminous dark!
reads the ancient tread of civilization's roots
deeply stretched and wrapped
around all futures here before this wall
stand the unshadowed contorted strangers
viewing these countless souls in check
travesty's crowned majestic dark
by all intended mercy pleading
lost,apotheosis lost -
upon civilization's towering cradle
lost amidst these ruins
humanity's sword left unconquered
the shape history's short and bittersweet
soul is destiny's salient sculpting
carved here -
upon this wall
weeping,weeping,weeping -

tyranny betrayed!
obliquity take shape!
history's haunting chance
streams rivers of gold and blood
to mix! the heart and mind
of nations bearing the bloody soul of genius
pauses -- contemplating wings -
and thrives

                    a tree in the sea

transcendent!
low the sacred mists of destiny
fall secret dawn majestic hover
upon a place immortal 'ceived
imbued,changing,deep

born the mystics seething universe
governs a tree out far
beyond other vast oceans and miles distant
a sea born tree
questioned,towering,alone -

nestled here between weeps and ferrets
and history's private lines
cradles the essence of civilization's bloodied tears
saline drip upon the bosom wanting
bathes the unseen opportunities
where unborn suckling children
breed the business of nature's noblest breath
bound from secret roots
fruited,unsorrowed,free
these ascendent fertile nations
climb to fruit and labor
and pinch eternity's rising bottom
climb to stretch and merit each branch
every line and crevice ruptures
a city,a state, a nation now exists!

seeds jubilation errant!
there is abundance -
raucous cultured,jestered fair
spouts its rainbowed wings embodies
every limb,each versicolored pallet
of passion and torment coupled wisely
nature's uncharted twist
dense with leaves and twigs
reading of destiny's multipitted choice
core of the eye of knot is searched
pierce the center,unsearched
eye of the peacock,stretched retort
looking out from this winged majestic colored black
fanning all futured unrelenting suns

to shower and seep these limbs
all hued envigoration expand
beyond all limits ponderous,unlived
its reach in finality's infinite trust
impelled,aghast,manifest

here upon these succeeding limbs
vestige foliage hangs a dew
nourish petty union drips
bonding eternity's roots and 'scendents
gentle tips undress profound
outpouring naked all scales weighs carnage
justice open floodgates destined profound
dripping dewy aggressive seduction pour
open,raw,seized and flourished
here nations breed and speak
tongues of every human speck
wag and carry the sad droopy expression
of humanity's tired protracted visage
still errant! still engaged
still motion portrays

vital seasons now wind
judicatory sapling bleeds all sides profound
entanglements whisper and cry
eternity's nuances despair and flow
outwards a sea of forevers engulf
the all too simple move by move
by illustrious monumental simple
glazened,wizened wisdom personifies
perpetuity's grand unseasoned line
delineates a nation unencumbered
a forest of these trees expounds
in different seas alone,unique
rooted deep an encore resolve
civilization's innumerable ties!

the eyes are green and fixed
upon a sun ten billion miles seen this night
kissing back with fire,centuries
alone,queen dark beauty is centered
        - forever

her naked form lies here,desert
fawning skies of black leopard silk
competition's illumination propose -
let her century come rise
above this heated jeweled extreme
mixing perpetuity's oxen stride
daring pointed star's compare
the age of beauty's incarnate
descent like a hawk's full swooping grasp
of treasures dreamed and scooped out
just beyond all eternity's bargain-reach
are diamonds formed of sand and blood
textures luminous life's pirouettes
water a thirst unquenched millenniums
now fertile drops imbue this queen
upon her reed and gilded desert
reigns an ancient trade of war and pity
risen out from mud and lust
a civilization bathes this light
this prescient distant untarnished gem
light-years distant comes its aura
simple,direct -searching

the age of forever is challenged
beauty ascent
commingle,seduce and conquer
earth goddess is proud to star contrast
soul to soil
all slaves buried rich
rise reflection ray's blossomed spectrum
mind engaged to straddle and ride
density peers its unknown pose
mockingbird cast -- a star's reflect!
cornered to open,daring -eternal
        impass!

brief,the eyes of eternity meet
the withered mortal truant
only transcendent need apply
storm to passion -art at last
weepy storm -teary passion,
clash!
eternity's weighty propose
suggests a silent tenor of genius
bearer propensity of light -burst
tragedy propels!
luminous exhaustion descends
blinding venus,poisoned art
brightly feathered winged sage
ascend toward this burning star
surmise!

manifests!
untinged descent to core
where civilization's soil is blood
dripping down to mortal scrappings
awash a desert monarch's royal flesh
dreamily,passionate,arduous pursuit
of equal bearing reputation foils
even a beauty so rich
compete still mortal depths subjected tinge
reality's conflicting murderous bearing
of limitations born ignored
spirit rise! contempt knowledge profound
transformation ignite!
destiny's curious arousal peak
consummation align!
there is birth -

flock!
they rise above the fawning yellow
over shadowed souls,naked blue
fill a nation's morning sky
on aged winged edge of truth
a breath of ray
        -immortal

pigeoned!
the essence of eternity's flight
one pulls and tumbles
the others soar and roll
gilded tumbled white feathered feet
nestled disease slip winged soar
magic!
the soul is harnessed
awesome cooling changing flight
a bird has soared,tumbled and fallen
from throne to earth to mortal it rests

here,familiar feeding his family,
he rests

on this park bench
an old man tethers,autocracy!
his ancient skin whipped sun black
deep his destiny lacerates,he feeds
these feathered gods and goddesses
centuries flown a nation's
grief and victories
here in this center park,
the liquid plumes of destiny
rain his universe is at once benign
and volcanic erupt
where the feathers torn and smooth and wet
work their way through time's ingratiate folly
all dreams of flight born here
a civilization's idea is formed
flocked and risen

open fortress,invade!
now at his broken and laureled feet

each soul nibs and pecks
and feeds those mountainous
weak and crippled dreams
of legacy's hope,
and awful mysteries waited far
beyond a tenor universe
the next flight dares eternity
to show its dirty face and habits cleansed
before all these ennobled magistrates
to rabble all suspecting
sounds of nature's darkest reasons
unleashed!
symphonies of thunder and light
strike the treasons of insatiate grain and fever
infuse this kindly white whiskered soul
with nations and voids
filled,aspired
autocracies forming spectre rains
alone,awed -transcend!

uncaged!
these distant claws on fettered earth
beg to take sky and move
in flight eternity measures and scowls
what offense the universe pleads
arching its warp is spine to coil
and untingle the drip of
blood on wings tipped
in victory and defeat
where a man and his birds
dare to scatter insignificant crumbs
of random will
another day of destiny intones
the luminous unshadowed dawn
of nature's most daring probe
unwombs the soul emitting
hosting tribute,mastered!

                    mr. ralph

old mr. ralph
with his suitcase full of souls
where does he come from ?
old mr. ralph
rounding another corner,
starting over again -
what is he looking for ?
where is he going ?

deposite!
soul of souls
a universe unbent,out searching
shadowed by blood and power
wafts the smell of history's smoking musket
through destiny's turgid foray
into his tired eyes perceived
embattled longings,eternity marks
        -untapped!

errant!

the angry turn of a nation's tide
dwells the chase of cities and countries
handling deftly each clause of truth
into a case of souls,searched
nestled,rosebudding and thorned-
deep in its mortal bed
of dignity's clash with reality's drop
of soul and immortality
a universe weeps
all teary and posing lily white
dripping fresh delinquent blood
upon the lips of gods
mightily sipping
nectar so sweetly imbibed
by codes of ethics perjured
and perilous delight
remarked -understood,deplore

stalked!
by nature's unremitting passion
shake the greedy hand of peace
then spread the unencumbered read
of destiny's hostile polemic
without cause
this civilization melts deep obscurity's
curious alter,

choked,forever's throat
caught once again on the bone
of a nation's pride intrude
without the iron spined
will of conviction,character-married
destiny robust
haunts its tired spectre vision

crowned!
isle of eternity, held mythic
in profile shadowed time
mr. ralph stands its edge
sharpened by the primitive challenge
lost in a bloody storm of greedy aspirations
neatly uncoiled solicitation
standing over a universe
of possibilities so vast
this omni-tortured-spectrum
straddled between fact of past
suspect future and present risk
lies old mr. ralph peddling his new souls
seeking his value of eternity's
well packed case
another town,
another universe

                    man of leaves

a storm — unmastered!

a bolt of light — strike!

upon a leaf, upon a star — struck!

the cindered figure falls
against wind and rock
from high thin aired gasping mountain peak
this leaf tumbles, falling
falling,
                        - fallen,
the still of season
                        - is off!

down upon the soil
this leaf comes to feed
new flourish a nation breathes
its first singular breath
destiny fired,alone
the ash is silent
a webby universe figures its pause,naked
the silken violent womb
of nature's first counsil beckons

come ferocity-
nature growls and bites its bitter tongue
gathered pride all fallen
of nations of war and treaty
compromise congeals
the essence of civilization's haunting spectre,
appears-

assassin!
smoke and fire -take rise!
conciliation bereaved
comes this licensed form,unremitting
austerity soothes
legions of nations be calm
to form a man of leaves
manifest!

flesh!
these leaves take flesh
ashen wrinkled sheaths of wind
bleed out of season souls and destinies
purge an ideology
born nation vein bastard
deep these lines of haunt
summon nature's still salient singe
forever's spectre looms incautious
a thousand volunteers rise
from this collection burned ash
now army infinite mortal,immortal
spirits play heroic life
stature drawn nature's better
elements steal then surrender

all possibilities to the naked virtue
of a universe wonders
which step will prove
its preceeding impression-

founders,icons,demigods
fill the absence born of neglect
the empty taunt
of destiny and history
ignite one last virtue
impoverished alone,
then elevated-
a man of leaves

vast!
blink of an eye!
an ancient sapient,
corner seated on the edge
of a great calm,untroubled sea
overlooking his universe
        -ponders!

possession!
sagacity outreach!
breadth a universe
a left hand extends -out!
his ageless destinied palm unfurls
a diamond,a ruby,an emerald
a piece of coal
extends in palm,
then retreats! extends again
extant! then rests,open
three students muse
stones are four -
selection ----doubt!
then reaffirmation;
resolution abounds!
choice becomes -infinite select!

the first curious eye of youth
has greenly circumspect exclude -
the emerald!

the sage intones:
lift and envision -
what do you conceive?!

holding stone to eye to dawn:

"I see the populous masters
        without element

conflict marches out
from under a mercurial cloud
where serenity seeks its refuge
deep in the unfathomed veld

of its labyrinthine harvest
where the two coexist
both in perpetual pursuit of meadowed souls
blanket in doven wings
deep in forever's unprincipled insatiate belly-"

now the master intones:

ruby?
what concepts perceived engage?

stone to sun
the colten eyes fill with blood:

"war uncharted!
conquer and defeat,
calamity unbounds!
rival peace's contentions vary
innumberable spirits,profit and scarred
deep the lash omaciate frames
upon societies all vulgar and proper
where incautious nestled dreams
succeed and fail miserably whipped
into an army's beleaguered surrender
too wary,continuity breaks,
valiant but untried -"

and lustrous multi-dimensioned star-
how vision the world's gleam?
diamonds of diamonds?!

"cold
the hearted pulse of passion dims
antiseptic bloodless histories
repeat without measure
of dramas great with torment
of unbearable desire and loss,
of hearts ripped out from love's tender coddle
here feed a softer quieter rainbow
void of bridges yet to cross
empty of aspirations,breathes ascent
of desperation's bottomless fall
in this cool contain
ventless movement varies only in degree
with immediate purpose,purposed-
all signs of life content-"

with his holding still unclutched
only a small of coal remains,
the wizard sums:

now we arrive at the beginning-
peer closely the core of black
we sunrise passers glaze deeply,four
here we are mirrored-
our reflection,our image
the soul of eternity is cast!

                         julie
                (diary of a dead hooker)

whore!
one last plummet
into eternity's veins
this fleshy sorrow relieves its realm
naked victory pauper triumph
stretched,thundered   -over!

whipped!
of royalty and gods
this bloody cloak is flushed
bathed in opportunity's
secret wishing wailing story
floods destiny of nations so few propose
a harmony gleaned of everything mortal
not common gutter wormy nest
unjudgy glistened purity springs
from ancient snares webbed tighter than tight
of feverish swans beauty night propose
from eternity's well probed depths
wrenches the soul
of nature's glamorous thread discovered
reeks the foul stenchy odor
of clench fisted destiny
and nature's opposition poised
clever,disguised,unrelenting

unbiased sweet soul of sensuous chaos
courting darkness gentle wary
bright lit chorus eternity's fire
ignited this one spectre brief aflame
burning brightly countless nights
wicked,proud,accustomed
nature's mystic comes her mercy
her sweet unwilling tattered child
beaming calm unnatural resolve
her services rendered sweetly

service!
upon the courts of pomp
and fertile miscellaneous   undreamed
there rests this ancient lady

her battered corpse now cold,
her breathy spirit hot,unyielding
grasps eternity's breasts to hold
firm the mark,remembered
deep upon each soul torched
scarred black-
lash for lash
spit for tangled spit
now immortaled upon the count
nature's log,recorded,dated
signed-

                    an empty street

a paper rustles
        newsy,refuse
the foul of city lingers
        naked,sovereign
the soul of anarchy
        whispers,weeping
a rain on everything appears
        then vanishes

dawn!
light's first singular ray
glissening all tracing passages
a trillion points converge this street
here we shake hands with destiny
here a mortal kisses eternity
smack on the lips
pure - raw
nerves of passion traffic
greetings destined, fortuitous
vegetable vendors,soldiers
dicker and march
time after time after
eternity pressing   up against
routine's intoxicating seduction
cored -
there is life!

crossroads!

naked virgins meet their spouse
and soul the air of passing,engaged
creates!
rainbows arcked of spirits
dancing,trading,laughing,killing
the flesh again and again
restored,resplenished streets
are pleading more and more and more
eternity full breathed,
unharnessed nature rides her storm
on thunder and quiet
on dark and light
each horse securely blending

into reality's monumental empire
of sinewy simplicity and unfailing forever
as one entity in continual pursuit
of destiny time and solemn appease
regains-

sunset crashes
deep into yesterday's womb
spills the irresistible residue of specters
slinking tears of all past recriminations
to fill with horror
at tomorrow's prospects
yet another time is set to rest
comfortably niching
its way into this streetsy fabric
of motion,time and future reside

                    melvin and his mountain

in the shadow of wings
in the shadow of a great mountain
far below its peak
stood melvin

as melvin peered
eagles circled and cut
and scraped and shaped
each dive,every wing
another grade closer
the eyes of melvin soared
and winged deeper shaping
sculpturing a yet unrecognizable form

melvin patiently,precipitously perceived

destiny!

circuitous eagles master wings
this mountain vast of centuries
tales innumerable rains and thunders
seize and make!
history -take!
capture and finesse time's indelible prison
forever take hold!
immortality ignites with each lightning strike
a wealth of melvin is cause-

a cloud bursts
crying melvin's hopeless hoping
incautious soul a flitting dare
a pounding eagle's chest
as one giant stroke
of deity and nature a millennium's mightiest
wing carves one thousand years
an eagle's brush
of soil and flesh a figure of stone
feather tip wounding cavernous perch is wash
of ancient blood of gods on earth
spills pain and glory swiping spiney veins
outstretch a gusty breath
of sorrow and gold and wind

apotheosis blows
through trees of spirits dripping
upon the slopes of ravaged native green
thrashing,howling tribal rage
turns soft benign,a whisper
of sacred dance on wind
travels the secret denizens
of life and death's perpetual swing
told upon a great mountain carved
slowly,cautiously,dangerously
scraped by wing after melvin wing's
a face becomes the crowning drive
an eagle's feather drifts

melvin ponders-
this visage grand,extolled,natured
winged more centuries than believed
countless bursts of weathered time on time
face to nature's multiple face
here carves one distinct,unmatchable form
of melvin,by his eagles,
high on a mountain

                              lover

he died a broken heart
walking toward the sunset
looking back
his life reflects:

blistering rubescent fire
sinking into the milieu of wonder
tell the tales upon these eyes
of mistress prolific splendid mate
giver of life,taker of pain
of back and mind breaking labor
so tired of stress
of storm upon storm upon the soul
serves only enlightened
one more year of destiny
one more time of memory
burning all life's passions
plucking out nature's
closely bosomed guarded secret
of awesome beauty,and equal dreams
the sense of eternity
seized in a hail of life

upon these lips kissed eternity's first naked breath
feeding genius pillared nest
fertile lover,childrens station
mother lover,alter soul
unbridled passion meetings come
a million times uncompromised
sheltered storms all ages
calmed the tides relentless suck
into maelstroms and rips ripping out
the rope pulls back
the bond unbroken
the ground under -still firm,terra
with the uncommon roar
of distilled silence

tired,that labored spine in contention
unshattered,dignities,peered related
the center of this universe
comes to rest upon the inevitable

tableau of perpetuity's engraved satin invite
into death's irretrievable harvest
waiting in the calculated whisper of superiority
garnished by high memory
of love's well earned season of sleep

52

spicey!

a host of blue jays singing victory,
bellowing the garnished sharps
of rainbows over a garden
a morning garden
a garden of noble austerity
and reckless aband'
of a hope spilled spring
filled from the juicy nectar
of gods untarnished
of destinies alarmed
soil rich,
souled from earth's wombiest center
the core-
what a garden!

early dawn
ripe of civilization's nastiest details
wings paragon and virtue
upon the nest,the cradle
the virginial promise
of destiny's unmet canopy
over a nation's mournful roots
poorly attached in soil unharnessed
in earth's mineral attack!
on a dewy pyre of morning glories
glistening eternity's teary weight
born threshold on seasons of rival treats
a simple quiet notch of bouquets
un'borted,posed firm in the thrash of power
conceals these destinies yet unfirmed
molding,cutting polish design
nature scoffs and tunes this energy
fired from her plumiest depths
toward soil atop her full bosomed attain
then leaps!

over eternity!
wings passion and hope
stocks of nature's best designs
soar over horizons

bursting with
autonomy's self reliant constraint
ripe only picking wishing
where stars and blue skies
converge and call refrain
history barks her wild dogs
caught in the wild thicket
of empty destiny and profound silence
nestles close to the wheezing strain
of one more monumental growth
stewed on originality's tender shores
rooted deep in sovereignty's hard fought serene
propose!

autumn's limitations cavort -
exceed!

the oncoming of winter's rival contentions
vary a gathering of varieties
of every breed mobile or rooted
fight for soil,rich for sport of sun
invigor one mighty stand
for time and nature carry
this burden,their souls respectively
valued top and below
right through all merciless weathered beatings
to the core   -absolute!

                henry: love letters to destiny

he looked at seasons
full of birds and trees
dense with history
packed with sounds - infinite
he stood the stars in wonder
viewed,his aspirations soared-

hallmark!
eternity whispers sweet nothings
of immortality blue as skies
and oceans pastured deep,
nature returns to nature
flooded bloody mortal wings
lift and match rose to soul
to twig to branch
and branch to soil and blush
with all seasons blossomed range
wintry flowers blooming wicked
fall's significant triumph
over death of summer's blistered
heat of spring's rise and dance
of celebrations conceived of bouquets of genius
burgeoned every step imbued
each banquet powers effuse
black orchids and lilies green
incalculable suns varied as much in aura
repose -

henry tempts the imitation stride
of nature's rapid endless beat
to this wavy elevated posture
its peaky crest for only a short
crash and pound create
equal her perfection
briefly flesh
so flabby vulnerable
pathetic this contemptuous reach
unjudged accepted buffoonery
nature herself mimics the mimic
with laughter rails her satiate amuse
she muses generously henry's tempt
of fate and mechanics,wishing,hoping

tempermental,monumental grain
of sand so insignificant yet
each great mystery persists
and mystifies every ancient code
modified still,unspoken,vague
precise the unflattered key,
brazen henry questions and wonders
still-

what if -
one secret revealed -is a match!
of wits and solemn achieve
cornered on the edge
of a universe so grand
would nature tolerate one space filled
with innumerable poses
persistently searched,
ultimately pathed,
would perhaps nudge the odds
closer to close so close
that henry and nature
might for a brief spectacular moment
be at one!